The First Twenty-Five

The First Twenty-Five

*An Oral History of the Desegregation
of Little Rock's Public Junior High Schools*

Edited by LaVerne Bell-Tolliver

The University of Arkansas Press
Fayetteville
2017

ISBN: 978-1-68226-047-0
eISBN: 978-1-61075-624-2

22   21   20   19   18   5   4   3   2   1

Designed by Liz Lester

This project is supported by a social-justice advocacy grant from the
Second Presbyterian Church in Little Rock, Arkansas, by an African American
Heritage grant from the Arkansas Humanities Council, and by the
Gordon and Izola Morgan Publication Fund.

⊖ The paper used in this publication meets the minimum requirements
of the American National Standard for Permanence of Paper
for Printed Library Materials Z39.48-1984.

Library of Congress Control Number: 2017941941

This book is dedicated in memory of my parents, Louis Anthony and Ruby Jewel Fleming Bell. My mother, in fact, asked me to do so long ago. It took me some time, however, to consider the fact that this topic might have meaning and value for others. I'm therefore grateful that my parents encouraged me to tell the story.

This book is also dedicated to my children and their spouses, to my five wonderful grandchildren, and to the entire Bell and Fleming family clan for your tireless support and love you send from generation to generations of family. Thank you for being and doing family.

CONTENTS

III   Conclusion

FOREWORD

Dr. LaVerne Bell-Tolliver has rescued from the memories of eighteen African Americans their experiences desegregating junior high schools. A half century ago they were the first African American students to enroll in five previously all-White junior high schools in Little Rock, Arkansas. They were called on to break down long-standing racial barriers while in their early teen years, a developmental stage that for most youth brings major emotional vulnerability.

In contrast to the experiences of the Little Rock Nine, who were the first to cross the color line at Little Rock Central High School, the enrollment of these junior high teens received little media coverage at the time, and since then their experiences have received little attention by scholars. Although these young teens had good academic records, which were one reason they were selected by school officials for their trailblazing roles, they were babes in the woods surrounded by the wolves of centuries-old racial prejudice and discrimination.

In the case of the young LaVerne Bell-Tolliver, she did not volunteer for the role at Forest Heights Junior High School in Little Rock, Arkansas. Her parents made that decision, which separated her from Paul Dunbar Junior High, an African American legacy school, where she would have enrolled with her friends.

I am especially pleased to read LaVerne's story because I was one of the first, along with eighteen to twenty faculty and staff colleagues at the University of Arkansas at Little Rock, to ever hear LaVerne tell it publicly. LaVerne was like war veterans and others who have suffered trauma but do not talk about it, do not want to talk about it, are afraid to talk about it—but who need to talk about it, for the sake of the rest of us as well as themselves.

In 2007, I sent a message across campus that I would like to talk with a group of faculty and staff members about the economics of race. We did not finish the discussion when we first met, so we decided to meet again the following week. The Monday afternoon meetings of this voluntary group continued into my final year as chancellor in 2015–2016. The twenty or so who showed up for the first meeting evolved into the Chancellor's Committee on Race and Ethnicity. In weekly meetings, this group covered a multitude of subjects and events related to race and also developed the plans for the UALR Institute on Race and Ethnicity. Everyone in the group learned immensely from each other. LaVerne Bell-Tolliver was a charter member of this group and one of its major contributors. It was with this group that she first publicly shared her Forest Heights story. All of us listening to it knew we were hearing a significant story and were honored that LaVerne was willing to share it with us.

LaVerne Bell-Tolliver today is an adult of faith, impeccable character, and dignity. She also is a person with passion to do whatever she can to move the community and country forward toward the beloved community, the more perfect union. In her chosen profession, social work, she has worked with stressed families and persons who were suffering and confused and isolated and silenced as a result of their circumstances, or their own choices, or both. She and the other children whose stories appear in this volume were put through the fire themselves, and they survived, and in different ways they have thrived in showing others how to make a difficult human journey.

The reader will encounter similarities and differences in the experiences of eighteen young teens that will provide the stuff of reflection and of better understanding as people of goodwill try to bring along their fellow citizens in the ongoing struggle for racial equality and justice.

This volume is rich in information and insight into what was going on fifty years ago in the desegregation of schools across the country. What one sees in the experiences of these eighteen students is that the schools, specifically school officials charged with desegregating the public schools, were not prepared for it. The school administrators were not prepared. The teachers were not prepared. The White students were not prepared. The African American students, one can infer from this volume, were the best prepared, thanks to families and churches and civil rights organizations that wanted them to succeed. Yet they were not prepared either for the circumstances they would face.

Outside of school, LaVerne had a solid family and a caring church.

Inside school, LaVerne was without friends in what for her was a cold place. She was socially and physically isolated, with teachers who made her feel conspicuous and who at the same time acted as though she was not in the classroom. Eventually it was in music that she found a voice.

For all of the eighteen African American students, their experiences were confusing, hurtful, belittling, sometimes frightening, and silencing. Going through the experiences and surviving them made them stronger, but they also incurred wounds that are not likely ever to heal completely. We should thank LaVerne Bell-Tolliver and all of the eighteen for telling us what it was like, as children, to be on the very front lines of the Civil Rights Movement. We must salute them for not becoming so discouraged and embittered that they could not handle adulthood and fight the good fight for racial justice.

Joel E. Anderson
Chancellor-Emeritus
University of Arkansas at Little Rock

ACKNOWLEDGMENTS

I'm so grateful to these former students who shared their stories. They have filled in many gaps in information. News articles, school board records, and even court documents can only supply certain amounts and types of information. These former students were invaluable in explaining their ideas of how certain things, such as the selection process and their decisions about desegregation, took place. They shared their memories, their emotions, and their hopes for the future. Thanks, all of you courageous people!

I also wish to thank the contributors to this book: John Kirk and Vicki Lind, both of the University of Arkansas at Little Rock (UALR). When I think of my own experience as a young person who entered an otherwise all-Caucasian junior high school, my memories, questions, and feelings could easily overwhelm the experiences of others. For that reason, I'm grateful to have these cocontributors on board to assist with the entire project. Their objectivity about this material allowed richer meaning and themes to come forth than what might otherwise have been seen through my eyes. Thanks is also extended to Charles Johnson and Carolyn Scribner, both of whom were members of the 1962 class of West Side Junior High. Charles helped me to locate at least six of the eighteen members of the first twenty-five, and Carolyn requested to be interviewed. Because the length of this current manuscript exceeded my opportunity to include her information into this book, her transcript may be found at the Butler Center for Arkansas Studies.

Thanks is also extended to my wonderful graduate assistant, Rachel Lindstom, who provided help for so many tasks associated with this book. Thank you, staff of Professional Typing Service, for assisting with the interview transcripts and final prepartion of the manuscript.

The staff at the Arkansas Studies Institute, including the Butler Center and the Central Arkansas Library System, along with the UALR Center for Arkansas History & Culture, were so helpful. Anna Lancaster assisted me with everything from teaching me how to operate my digital recorder and the video camera she loaned me from the center, to putting together a DVD of slices of the interviews! Rhonda Stewart and all of the historians and archival assistants went above and beyond the task of finding just the material I needed to bring this manuscript to completion. They even pointed me in the direction of the UA Fayetteville Library, where I completed my work. All of you are wonderful!

This book is made possible in part because of the generous support received from the following: African American Heritage Grant of the Arkansas Humanities Council; Second Presbyterian Church, Little Rock, Arkansas (subvention funds); Butler Center for Arkansas Studies; Rhonda and Tracy Homes, Sr.; Chancellor Joel Anderson and the University of Arkansas at Little Rock; the Committee on Race and Ethnicity; the Joel E. Anderson Institute on Race and Ethnicity; and the UALR School of Social Work.

Overview

INTRODUCTION

On May 23, 1961, the Little Rock School Board designated twenty-five students to be the first African Americans (then called "Negroes" or "Coloreds") to attend four of the five public Little Rock junior high schools. By the first day of school, September 5, 1961, one of those students had submitted a request to be transferred to Dunbar Junior High School, the all–African American public school. The fifth junior high school was desegregated during the 1962–1963 school year. The purpose of this book is to allow the stories of those courageus students who desegregated East Side, Forest Heights, Pulaski Heights, Southwest, and West Side Junior High Schools to be heard in their own way and from their perspectives.

Much has been written about the historical desegregation of Little Rock Central High School by nine African Americans. History has been silent, however, about the desegregation of the five all-White junior high schools. Newspaper articles and research through literature, court records, reviews of the records of Little Rock School Board meetings, and an interview from a civil rights activist of that time will allow us to explore the reason desegregation of the junior high schools occured when it did, and in that manner.

This book consists of a portion of the oral histories of those "first" students who were successfully located during this project. This oral history approach provides them with something they did not have in 1961 and 1962: the opportunity to break the silence. It will serve as a platform for them to share their perspectives of what it was like to enter places no other African Americans or "Negroes," the term commonly used at that time, had previously entered. To that end, this book will largely relate the junior high school experiences of these students, as told by them. Telling their story through their own lens affords them the opportunity to share their perspectives of what they saw, heard, and felt. These recorded interviews provide information about what these former students believe helped them move successfully through that academic time in their lives. They will also describe the extent to which the desegregation experience influenced their personal and professional lives over time.

The author. I, the author, am also one of the participants/former students. I was interviewed by one of the contributors to this book to tell my story in a manner that separated me from my regular role as researcher. For that very reason, the contributor also interviewed my sister, who desegregated one of the other junior high schools. Efforts were made to maintain as much neutrality as possible during the interview process to allow each interviewee to tell their stories in their own way.

I used a research approach that examines how the student participants, their families, and their community were influenced by school desegregation. We also considered how the students who desegregated the schools coped or dealt with this potentially stressful situation that they encountered on a daily basis. Please refer to appendix 1 for more information about the research methods used in this book.

I am a social worker, not a historian. This is important for readers to know because historians will have much more knowledge about how to conduct historical research than I have. I am much more comfortable with interviewing the students, listening for themes that resonate with the majority of them, and reporting about those than I am with sifting through historical information. Nevertheless, given the fact that I was driven to understand that time in history, I searched for information that helped me to make sense of what happened to me and to others as members of the twenty-five. Newspaper articles, legal decisions, and the recently released (2014) minutes of the Little Rock School Board from that era were the primary sources of material that were found to be of help in piecing together the puzzle of how junior high desegregation took place.

We have questions. Are there answers? I initially hoped to find answers to several questions that had lingered in my mind for years by conducting a search of historical data and legal documents. I also hoped to discover answers from the interviews of the participants. Other questions arose, however, as a result of the responses received during the interviews. The general questions explored were:

1. What was the reason the entire school district was not being simultaneously desegregated?

2. What was the method of implementing desegregation of the junior high schools in 1961?

3. How did the students' parents and other important figures prepare them to desegregate the schools? Were they given the opportunity to make a decision about whether to attend that school?

4. What was their perception of the level or quality of education they received in the junior high school, perhaps as compared to what was received in their elementary school?

5. How did attending their predominantly White junior high school influence their lives as adults?

This book will first provide a contextual backdrop to the school desegregation process. In chapter 1, we will briefly explore the Arkansas response to the *Brown v. Board of Education* Supreme Court ruling and the subsequent Arkansas court decisions that resulted when the state delayed with desegregation. The original plan of desegregation developed by the Little Rock School Board, called the Blossom Plan, will be described. Finally, we will provide a very brief overview of the desegregation of Central High School by the now famous Little Rock Nine. This chapter will in no way attempt to provide a detailed approach to that historical time, as it has been amply covered in other forms of literature. The Central High Crisis, important in its own right, is also an integral element that led to what is identified as phase two of Little Rock's desegregation process.

Chapter 2 launches the discussion about phase two of the Little Rock public school desegregation, that of the junior high schools. The desegregation process of the first four schools in 1961 and the final one in 1962 is discussed. Also covered is the attempt made by thirty-nine students to desegregate the junior high schools in 1960, and the successful campaign made by the school district to delay desegregation in the junior high schools. The original date indicated by the school board and approved by the federal district courts to begin junior high desegregation was 1960. Also included is content of some of the appeals hearings of students who attempted to enroll into the schools.

The next few chapters consist of the actual stories of the former students as told through their memories of that time. Chapter 3 is devoted to six of the nine students who desegregated East Side. Chapter 4 highlights the one student who attended Forest Heights. Chapter 5 features the two students who desegregated Pulaski Heights, while chapter 6 does the same with the two students placed at Southwest. Finally, chapter 7 concentrates on seven of the twelve students who were initially identified as desegregating West Side Junior High. One of those students did not attend the school assigned. That information surfaced over the course of gathering the data for this book.

A cautionary disclaimer is offered: As the schools desegregated in 1960 and 1961, it is realistic to point out that some of the participants' memories of things may be clouded by the passage of time. It is also important to mention that several of the participants indicated they actively repressed memories of the pain involved with the experiences they shared. Nevertheless, these stories were their recollections of what occurred and how they felt, and their recognition of how those events influenced their lives.

Chapter 8 provides information concerning significant findings that emerged from the students' responses to the final three research questions that are listed at the beginning of the book. The first two questions are addressed in chapters 1 and 2. Chapter 9 offers recommendations by these former students for parents, educators, and members of the community.

One final word prior to moving forward in this book has to do with the use of various racial terms. Readers will see the words "Negro," "Colored," "Nigras," "Black," and "African American." All of these terms have been used to describe African Americans. During the 1950s and 1960s, however, the names "Negro" or "Colored" were in use by both African Americans and Caucasians. "Nigras" seemed to be a slightly less derogatory form of the word "Nigger." Nevertheless, it was just as derogatory as the latter word. Those expressions were specifically found in the documents reviewed during the process of gathering and interpreting research for this book. The more recent and perhaps more politically correct term, "N-word," was not in use during the 1960s and does not adequately describe the experience of African Americans during the time of school desegregation. It will therefore not be used in this book. The word "White" was used for the dominant culture. That term is still in use today but is also substituted occasionally with "Caucasian" or "European American." Readers will see these expressions used in this book.

Reading audience. Readers who love to fill in gaps concerning history in general or civil rights history more specifically will enjoy reading this book. Adults, parents, grandparents, and educators may enjoy sharing this information with children and youth in a way that they can understand it, for it is frequently said that a people who don't know their history are doomed to repeat it.

It is hoped that this book will have value for families of the twenty-first century. Although the times have changed since the 1960s, some things remain the same. Although the setting is in Little Rock, Arkansas, and the subject is desegregation, the book may appeal to those who have experienced various types of rejection, including discrimination. Racism, hatred, and bullying, unfortunately, remain a part of what occurs in middle schools and beyond. This book may serve as a vehicle for exploring how to identify and solve such problems in a constructive manner.

CHAPTER 1

Setting the Context

To fully comprehend the stories of the African American students who first attended the White junior high schools in Little Rock, the context is established by exploring what was occurring before and during that time. For instance, only the seventh grade was desegregated in the junior high schools in 1961. This chapter provides the answer to one of our original questions: "What was the reason the entire school district was not being simultaneously desegregated?"

Arkansas's Response to *Brown v. Board of Education*

When the Supreme Court of the United States unanimously ruled on May 17, 1954, that "segregation of itself deprives Negro children of equal opportunities" (*Brown v. Board of Education* 1954), and ordered integration of public schools to proceed, Arkansas governor Francis Cherry voiced his opinion that there would be no problem with the state having to comply with the court order. His opinion seemed to verbally support a belief that the state would be able to find a way to meet the requirements within a year of that ruling. He disagreed with the proponents of fighting the court order and appeared to want to maintain racial harmony. In the article, titled "Cherry Says Arkansas to Meet Requirements" (*Arkansas Democrat*, May 18, 1954a), the writer stated the governor "hoped that the problem could be solved 'without incidents' and he expressed the hope that 'this matter does not set back the advancement by Negro people in Arkansas in recent years.'"

Based on Governor Cherry's early statements, Arkansas appeared to be off to a positive start toward desegregating the schools within a year. Indeed, desegregation had already been achieved in some schools within Arkansas—including Fayetteville, Charleston, Hoxie, Fort Smith, and Van Buren—prior to the 1957 Central High desegregation (*Fort Worth Herald Tribune*, September 1, 1957). Some of these included smaller school districts that desired to immediately carry out the order from the Supreme Court because they had very small African American populations living in their areas. Those school districts were losing a great deal of money busing children to atttend segregated schools in districts located miles away from home, or were paying for private educations of other African American students (Kirk, 2011). Nevertheless, school districts such as Charleston and Fayetteville (1954), Hoxie (1955), and Bentonville (1956) began to place African American students into the public White school system (Kirk 2011).

What went wrong with desegregation in the other areas of the state? One of the main setbacks occurred when Cherry's position as governor was upset in the very next elction. He was in office for only one term, 1953–1955. Cherry, already struggling because of decisions he had made in other areas, was in a runoff for the governor's race for reelection at the time of the ruling of *Brown v. Board of Education* (Dougan 2016). Second, although Cherry voiced a positive sentiment toward desegregation immediately following the Supreme Court's decision, he was primarily silent on that issue until the court made the ruling, at which point he voiced his opinion that desegregation would occur smoothly. Gubernatorial candidate Orval Faubus, on the other hand, warned that "any sudden integration would disturb the state's harmonious race relations" (Dougan 2016), thus seeding the likelihood that there would most certainly be problems if desegregation was to occur in Arkansas. Although this issue alone did not lead to Cherry's defeat, it may have affected it.

A third reason for the setback of school desegregation was the fact that many people wanted to maintain segregation, including those involved in the growing number of citizens' councils that were being launched in various parts of Arkansas. Campaigns were formed in such towns as Van Buren, Sheridan, and Charleston in an attempt to either prevent desegregation or re-segregate the districts. Many elected officials from Arkansas opposed desegregation. By 1956, all eight members of Arkansas's delegation to the United States Congress voted for the Southern Manifesto—a document opposing racial integration of public places. They were joined by ninety-three other members of the US Senate and the House of Representatives. Elected members of the Arkansas legislature also passed many bills to forestall desegregation (Kirk 2011, 233). The Arkansas legisture introduced and approved such bills as HB 488 into the Arkansas House of Representatives (Valachovic 1955). This measure sought to maintain segregation in the public schools of Arkansas. Ernest Valachovic, a writer at the *Arkansas Gazette*, indicated that Negro leaders launched an appeal to get members of the senate to vote against this measure. Although they also attempted to meet with the new Governor, Orval Faubus, they could not have known at the time just how staunchly he was in favor of maintaining segregation in the schools.

The decision of the Supreme Court in what has become known as Brown II appeared to cloud the matter of desegregation to some extent. Although Chief Justice Earl Warren affirmed the court's original statement that "racial discrimination in public education is unconstitutional," he basically left the decision as to *how swiftly* each local district could achieve desegregation status up to the lower courts and school administrations by explaining that districts and school authorities might have various types of problems they may need to address before they could fully implement desegregation. The bottom line that the Supreme Court placed was that lower courts would have to determine whether the districts were operating in good faith in their plans to desegregte the schools. The "burden of proof" would be placed upon the school districts to argue that the delay was legitimate (*Brown v. Board of Education* 1955).

Aaron v. Cooper. Tired of waiting for the state of Arkansas to begin the process of desgregating, as promised by former Governor Cherry, a group of students attempted to desegregate the public schools in Little Rock. On January 23, 1956, twenty-seven Negro children appeared at various White schools to apply for midyear transfers (Forster 1960). They were turned away and ultimately referred to Virgil Blossom, the superintendent of the school district. The students were not allowed to register in any of the schools. Instead, they were informed of the fact that the school board was working on a plan to desegregate. On February 8, 1956, thirty-three children, through their guardians, filed a complaint in the US District Court for the Eastern District of

Arkansas, Western Division "against President and Secretary of the Board of Directors of Little Rock School District; the Superintendent of Little Rock School District; and the Little Rock School District itself" (*Arkansas Gazette*, August 29, 1956). The same news issue identified the case as "John Aaron et al., . . . Plantiffs v. Civil action No. 3113. Wm. G. Cooper, et al., Defendants." The name of the first child in the suit was John Aaron. The name of the president of the school board was Dr. William Cooper; thus the name of the original case became known as *Aaron v. Cooper*. Subsequent case names changed for the names of new school board presidents (Forster 1960). The original case was tried before Judge John E. Miller on August 15, 1956, and the opinion was rendered by him on August 28, 1956 (*Aaron v. Cooper* 1956). The students, or plaintiffs in the suit, argued that they were being denied their right to attend desegregated schools solely on the basis of their color or race and that this was keeping them from pursuing the right to have the level of education guaranteed them by the Constitution. They argued that the defendants, or the school board, were depriving them of their rights (*Arkansas Gazette*, August 29, 1956; *Aaron v. Cooper* 1956).

Ultimately Judge Miller, recommended for this position by Governor Faubus, issued a judgement primarily in favor of the defendants (private communication on January 27, 1956, and April 16, 1957, from Governor Faubus to then-citizen Winthrop Rockefeller). He ruled that the defendants were not attempting to keep the educational institutions segregated. Instead, his judgment was that the defendants were doing what was necessary to bring about an integrated system (*Aaron v. Cooper* 1956).

On August 28, 1956, Judge Miller found that the Little Rock School Board had developed an appropriate plan of desegregation, which he considered as the only real argument of the plaintiffs against the defendants. Judge Miller therefore approved that desegregation plan and denied the injunction of the plantiffs, citing the fact that he considered the testimony of the defendant, the superintendent of schools, to be "convincing." Miller believed the school district was doing all that it could to bring about "a plan that will lead to an *effective and gradual* adjustment of the problem, and ultimately bring about a school system not based on color distinctions" (*Arkansas Gazette*, August 29, 1956; emphasis added).

Arkansas Legislature Challenges
the United States Supreme Court

Legal action pertaining to the matter of segregation versus desegregation was taking place simultaneously at both the Arkansas judicial and
legislative levels. Such bills led to acts that reinforced states' rights over
the rulings of the Supreme Court. The rationale given was that the
judgments were out of line with the Constitution of the United States.
Governor Faubus wanted a state sovereignty commission, armed with
broad, sweeping powers to maintain segregation. Each amendment was
ultimately overturned; however, the governor and legislative body of
that time clearly demonstrated their desire to challenge the right of the
federal government to supersede the desire of the state of Arkansas
to maintain segregation. (See appendix 2 for more details about the
amendments.)

The School Board's Plan (Blossom):
The Phases of Desegregation

What was the "plan" Judge Miller mentioned? The Little Rock School
Board adopted a plan of desegregation on May 24, 1955. The original plan, *Little Rock Board of Education's Plan of School Integration*, also
known as the Blossom Plan because it was developed during the time of
Superintendent Virgil Blossom, offered three primary recommendations
to take place for this "most difficult educational problem of our time" to
be resolved (1956, 1; *Arkansas Gazette,* August 29, 1956). First, the school
board stressed the need of the school district to build additional schools—
"three senior high schools and six junior high schools"—to accommodate the "time" aspect of integration. In other words, until those schools
were completed, full integration could not take place (*Arkansas Gazette,*
August 29, 1956). Second, the school board believed that desegregation
needed to begin *gradually,* with the entry of Negro students to the White
high schools (FBI: Little Rock Crisis Reports: UALR 0044, Box 1, File 10,
Director's Brief 2673, Volume I, File 3, Chronology page B1). The rationale given by the superintendent was, "Due to the complexity of this
problem, an orderly systematically planned process should be followed"

(*Plan of School Integration* 1956, 1). Third, the school board argued that they needed to wait on a "proper time and method for the integration of the schools of Little Rock School District in a manner consistent with the law as finally interpreted by the Supreme Court and acceptable to both races" (*Arkansas Gazette*, August 29, 1956). The board essentially delayed the timing of desegregation by rationalizing that the ball was in the court of the Supreme Court (FBI: Little Rock Crisis Reports: UALR 0044, Box 1 File 10:2673 Director's Brief, Volume II: UALR Exhibit 3: Little Rock School Board plan of gradual integration). The board proposed that desegregation not begin until the 1957–1958 school year, at which time it should begin at the high school level. This idea was based on their publicly expressed opinion that, while additional schools needed to be constructed at all levels, the ninth through twelfth grades would require fewer new schools and teachers. They proposed that the second phase of desegregation would begin at the junior-high level in 1960, "following successful integration at the senior high school level." Finally, "following successful integration at the junior high school level," desegregation would be implemented at the elementary school level in the third phase in 1963, (*Arkansas Gazette*, August 29, 1956) or "two or three years thereafter" (Minutes, March 21, 1960, 1; *Aaron v. Tucker* 1960). Denying charges that they were delaying the process of desegregating, the board objected to beginning the process simultaneously, arguing that they wanted to benefit from their experience by beginning desegregation first at the high school level (FBI: Little Rock Crisis Reports: UALR 0044, Box 1 File 10, Director's Brief 2673, Volume II: UALR Exhibit 3: Little Rock School Board plan of gradual integration).

The ruling of Judge John E. Miller to approve the Little Rock School Board's request for gradual integration in essence meant this plan allowed the schools to slowly desegregate over a period of a minimum of ten years, beginning in 1957 (Frick 1956).

Desegregation Begins at Central High School

As school was preparing to open in September of 1957, the Little Rock School Board made the decision to move forward with the desegregation plan. Unfortunately, Governor Orval Faubus, the Mothers League of Central High, and others attempted to block this action. Their rationale was that violence would erupt. "They warned that violence, bloodshed and rioting might break out if the schools were integrated" (Fine 1957a). The fact that Faubus had previously promised the citizens of Arkansas that he would never support integration may have prompted him to use language that might incite or encourage violence. "Segregation, in his opinion, is a sociological problem, rather than a political issue. But he makes the most of it when he declares: 'There will be no enforced integregation in the public schools of Arkansas, as long as I am your governor'" (Foreman 1956). Nevertheless, the school board initially began to move forward with the attempt to desegregate the schools.

On August 31, 1957, Judge Ronald Davies issued an order preventing anyone from halting the desegregation process (Forster 1960; Fine 1957a; *Forth Worth Herald Tribune*, September 1, 1957; FBI: Little Rock Crisis Reports, November 25, 1957). Not satisfied with the ruling of the federal court, and acting in defiance of Judge Davies's warning not to interfere with the court order (*Forth Worth Herald Tribune*, September 1, 1957), Faubus "declared a state of emergency" and ordered seventy National Guardsmen to bar the Negro students from attending Central High School (Miller 1957, 1). His statement in the press conference, according to the *World Telegram & Sun*, continued to voice his desire to prevent violence. On the other hand, L. C. Bates, the publisher of the *Arkansas State Press* and the husband of Daisy Bates, president of the local NAACP, offered a different perspective about the matter: "If we have violence, my feeling is that it can be laid directly to the governor" (Miller 1957, 1).

On September 5, 1957, the school board petitioned the federal district court to set aside the integration ruling, thus reversing the decision it had made only a week earlier (Fine 1957b). At that time, the board explained that it was concerned about the presence of the National Guard, the fact that the Negro students were barred from entering the school earlier during the week (*Daily News*, September 5, 1957), and the growing racial tension in the White Little Rock community.

President Dwight David Eisenhower also took action on September 5, 1957, when he sent a telegram to Governor Faubus, essentially warning him of the action Eisenhower would take, "by every legal means at [his] command," if Faubus did not comply with the court order (Lawrence 1957). This decision of a governor to act in defiance of both a federal court and a president could have set a dangerous precedent for every state of the union. Perhaps for that reason, and to restore order, the president carried out his warning to the governor. Ultimately, the presidential act allowed the nine African Americans to begin the stormy and tumultuous process of enterng Central High. The govenor, citing unrest and instability, then closed the public high schools for the entire 1958–1959 school year, under the authority of Act 4 of the Second Extraordinary Session of the General Assembly of Arkansas (*Aaron v. Tucker* 1960). Please see appendix 2 for additional information on Act 4. Ultimately, the defendants were permanently enjoined from impeding the progress of desegregation in the Little Rock public schools (Minutes, March 21, 1960, 4, 5). Public high schools in Little Rock reopened for the 1959–1960 school year.

CHAPTER 2

PHASE TWO:
Historical Introduction
Junior High Desegregation

This chapter reports information about phase two of the desegregation plan: the desegregation of the Little Rock public junior high schools, grades seven through nine. The second research question, "What brought about the specific method for carrying out the desegregation of the junior high schools in 1961?" will be answered. Many students, parents, and community activist experienced failures and disappointments in 1960 as junior high student applicants attempted to desegregate those schools. We will describe that event.

We will briefly review the role civic organizations played in preparing African American students to desegregate the junior high schools, thus exploring a bit of the response to research question three, "How did the students' parents and other important figures prepare them to desegregate the schools?" Finally, the official procedure of the school district for selecting African American students who would desegregate the schools will be addressed here. Later chapters will reveal the beliefs or ideas of those students about this process.

Postponement of Desegregation to Junior High Schools

According to the plan of the school board, the desegregation of the Little Rock junior high schools was originally slated to begin in the 1960–1961 school year. Families and members of the African American community attempted to follow this process. The June 14, 1960, *Arkansas Gazette* reported "39 Negroes Seek Integration in Fall at Jr.

High Level." The school board, with several new members ultimately replacing the 1956 board members who resigned following the approval of the Arkansas Plan (*Aaron v. Tucker* 1960), had already begun, however, to take steps to halt or delay the original process of launching desegregation in the junior high schools. The board approved a resolution on March 21, 1960, to prevent the move to desegregate the junior high schools in the fall of that year:

> Section 4. That the Board will not move to phase two of the Court approved plan (that is, junior high schools, grades 7 to 9) in September, 1960. Phase one has not been successfully completed and will not be successfully completed at the end of the current school year. (Minutes, March 21, 1960, 5)

The board offered three reasons in the resolution to support this delay: (1) the high schools were closed in the 1958–1959 school year due to the "adverse circumstances" that occurred during the time of desegregation of Central High School; (2) the board, as of March 21, 1960, had no time to evaluate the results of the 1959–1960 school year; (3) the board needed to complete the evaluation of the process in order to determine what could be learned from the desegregation experience.

The resolution also included the decision of the board to "follow the Arkansas Pupil Assignment Law (Act No. 461 of 1959) and its regulations adopted thereunder, and students will be assigned and reassigned throughout the schools of the District in accordance with said regulations, but there will be no desegregation except in accordance with the phases of the Court approved plan" (Minutes, March 21, 1960, 4; *Norwood v. Tucker* 1961). The Pupil Assignment Law appeared to be an obvious effort used by the school district and other parties to delay full-scale desesegregation as long as possible.

The Little Rock Board of Education scheduled meetings for each of the students who appealed their denials, and the decision was ultimately made to deny all thirty-nine of the students who applied to attend the junior high schools. The students cited overcrowded schools, the fact that they lived closer to the White junior high than to Dunbar, better or more course offerings, newer textbooks, and many other reasons for their request to transfer to the schools listed on their applications. The board, however, challenged those reasons, frequently stating that the students' or parents' information was faulty. A transcript of a student's appeal from such a meeting follows. The names of the student and parents have been omitted.

Stated Reason for Request: "Dunbar is the only colored Junior High School in Little Rock and it is entirely too crowded and it doesn't offer enough subjects."

Present for hearing: the student, his parents, and attorney Harold B. Anderson

Board: (addresses student) How old are you?

Student: 13

After the board reviewed the stated reasons for the reassignment request, Mr. [Everett] Tucker [Jr., President] asked those present for the hearing if they had any additional information they would like to present.

Student: Dunbar doesn't have enough subjects.

Board to Mr. Powell: [Superintendent of Schools] Would you like to comment on this?

Mr. Powell: The curriculum is the same at both schools.

Board to student & parents: Are you sure of that?

Student: I thought Dunbar was so crowded you couldn't learn enough of the subjects they gave us. You could learn more if it wasn't so crowded.

Board: What grades did you make?

Student: "As" and "Bs"

Board: Were you advised by anyone in your request for reassignment?

Student: By Mr. Walker.

Board: Did he have some meetings with a group of you?

Student: Once or twice.

Board: At Dunbar Community Center?

Student: Yes, sir.

Board: Do you live close to Dunbar?

Student: One block.

Board: How do your parents feel about your request?

Parent: I would feel satisfied if he wanted to go. In fact, I feel it would be better for him.

Board: Do you have other children?

Mother: Yes. One daughter who has finished college, and one daughter entering college. (Minutes, July 12, 1960, 19–20)

Desegregation of the public Little Rock junior high schools, therefore, began in 1961, with the gradual desegregation of the junior high seventh grade classes. In 1962, the Little Rock School District increased the number of junior high students in the eighth grade by allowing additional students to attend that grade as well as grades seven and ten through twelve. The ninth grade would naturally integrate the following year (Garrison 1962).

School Board Selection of Students
ARKANSAS PUPIL ASSIGNMENT LAW (ACT 461 OF 1959)

The question of who made the selection of the students to attend the junior high school was answered by the *Arkansas Democrat*, by the school board, and by *Aaron v. Tucker* (1960). The superintendent of schools and the Little Rock School Board were ultimately responsible for making the decision to identify which students be assigned to attend the junior high schools (*Aaron v. Tucker* 1960). Although Forster (1961) indicated, "Without stating a policy on the junior-high level, the Negroes were simply included in the assignments of 22,000 pupils to the schools they will attend next fall," the board operated under the court-approved Arkansas plan and the Pupil Assignment Law.

Forster's May 25, 1961, article indicated that the board voted to desegregate four of the five junior high schools, as no one applied to desegregate Pulaski Heights, the fifth school, during 1961. Although students and their parents attempted to desegregate several Little Rock schools as early as 1956, no mention was made of students attempting to apply to attend Pulaski Heights or of them being assigned to attend that school prior to 1962. Instead, parents and their children, arguing for immediate desegregation at all levels, applied to schools that were in close proximity to their homes (*Aaron v. Cooper* 1956). Those schools included "Central High School, Technical High School, Forest Heights Junior High School, and Forest Park Elementary School."

The Pupil Assignment Law Act No. 461 of 1959 outlined the process of assigning pupils to the public schools of the Little Rock School District. Included in this law were the matters of the assignment, reassignment, appeals, and qualifications for selection to these schools. The assignment law (see appendix 3) went into efftect for the 1959–1960 school year; however, the procedure was also outlined for subsequent years (*Aaron v. Tucker* 1960). Criteria that were utilized for assignment did not mention race, as race was not to be used as criteria in determining assignment of students to the schools (*Aaron v. Cooper* 1956). The onus was placed on the Little Rock School Board to demonstrate only that they were not discriminating based on race.

Aaron v. Tucker identified the sixteen placement criteria identified in the Pupil Assignment Law:

1. Available room and teaching capacity in the various schools;
2. Availability of transportation facilities;
3. The effect of the admission of new pupils upon established or proposed academic programs;
4. The suitability of established curricula for particular pupils;
5. The adequacy of the pupil's academic preparation for admission to a particular school and curriculum;
6. The scholastic aptitude and relative intelligence or mental energy or ability of the pupil;
7. The psychological qualifications of the pupil for the type of teaching and associations involved;
8. The effect of admission of the pupil upon the academic progress of other students in a particular school or facility thereof;
9. The effect of admission upon prevailing academic standards at a particular school;
10. The psychological effect upon the pupil of attendance at a particular school;
11. The possibility of breaches of the peace or ill will or economic retaliation within the community;
12. The home environment of the pupil;

13. The maintenance or severance of established and psychological relationships with other pupils and with teachers;

14. The choice and interests of the pupil;

15. The morals, conduct, health, and personal standards of the pupil;

16. The request or consent of parents or guardians and the reasons assigned therefor. (Aaron v. Tucker 1960)

Across the state of Arkansas, testing of African American students became a part of the criteria in many school districts for determining who would be capable of studying with Caucasian students. Tests targeted both academic achievement and personality. Dollarway School District administered their two tests to all African American students within their district: (1) the Metropolitan Readiness Test and (2) the California Test of Mental Maturity, Pre-primary (*Dove v. Parham* 1961).

Tests were also reportedly given to all ninth grade students in the Little Rock public schools beginning in 1960 to determine which students were qualitified to attend a majority-Caucasion school. Although race was not to be considered as a factor for school selection, only African American student placements in Caucasian schools, however, were determined as a result of the outcome of the tests. In an article titled "Fall Integration May be Limited to 12 Negroes: School Board Bases New Assignments on Preference, Test," the *Arkansas Gazette* stated that all ninth grade students of both races began taking a standardized "psychological" or "personality" test—both terms were used in the article—that apparently determined whether students would be deemed capable of understanding information that would allow them to perform appropriately. This test was one of the sixteen criteria, not including race, to be used in assigning African American children to schools under the pupil placement law (*Arkansas Gazette*, May 21, 1960).

THE LIMIT OF JUNIOR HIGH STUDENTS
ALLOWED TO DESEGREGATE EACH YEAR

The culling from eighty-four to twenty-five. Bobbie Forster reported in the May 25, 1961, *Arkansas Democrat* that out of a possible eighty-four applicants, twenty-five Negro sixth grade students were approved to be the first to desegregate four of the five junior high schools. No African American student applied during that year to attend Pulaski Heights Junior High (*Arkansas Democrat*, September 4, 1961). US district court judge Gordon E. Young approved the plan of limiting the total enrollment of Negro students to forty-eight in the entirety of Little Rock School District's previously all-White schools. Young indicated that the school board was showing there was no prejudice involved and that they were making a good faith effort to desegregate the district (*Arkansas Democrat*, September 10, 1961).

Errors in print. Some errors or updates occurred in the overall reporting of the total number of African American students who enrolled and attended these schools. Twenty-four Negro students were expected to enroll in the junior high schools as early as the opening day of class (*Arkansas Gazette*, September 5, 1961). The September 6, 1961, *Gazette* reported an error with the overall total count; two students rather than one did not report to their assigned schools. Whereas the May 25, 1961, *Democrat* indicated that twelve students would enroll at West Side, the September 6, 1961, *Democrat* reported that eleven actually enrolled. Felton Walker, assigned to West Side, did not attend that school (personal communication 2014).

The September 6, 1961, *Arkansas Gazette* reported that one of the original twenty-five who was selected submitted a request to return to the Negro school, Dunbar Junior High (1). On June 5, 1961, Ida Marie Butler and her parents, Mr. and Mrs. L. Tucker, submitted a request for her to be reassigned from Forest Heights Junior to Dunbar Junior High for the 1961–1962 school year. Mrs. Tucker explained as her rationale, "I did not sign the preference sheet. I could not get my child to Forest Heights because of transportation difficulties" (Minutes, June 28, 1961, 29). When the board approved that request, one student, rather than two as stated in the May paper, enrolled.

The names of the remaining students who first desegregated the public Little Rock junior high schools according to the May 25, 1961, *Arkansas Democrat*, minus their newspaper-published addresses, include: East Side (nine)—Equilla Banks, Alfreda Brown, Larry Davis, Myrna Davis, Linda Eskridge (or Brown), Shirley Hickman, Sarah E. Jordan, Jessie Walker, and Glenda Wilson; West Side (eleven)—Clarence

Johnson, Alice Joiner, Kenneth Jones, Gary Ledbetter, Betty McCoy, Brenda Sims, Sandra Smith, Nathan Summerfield, Alvin Terry, Dianne Threet, and Joyce Williams; Forest Heights (one)—LaVerne Bell; and Southwest (two)—Henry Rodgers and Wilbunette Walls. The total enrolled for the 1961–1962 school year was twenty-three.

For more than two days, both the *Arkansas Gazette* and *Democrat* newspapers seemed to heavily emphasize that the desegregation of the junior high schools was "quiet" (*Arkansas Democrat*, September 5, 1961, 1; *Arkansas Gazette*, September 6, 1961, 1, and September 10, 1961, 4E;), "peaceful" (*Arkansas Gazette*, September 6, 1961, 4A; *Arkansas Democrat*, September 10, 4E), or "normal" (*Arkansas Democrat*, September 6, 1961; *Arkansas Gazette*, September 6, 1961, 4A). This report of "quiet" was dramatically different from the descriptions offered by the students in their interviews. According to the newspaper reports, African American students arrived either singly or—as in the case of West Side—with larger groups in cars. Although police were present at both East Side and West Side Junior High Schools, no unruly incidences occurred (*Arkansas Democrat*, September 5, 1961, 2; *Arkansas Gazette*, 1). The police returned to performing regular tasks within an hour of the school opening. This was in contrast to the uproar surrounding the 1957 desegration of Central High School, which was ultimately heard around the world.

The enrollment of Negro students slowly increased during the 1962–1963 school year. Two students enrolled in the previously all-White Pulaski Heights Junior High School for the fall 1962–1963 school year. Although the information concerning the number enrolled was published (*Arkansas Gazette*, September 30, 1962), the names were with-held. Those names, however, were Kathleen Bell and Pinkie Thompson.

The Little Rock School District continued its practice of desegregating the junior-high level one grade at a time. Thus, for the 1962–1963 school year, there were seventy-one Negroes in attendance in the high schools and junior highs combined, with a total of twenty-eight attending the high schools: Central (twenty), Hall (six), and Technical (two); and forty-three attending the junior highs: East Side (eighteen), West Side (twenty), Southwest (two), Pulaski Heights (two) and Forest Heights (one) (*Arkansas Gazette*, September 30, 1962).

The eighth grade was basically desegregated when the seventh graders from the previous year enrolled, although no African American seventh graders arrived at Forest Heights or Southwest. In fact, although the *Arkansas Gazette* (September 30, 1962) reported that two students would be in attendance at Southwest, interviews with the participants indicated one of the original two students transferred to Dunbar Junior High School. Also, participant interviews from the students attending East Side indicated that the two male students departed from the school within their first year.

It was the plan of the Little Rock School Board to continue to slowly integrate African American students for approximately ten years, until the elementary schools were desegregated. The Arkansas plan was designed to allow small numbers of students to enter any school, thus preventing a major change in student composition. It was not until the Civil Rights Act of 1964 (Title VII) was passed that larger numbers and higher percentages of students began attending the Little Rock public schools. The Civil Rights Act enforced equal access to public education, among a number of other rights for all United States citizens (US Equal Employment Opportunity Commission 2015).

II Our Stories

The next chapters are the heart of this book. The former students will tell their stories of desegregating the public Little Rock junior high schools. For some of them, this was their first time talking at all about what they experienced. You will discover that some of the students' perspectives, particularly concerning the selection process, will be different from the stated account of the school board or the Pupil Assignment Law. It is important to understand that although these former students' understandings of such issues at the time did not align themselves with historical data, both are of equal value in this book, in that the students' perspective of what happened to them at the time tended to guide their future lives. Also true is the fact that historical data is largely written from the position of the writer and from the dominant culture in positions of power.

Although you will become aware of some similarities from a few of these students, you will also read their unique stories as they focused on their familial backgrounds, socioeconomic statuses, internal strengths, or other factors that made them distinctly able to move through this school.

Two final comments are offered before proceeding with the interview transcripts. First, although you will read questions the interviewer asked the participant, other questions are eliminated to facilitate a smoother reading opportunity and minimize distractions from hearing the main story. Second, due to the length of some of the interviews, readers will not be able to read the full narratives of every participant. The transcripts may be viewed in their entirety upon the publication of this book at the University of Arkansas Center for History and Culture, Arkansas Studies Institute, 407 President Clinton Avenue, Little Rock, Arkansas, 72201 (http://ualr.edu/cahc/). Oral interviews of almost every interview are also available at the center.

CHAPTER 3

East Side Junior High School

Nine students were assigned to attend/desegregate East Side Junior High School in 1961. They were Equila Banks, Alfreda Brown, Larry Davis, Myrna Davis, Linda Eskridge (also known as Brown), Shirley Hickman, Sarah E Jordan, Jessie Walker, and Glenda Wilson (*Arkansas Democrat*, May 25, 1961; Minutes, Executive Session, May 23, 1961). In this chapter you will read the experiences of six of these students, all female. Although some of the participants who were interviewed remembered that Larry and Jessie attended the school for at least one year, they also remembered that neither of them completed the ninth grade with them. A few students remembered Linda Eskridge Brown; however, no one knew of her whereabouts. All attempts to locate these three persons failed. Interestingly, in spite of the relatively small number of African American students who originally attended the school, participants will have different ideas about the number of original nine students who actually enrolled and attended.

Equilla Banks Webb

*"We may have looked passive from the outside,
we were real warriors from the inside."*

My name is Equilla Banks Webb. I was born in Little Rock, Arkansas. My parents were Ray Banks Sr. and Evelyn Smith Banks. I have a brother, Ray Banks Jr., who's five years younger. I have a half-brother but who was not actually in our home. I grew up in Little Rock, and I actually lived in what is known as the East End, which is kind of the wrong side of the track. I attended Carver Elementary School. We stayed in the East End all during my junior high years, and we eventually moved in . . . I think I was a junior in high school when we moved to the West End.

What made you say, "The wrong side of the track?"

Well . . . it's mostly poor people, poor Blacks, poor Whites. It was close to the airport; it was about two blocks from the airport and most of the residents there lived in poor, rundown houses. Not very many professional people at all, you know. It had a pretty bad reputation . . . When I was growing up, I didn't realize that. . . . I didn't realize, really, the negativity until I started attending East Side and saw how other people lived.

What junior high school [did you attend]?

East Side Junior High School. I started there in the seventh grade in 1961 . . . Well, there were seven of us. Well, it said on your list eight, but it was one young man I'm just not familiar with. But seven of us attended.

Do you remember [his] name?

I think it was Larry Davis. I do remember him. He didn't finish with us, but he did attend . . .

Did you know the others before you began school?

I did not. I was the only one from the East End going there. Everyone I met for the first time.

How did you happen to arrive at the school on that particular day?

My dad . . . it's kind of a long story. What happened was that my mother bought me a new dress to go there, and she laid it out on the bed and the cat urinated on the dress. . . . so I was trying to get the smell out and . . . trying to clean it up . . . it was all I had. And, so I was late leaving, and my dad actually drove me . . . and he was so nervous about it, he parked a couple of blocks from the school and walked me up to the school. And so I was late getting there, but you know, it was a providence. I learned later from Myrna that there was like a mob there, awaiting them. Well, I missed all of that. I was late because of the cat. . . . I can't remember if he actually took me inside, but I think it was a teacher or the principal, someone met us. . . . When he knew I was safe, then he walked back to the car.

Did he share with you why he was nervous?

No, he didn't have to . . . you know, I was aware of the Central High

School situation. In fact, that was one of the reasons that it was my intent to go to Central High School. And, well, I'll just tell you the story.

When I was eight years old, my dad and I watched the mob violence and everything on TV. And I looked at him, and it just . . . angered me and I just felt so defiant at that moment. And . . . I looked at him and I said, "Dad, I'm gonna go to Central High one day." So that was my aim, from the time I was eight, to go to Central. . . . I guess that was going to be my contribution. So what happened was that when I was in the sixth grade, and I was supposed to go to Dunbar. And . . . they have those visits. . . . I thought, "I'm not going to that school." But at that point, I didn't know where I was going to go. So a couple of weeks later was when they told us in school . . . about the desegregation plan. So I chose the school closest to me—East Side. And I took the information to my parents, and my dad of course agreed. But I had no clue what I was getting myself into . . . but I had planned all along to go to Central. So when this plan, when this opportunity came up, I signed up for it.

You mentioned that someone told you about the desegregation plan. Was that in a class?

It was. . . . At the time we had our . . . our homeroom teachers. They came in and they talked about the plan to desegregate the schools. And I was all for it. And there was one other gal from Carver. I think her name was Ida Butler, but she dropped out before the first day of class.

Did you know Ida Butler?

I knew her from school.

She was one of the people on the list.

Oh, okay. . . . She didn't attend East Side. So I don't know if she attended another school or not, but I think I remember her dropping out.

You mentioned wanting to go to Central, and watching that situation on TV. Talk a little bit more about what was going on . . . that made you decide, "This is the place I need to be."

I think it was the mob around Elizabeth Eckford . . . that they showed, and it just angered me. . . . It was just . . . that spirit of, "I'm gonna show them" . . . at eight years old. . . . I still pretty much have that kind of attitude . . . I really don't know what drove me to do it, but I knew I had to do something. You know, it was going to be my contribution. So that's why I did it, and my dad, bless his heart, he just nodded.

So it sounds like, when you went home . . . they discussed it. Your dad at least said . . . "Okay?"

My dad said—there was really no discussion. . . . You could probably figure out . . . I was a daddy's girl when my dad was alive. But I told him what I wanted to do, and he said, "Okay." My mom didn't say much of anything.

Was she supportive of you?

No, no. My mom was never supportive of education. . . . She dropped out of school in the sixth grade, and she was always saying, "Don't be an educated fool," even though she went to a private school, St. Bartholomew. My dad, on the other hand, was very poor. He finished his high school after he had gone to the Navy. He came back and went to night school to finish high school. So education was very important to him, and he . . . and my uncle, they always stressed, "You gotta get a good education. You gotta take care of yourself. You gotta . . ."

So you received two competing, conflicting messages . . . but being a dad's girl . . .

Yeah. . . . I listened to my dad.

So that was the reason he was walking you to the school?

Right.

Do you remember your dad doing or saying anything, or other people, to prepare you for the process of desegregating?

That summer, the community leaders contacted my parents, and they had a meeting at Dunbar Community Center . . . the Urban League, was part of it . . . and there was a Mr. Jordan who was like a mail carrier, but I'm not sure . . . if he was part of the group or not. But I also met Joyce Williams there. . . . We met at the Dunbar Community Center, and they sat with us and told us what to expect. . . . They weren't expecting any violence . . . They just said that we would be watched, and they let us know that . . . we had to represent the race well. If we did poorly, there would be no class after us.

Oh, wow. No pressure there.

Yeah! At twelve years old, you know. "You gotta do this right. We don't want them to have any excuse not to keep the plan going. If you go, and you do poorly or you act poorly, then they will have that excuse and say, 'We'll just leave the school segregated.'" You know.

Do you remember . . . having relatively good grades in the elementary school?

I had great grades . . . I was really a good student. . . . That was part of the qualification. Plus . . . I was a good citizen at school. I loved school. I loved learning. There was no problem with my being chosen.

You mention the word "chosen." Now what do you mean by that?

We submitted the paperwork, I guess, to the school board. They decided whether or not you would be one of the chosen ones . . . You know, it wasn't automatic. . . . If you had poor grades, or if . . . you were a problem student, behavior-wise . . . there was no way you were going to go there.

What experiences did you have with the White community before coming to the junior high school?

It was a little bit limited. . . . There were Whites living and working in the East End . . . but we really didn't associate with them very much. . . . We were two blocks from the airport. We lived across the street from some Whites, but their backyard faced our front yard. . . . My parents managed [a] twelve-unit apartment complex that was owned by my father's employer—Central Flying Service. They had been Army barracks in World War II, but after that, they were converted to studio apartments. . . . A third of those apartments, dad rented to our relatives. . . . There had been Whites there before, but the employer moved the Whites out . . . and moved in my dad and our family. . . . It was like a duplex. The White families had . . . both sides; but they told dad he had to pay thirty dollars a month to have the second side. So we lived in one side—it was like shotgun. It was three rooms, but there were . . . only four of us, to start with. . . .

Across the street, there were . . . a row of White families, but we faced their backyard. . . . There was one little girl named Sharon. I guess we were about nine, and we kind of discovered each other. . . . We started playing together, until her brother saw . . . and we would go to each other's house. . . . But when her brother noticed that, he put a stop to it. . . . He was not very nice. . . . What's interesting—when I went to East Side, I saw Sharon. . . . We spoke, and we were cordial, and she told me . . . , "You know, I am so proud of you." . . .

There were merchants there on Sixth Street. They had the stores, and there were Jewish people there, although I really had no concept of Jews versus other Whites . . . I avoided Whites. There were a couple of incidences. Once I was walking along the road and . . . a group of White men drove by and saw this young Black child. And so one of them, a big heavyset fat guy, rolled the window down and cursed the little boy out. I thought, "That was ugly." But then I noticed that his companions were very displeased with him . . . for doing that. And . . . there was kind of like a nightclub around the corner from where we lived, called Stewart's. I would go there; in the daytime he would sell these greasy hot dogs for seventy-five cents. So it was always my treat to go there and get one. One day I went there, and this White man was sitting around talking to them, and he was talking about how our plans to integrate anything would fail, that we . . . could never win. . . . There were Black men listening to him, and they were being polite and all of that. . . . He was trying to advise against . . . any kind of desegregation plan. . . . He felt it would ultimately fail. And that stirred something up in me too, just like watching those mobs. . . . I don't know if it was a rebellious spirit . . . but I wanted to prove him wrong. . . .

There was another experience we had. I mentioned my father's employer, Central Flying Service. The owner was Claude Holbert. Mr. Holbert, my dad said, was Jewish. I don't know if that was true or not, but I know he was very fair to my dad. My dad would take my brother and I to his job, and meet with Mr. Holbert and his family, and he was essentially showing us off. And Mr. Holbert was always nice, and he always complimented us. My dad was really fair, my mom was really dark. And so my brother and I were kind of in the middle color wise. Mr. Holbert thought that was the coolest thing and that we were just the best looking kids. And he would tell us that, "Oh you're—you're just so pretty. . . . Oh, I just love your color." Yeah, yeah, and so we just were thankful . . . That was very positive. . . . So that was the experience. Otherwise . . . we'd see the Whites, but we didn't associate with them.

So, with those experiences, you entered East Side?

Yes. Very naive.

What kind of experiences did you have once you began entering on the day that your dad walked you hand in hand to East Side?

There was one thing I forgot to mention that was really important. Mr. Ozell Sutton . . . the head of the Arkansas Council on Human

Relations, contacted my family and had dinner with me and my family . . . It was an interracial group. . . . Ozell Sutton [w]as the first African American reporter for the *Arkansas*—I think it was the *Democrat*.

Ozell Sutton had . . . a White woman sit with us and we ate. . . . That was the first White person . . . who was very cordial, who sat and who talked. I don't really remember what she said. I just remember she was so pleasant. And then Mr. Sutton came over and talked to my mom . . . He was very supportive and saying that he would check back and this woman was so . . . cordial, and so nice. I was just so impressed . . . They let me know that they were behind my decision, and that they would be following up. So I wanted to mention that . . . And back to my dad. You had mentioned something about . . . our addresses being published in the newspaper. . . . Shortly after I decided to go to East Side, that summer my dad, who had been working there at Central Flying Service, I think since I was six, so it must have been about six years. . . . My dad would service the planes . . . Clean the planes up and all that. He did that in the daytime, and he had a crew, and he was a supervisor. Well after . . . I announced that I was going to East Side, he got demoted to janitor, and he worked like, from ten at night until six am in the morning, and he never complained. . . . My dad always said that he liked it that way—he didn't have to deal with anybody else—but I know it was painful for him. He worked there until I think it was 1980 . . . when he retired. . . . At any rate, my dad was demoted. So, that's one thing that happened; essentially what happened was all hell broke out on my family. I was not prepared for it by my family or anyone. . . . Years later I wonder if it was orchestrated.

My mom bought me a dress. She borrowed the money from my grandfather. My grandparents—her parents—were deaf-mute, and my grandfather was a . . . house painter. He rode a bicycle . . . In the East End, everybody knew each other. Well, shortly after I decided to go to East Side, my granddad was hit by a car as he rode his bicycle. . . . Everybody knew he was deaf. So he . . . lived a couple of months after that, and he died from complications of that. He caught pneumonia and passed away. And my grandmother, who was living by herself, moved in—remember we were in these three rooms. . . . She couldn't live on her own, being deaf-mute. So that was good news and bad news.

I was in homeroom with Alfreda and Linda Brown; and so I met

Myrna and Glenda. And I don't remember meeting Sarah Jordan at that time, but Larry Davis. So, I met a few of them. And so I was really impressed by them. . . . I thought they were the most beautiful women in the world. . . . Myrna and I were these little tiny skinny girls, but Myrna and I hit it off right away. So much of that day was kind of a blur. . . . I'll just give you some of the highlights. . . . My homeroom teacher was . . . the music teacher. These boys started harassing me in homeroom. One in particular I grew to hate. He . . . picked on me. He would harass me every day—and a couple of the other boys. And I just realized after going through my notes: my homeroom teacher always delayed coming in. She always came in at the very last minute. . . . After a while though—I've always been timid—I started kind of talking back to them. And other people would say, "Leave her alone."

I think Alfreda and then other White people started saying that. . . . So, that was one of the experiences. . . . I had a teacher . . . we had a pop quiz. I missed a couple of . . . the questions. She gave me a D. I showed my dad, he was furious, and he said that should not be a D. So I was talking to this little White boy in the class, and I asked to see his work. He missed more and he got a B. So I think she changed my grade, but I think that I confronted her about it. And I said, "You know this little boy, he missed more than I did. Why did I get a D and he got a B?" And I remember her being really angry . . . I was really a good student. I . . . loved to learn. It wasn't about grades to me . . .

I had some teachers who were really good. There was one in particular [name withheld]. He was kind of an outsider too. He had an accent. . . . I think he was like a coach. He . . . taught science I think, and . . . he coached some sport. . . . But he was always nice to me—until one day when I was in the nurse's office because I started feeling sick. . . . I was just tearful—everything just came to a point, all the pressure—and I started to cry. . . . He was not supportive at all. I heard later someone said he made fun of me in class, and I thought, "He's not my friend." But even though he said that, years later when I graduated from Central, I sent him a thank you card for the times he was nice. . . .

I started getting bullied whenever I was in the hallway—between classes. These groups of White boys would bully me. Call me names . . . follow behind me. . . . Be threatening. Big White boys . . . and I was a little girl. I had no peace between classes. If I was with a group, that was okay. But if I was by myself . . . to go to the restroom or anything, they would be threatening.

In the East End, this group of Black boys started bullying me. . . . They had always ignored me. Big—they were thugs . . . would start following me wherever I went. . . . They had no interest in me whatsoever until I started going to East Side. And then one day—I like to go to Stewart's and get my hot dogs—I went there, and was walking back home. This man walked up to me and threatened, "I'm gonna rape you." . . . That just scared me, and I thought, "Oh my gosh," you know, and I didn't even know this man. When I walked around the corner, I saw my cousin who we call Buck. His name is Ulysses. When he saw my face, he asked me what happened, what was wrong. And I told him what that man said and he said, "Point him out to me." And I pointed him out to him, he said, "Don't you worry about a thing. Don't you worry about it." The next time I saw that guy, he saw me . . . (laughing) . . . he crossed to the other side of the street. He did not bother me again. . . .

I told you about these bullying Black boys. That went on until one day I had another cousin . . . Michael Burns, who's a gentle soul himself, we were walking along. These boys started bullying me, and he . . . turned around and went after them. He told them, "Don't you mess with my cousin." He said "We got a big family. . . . We know where you live" (laughing). That cut it out . . .

Then my mother just started . . . acting out. My mom, from what I know about psychology and everything, had a personality disorder anyway. She didn't finish school. My relationship with her was not good anyway. At her very best, she was neglectful. At her very worst, she was abusive. I know part of that was—she liked being the center of attention. Essentially, she had me so that she could marry my dad. But after I was born, she had no use for me, so she didn't teach me the basics of anything. So . . . [when] I went to school . . . I looked horrible, my hygiene was horrible. And my dad . . . worked, but I was my dad's girl. And so, in fact, a classmate at Carver said to me, when I told her where I was going, she goes, "Well I hope you dress better." In fact, my mom didn't believe in buying us clothes, and my dad would say, "Well let's buy the kids clothes." She'd say, "No we don't need to buy them anything; they're growing." . . . She bought herself stuff . . . but my dad was really supportive.

I mentioned my grandfather passing away and my grandmother moved in. Well, and she was deaf-mute, but she was a sweetheart. I just loved her. . . . My grandmother . . . was just warm and loving and supportive. . . . Even though I couldn't tell her everything that was going on . . . she hugged me and called me "baby." But she moved in, and that created another conflict.

My dad, even though he was a wonderful person, my dad had schizophrenia. He had a nervous breakdown in the Navy. . . . There are people in my family who have mental illness . . . But his experiences with the Navy brought it out. His last six months in were spent in a mental hospital in the Navy. Well, when he got out, he met my mom, and he married her, and she had these personality disorders. . . . She . . . used anything as a weapon. Well, my dad would not let her use corporal punishment, so she did it with mental and emotional abuse, you know—anything that wouldn't leave a mark. But . . . in school—so, all this happened, and my dad, of course, with my grandmother there, he was paranoid that she was watching it. So that created another conflict, and we're in these tiny, three rooms. I'm trying to go to school. I'm catching hell at school. I can't go out . . . "These bullies will bother me, and I gotta, gotta be nice. . . . I have to be a credit to the race."

But the good thing was, my new friends, Myrna and Glenda and Alfreda, were so accepting of me, so kind. I just dove into my studies. I spent every waking moment studying. The way I escaped was to go to the library. . . . I read everything.

My dad didn't have much money; but one of the White merchants on Sixth Street had a daughter who was about my age. I guess my dad had told him I needed clothes. Well she sold me her whole wardrobe for twenty-five dollars. And my dad paid, even down to the socks, everything. Really, awesome clothes. . . . So all of a sudden, I had all these clothes. . . . I was sharp. (Laughing.) I was sharp every day now. You know I had had that one dress. . . . All of these all at once. . . . My mother wouldn't do my hair, so my dad started . . . taking me to the beauty shop. The beauty shop was within walking distance . . . So dad was just my support team.

I threw myself into my studies, which I enjoyed. I started making the honor roll. At East Side, the honor roll was a big thing. They would have . . . these assemblies, and everybody who made honor roll had to come up on stage, and you had these huge buttons. It was . . . school colors were blue and white. We were the hornets. . . . I would bring it home to my dad; he was so proud of it. But I started noticing my buttons started going missing. He was wearing them on his suit to church. (Laughing.) "Honor roll," you know. And if you got it for the whole semester, you got this certain charm. And so he would wear my charms. He was so proud. . . . My dad . . . was so proud of me. . . . I had relatives, too, who were supportive; but there were other relatives who were not. One in particular said, "Well it's easy for you . . ." He said, "Well, I got on the honor roll too when I was in junior high, but when you get to high school, it's gonna be different. You're not gonna do it." Well when I got to high school, I kept it up. You know, he stopped speaking to me.

I have to admit, I did some self-promotion. . . . The people in the neighborhood, old ladies—who were like maids and janitors . . . would say, "Baby, I'm praying for you. How are you doing?" . . . "How are you doing?" And any time I was selling . . . candy bars and all, "Baby I don't want"—or magazines—"I don't want that, but here, baby, you take this, and just use this as a donation, baby." . . . They would pull out wrinkled up dollars . . . "Baby you take this, this is all I got; but you take this. . . . Baby, I'm praying."

I didn't even know what prayer meant. Even though my dad went to church, he never took us . . . I think that my mom didn't want us to go. And so he wouldn't go against her . . . I had neighbors who would come over and . . . essentially talk to me about . . . Jesus and all. That meant nothing to me. . . . Well, Hattie came down and said, "I want you to get with my daughter, she's about your age." Turns out her daughter and my cousin, Michael, were friends. I started hanging with them. She took me to church, and that's when I joined church. And my dad was proud of that. He went to my baptism; my mom didn't. She called church people "church-asses" . . . and that didn't endear me to her.

My dad . . . was being harassed at work. . . . He and mom were invited to this picnic. . . . One of the other supervisors . . . painted two chairs black and said, "That's where you two sit." . . . He was working really long hours . . . I don't know the details of it, but my mom had my dad committed to Fort Roots VA Hospital. She said, "Oh, your dad had a nervous breakdown." Well I never saw any evidence of that. . . . He was angry about that. He was in Fort Roots my second semester. He was the only person who would support me, and he wasn't there . . . and she started running around . . . with men. She was never there. She was supposed to come and pick me up from school; she'd come there drunk . . . She was always abusive anyway. . . . My dad was essentially a disabled veteran. [He] got money sent; and I found out later, my brother and I got allotments, but we never saw them . . . The good thing about it, my grandmother was there. So you know, it was just God's providence . . . my grandmother was there. My mom just kind of went off . . .

How long was your dad in the hospital?

Only two months; but when he got back, he was so angry with her. . . . He would beat her and ask her, "Bitch, why did you, why did you have me committed?" . . . The most embarrassing thing for him was that he was considered legally incompetent. He tried to get a divorce, and he could not get a divorce. . . . My own mother was so angry that I was on the honor roll, that my dad was supportive. . . . After that's when she had my dad committed. . . . I really dove into my studies. . . . She treated me like an enemy up until she died.

Our house was chaos. It was chaos at school, chaos at home. I escaped to the library. I started visiting my friends—Alfreda, Myrna, and Glenda—on Saturdays. I did whatever I could to be away from all of that . . . I would catch the bus and spend the Saturdays with them, and it would upset Freda's mom. Freda had chores. (Laughing.) And she would say "Don't you have chores?" Well, no. My mom never taught me anything. She never . . . I didn't know how to do anything. So I said, "No, I didn't have chores." I was never taught anything . . . none of those skills, and if I asked her she said, "I don't know" or "You should learn that at school." . . . Well, I started learning from my friends. . . . I started watching how they did things . . . and the books. I learned to such an extent that we had an open house at homeroom and this White girl said, "We want you to greet people. Your manners are so good." But . . . I had read the Miss Manners and the etiquette on what you should do . . . I realized that I could read, and find that out . . . So that was part of my first year.

In the classroom, I did well. . . . The teachers, they were okay. I had this one instructor, he was asking something about—I don't know if it was Booker T. Washington, George Washington Carver. . . . He asked a question. I said something, and he said I was wrong. These boys in front said, "You don't even know anything about . . . your own," and they were laughing at me in class. But I knew I was right. So I didn't say anything. So, the next day he [the teacher] came back. His face was red; he said, "I looked it up, and you were right." Yes. "You were right . . ." I loved to study. . . . Other teachers would . . . make snide remarks, but . . . my comeback was that I was a good student. In fact my first . . . six weeks . . . I had straight As and had only one B, and that B was in gym. (Laughs.) That B was in gym. I believe it was a B plus; and I believe she gave me a B plus so I couldn't have straight As. . . . The home economics teacher . . . called me aside, Mrs. [name witheld], called me aside, she said, "I want you to see something." She showed me my report card before it was, and she was so proud for a moment, and then she happened to look at me like, "Oh, you're Black." You know what I mean, and then her face changed. You know, she was proud of me as a student, and it was all, it was like she remembered, "Oh you're the enemy . . . I'm congratulating you." . . . She said, "She could have given you an A–, she could have so you could have straight As"; and then she looked at me, it was like, she, it clicked, "Oh, she's Black . . ."

One thing that . . . really changed the atmosphere that second semester. . . . The principal . . . had a local pastor, and I think it was like from Second Baptist Church or . . . a church that was nearby . . . The pastor would come in and preach messages to the whole student body . . . about loving and, and being kind. I would look around at the White students, and they looked ashamed. . . . He would talk to the whole student body, and gradually the atmosphere changed in the school . . . changed to be very positive. So, by the ninth grade, things were so positive . . . But that first year was like hell. . . . I believe I was just twelve years old . . . I believe the prayers of those washer women and my grandmother . . . and my dad, those prayers carried me. I don't know how I made it. I should have lost my mind, but I did not—and family who stuck up for me. So I understand how these kids are when they are bullied. . . . Bullies . . . pick on the people who they feel are going to make it. . . . So the only way they could stop me was to stop my mind . . . But it was the prayers of all those older people, and encouragement that carried me through.

You mentioned one young man who was in your classroom . . . who bullied you . . . and then the big guys that did it. . . . Did their behavior ever calm down?

After these . . . assemblies where we had the minister, they did. . . . School got better. . . . Overall, I thought they handled it well. Our school was so small that the school board was actually on the first floor, and we were on the second and the third floor. Most of the teachers were really good, impartial. They were okay.

In the seventh grade, the National Rifle Association gave shooting lessons at the school . . . My little twelve-year-old mind, I thought, "They're practicing to shoot Black people." I said, "You know what, if somebody's gonna shoot at me, then I'm gonna know how to shoot at them," so I signed up. I was the only Black person. When I showed up, they about fell over. And they had to do it! They had opened it up to everybody. . . . So that's another experience.

Another one was that I had problems; I didn't realize I was nearsighted until they tested at school. So, I got glasses and, and dad—of course he was the only one working, mom wasn't working—got my glasses from Dr. Townsend [African American optometrist and later an Arkansas state legislator]. It was my first time meeting him, and so I was impressed with him. It was just a very positive thing. Had I not gone to East Side, there [are] just an array of people I never would have met. So I met him, got my glasses, and so . . . I could see. . . . I was dressing well; I was learning how to take care of myself.

There was one thing they had at Dunbar Junior High School. They had this community meeting, Blacks and Whites, and they were going to talk about . . . race relations and how they could improve race relations. So . . . I got up there with my big mouth, and I said something about—and I was starting to get really militant. . . . we . . . had studied slavery and a lot of the White kids were feeling sad about it. . . . I got up . . . and I said, "You know, these White kids, you know, they're ashamed of slavery." I said, "We're the ones that should be ashamed of slavery we let it happen." . . . These White people said, "Well you don't like us." . . . One of the Black leaders interrupted before I could say, "Why should I like you? Why should I like you after . . ."—you know we were little kids, we had gone through hell just going to school . . . So that was something I'm kind of ashamed that I said; but I was getting militant . . . So that was a first year . . .

The students were nice, most of them, after they started calming down. And it wasn't everybody . . . it was these thugs. . . . I started catching the bus. These same thugs were riding in the car and yelled out, "There goes that good looking Nigger," and I thought "What? What's up with that?" . . . So after that, they were coming on to me. . . . I wasn't into all that. It just puzzled me. . . . I don't know if, if they just wanted my attention all that time with their harassment, I don't know. . . . I certainly wasn't interested.

One girl I really liked, Glenda Cale, she was on the honor roll. . . . I was in the Beta Club and the National Honor Society and . . . took Latin; so I was in all the honors stuff. And, well, those kids were okay. . . . They were in a different type of group, and they were okay. And Glenda Cale, I always thought, was really nice to me. Well, anybody who didn't call me names, I thought, was nice to me. We had these tournaments . . . and I think we went to Southwest for . . . volleyball tournaments, and people running track, and all of that.

I was [a] horrible athlete. I don't know why they chose me. I think it was my class . . . although I was pretty good at basketball. I played basketball with my cousins, so I was pretty good at basketball. In addition, Freda was a great athlete, so we did a lot of that. And that was very positive. . . . One negative thing is that Glenda and I went to—I don't know if, I think it was at Southwest—it was like a tournament, and it was just me and Glenda, and we were the only two Blacks of the group, but we wanted to see this basketball game. . . . These White boys high up in the bleachers started showering us with ice. There was nobody sitting around us. People moved out of the way . . . there was no place we could go. That was another time I prayed, "God help." An instructor came around and stopped them.

We got on the . . . newspaper staff. We were asked to join, and Mrs. Harper, who was a wonderful lady—she was the best teacher—she was the sponsor. The goal was to do interviews. So I interviewed teachers, and so that was very positive. It was me, Glenda, and Myrna who were on the paper staff. So we did that, and the students were very nice. I even went to . . . they had a conference at . . . Hendrix Teacher's College.

I . . . was the only Black who went there, but I went with a couple of the other girls . . . I always overdressed. I was dressed in this suit that had overlaid lace . . . but it had a couple of spots . . . So they said, "Ooh, we like that." Then they started picking it apart, "Oh you got this, you got that . . ." These were students . . . They were . . . started picking it apart. So I kind of . . . ignored them. But one thing, you know, that [was] very positive from my mother's experience—I told you about her negativity—I learned how to tune her out. I was used to being abused; I was used to verbal abuse. So, when I went to East Side, and got all that verbal abuse, I was used to it . . . And I knew how to just tune them out. And essentially . . . what my mom did made me tougher. . . . I cried easily, you know, and I'm still tenderhearted. But if something comes at me, I go inward.

Another thing—I got tunnel vision. I was determined. I was gonna finish school, I was going to do the best I could. I wasn't so much hung up on grades. I was going to be a credit to my people. Nobody was going to be able to blame me for stopping anything . . . So when he said that, I was focused. And plus, my association with . . . especially Myrna and I were really close . . . Her family . . . was better educated, and I learned from watching her—learned from watching and listening to the others.

I had said I promoted myself. When . . . all these older ladies were [saying], "I'm praying for you, I'm praying for you," and I thought, "Well, they should know how I'm doing. Well, how am I gonna tell them all?" . . . I was in the journalism club. Now I decided to write articles about myself, and put them in the Black newspaper . . . my pictures, my class picture. "Well they gotta know who it is." . . . Every time I got some kind of honor or something, I would write an article about myself, take my picture, and they would publish it in the newspaper. I wasn't doing it [because] I wanted people to applaud me. It was [because] all these older ladies had encouraged me, and I wanted them to know how I was doing. So I thought, well they should all know. Whenever I got on honor society, got [on the] honor roll, was elected to some office, whenever I did anything good, I would put it in the paper. Well . . . that didn't sit well with my mom either, but it sat well with my dad. He would get all the papers and he'd cut all the articles out and send them to all the relatives.

I was the only one in the East End that first year . . . Second year there were two more people, Jeanette Abraham and Versa Williams, and we carpooled. By the time I got to Central, there were so many Blacks from the East End at Central. My daughter actually was supposed to go to Central. And she was like, "Oh no, mom, I don't want go to Central. There are too many folks from the East End there." I'm from the East End! But they were able to continue, and they were able to go there.

It was important that we did what we did. And I said that of my background, of that abuse from my mom, I developed a mental toughness. That, and if somebody challenged me . . . I'm not the kind of person who would confront them, I'm not going to fight, but I do it in my own way. I'm not going to let you win. I'm not going to let you say, "Oh, you're gonna lose." You know, the moment you tell me I'm going to lose, that's when I really dig in my heels. So [student's name withheld] and all these guys, all they did was motivate me. I dug in my heels and I did really well. In fact . . . by our ninth grade, it was so peaceful in the school. . . . It was just a wonderful school to be in. And there was racial harmony.

So, the plan was a success at East Side Junior High School. I think Larry Davis had a problem with fighting some boys jumping him or something happened. But . . . I think he was gone the first or second semester; but after that, it was mostly girls . . . We did okay. I only had one incident where I borrowed the textbook of this girl, and I flipped through it. She was in the grade ahead of me, and I gave it back to her. She said I didn't give it back to her and I owed her money for the book. And I was worried about that, and how I'm gonna get money, so this other Black girl, and I don't know her name, stood up and said, "No, you've got that book!" And she went over there and picked it up. She said, "Here it is!" The White girl said, "Oh, you know I was just joking." I never spoke to that girl again.

And another incident that happened in the ninth grade: you know we had our class pictures and so . . . these White girls . . . you know, the popular ones, you know the beauty queens and all of that—so they wanted my picture, so I handed it to them. . . . I didn't know what they were going to do . . . So this guy—he was like the popular, "Mr. Big," you know, the athlete—came to me. I was leaving gym, he handed me my picture, and he told me, "They gave me this picture. They were thinking," he said. "They thought it was a joke." He said, "But I think you're just the most beautiful person in the world." And I thought, "Wow!" I said, "Thank you." And he said, "Here's your picture back." He said, "Don't worry about them." So that was really nice of him. . . . He was one of those really popular guys. . . . So it was things like that, the students were really nice . . .

I got some exposure to some other students—so, and overall . . . it was very positive for me coming from the East Side, never knowing that any of these things existed. And I met some really cool people. [We] eventually moved . . . from the East End to the West End. Dad was asking me one day about my friends, and I said, "Dad, all my friends' families own their own homes," and we were in this three-room duplex . . . and he said, "I gotta get my baby a house." . . . And when we . . . moved out of the East End, that's when things just really blossomed for me. That's when I met Mrs. Bates. I joined the NAACP. Myrna introduced me to Girl Scouts. I joined Girl Scouts with her. . . . We were talking about extracurricular. . . . There were a lot of things we could not do in school. I know Freda wanted to be a cheerleader, and they wouldn't let her. And she also wanted to run track, but they wouldn't let women do that. That never was important to me. I had no concept of junior high school. Neither of my parents had gone there. I had no concept. Nobody had told me what to expect. So I knew that I was going to study. . . . But Myrna introduced me to Mrs. Rush, whose husband had a liquor store in the East End . . . so I joined Girl Scouts . . . all Black, and so a lot of support there. . . . So that kind of released the stress. . . . I spent a lot of time with my new friends, and my family situation calmed down. So the eighth grade and ninth grade were really good. . . . and when I went to high school, Glenda introduced me to the NAACP and I met [Mr. and Mrs.] Bates. We did a voter drive . . . where we'd canvass all of Little Rock. The youth council . . . went to every house—they had voted down the poll tax . . . But it all started from East Side. . . . and my meeting these gals, and their introducing me to people.

And then . . . Hattie Peer took me to church. And . . . when I went to church, it was like heaven. People were nice. People were kind. I got in the choir. . . . I still spent as much time as possible away from home. But . . . I wasn't escaping; there was so much to do. . . . I met people at Girl Scouts. I met people at NAACP. And, you know, they always had some kind of meeting going on. And so it was just a great experience for me. In addition, I noticed my mother would back off . . . There was nothing to pick on. . . . I was a good student.

All these things kept you away from home . . .

Kept me away from home. I was with positive people. Mrs. Bates got me a job when I was seventeen. . . . I was on the Pix Staff, the yearbook staff, in high school. . . . High school was a very happy time for me. . . . I did really well in school. . . . I . . . think I was . . . number thirty-one or something like that, in a class of six hundred. . . . Central High School.

But to get back to junior high school . . . The school did so well. It was a pleasure going to school. By that time other kids were coming. . . . We did so well that what came next was a surprise. When we graduated from East Side, the school board ruled that—this is freedom of choice—they assigned us to high schools according to where we lived. They did not give us free choice as before. So that meant that every one of us except one was going back to Black schools. . . . Glenda was the only one to be assigned to Central.

We had to appeal. And that's another thing that happened that summer of our—after ninth grade—we all showed up at the school board, and we were each interviewed, and, I don't even remember the questions. . . . We had to go there with a parent, and I don't remember which parent went with me. . . . We had to essentially tell them why we wanted to go to Central. . . . And that's how I ended up at Central. But I was willing to go to Horace Mann . . . It was just too traumatic. Even though the last years at East Side were wonderful.

I still remember, and it damages you. And we were twelve years old . . . it was damaging. . . . I realize that now . . . and I just wanted to be normal . . . I was always popular at school. I just wanted to be normal . . . So I went ahead, and went to Central. You know it was the best decision for me.

You talked a little bit earlier about some of the strengths and resources . . . you had to complete your education. Some came out of the pain that you experienced . . . others might have been those innate resources.

Plus, a big thing too—a support system. There were people who supported me. And even just a kind word, just a hug—my dad was a big part of that . . . We were in a duplex, right next door were cousins . . .

and so they were very supportive. . . . A big extended family. . . . Very protective, very kind. They never really asked me what was going on; they were just kind.

And the praying washer women.

Praying, and sometimes my mother would—even before all this— she would say something somebody would overhear. They would confront her about it . . . and she'd say "I don't care, I . . ." this that or the other. They'd [say], "Well you shouldn't say this that or the other." So, yeah, they'd confront. They witnessed a lot of that stuff, and they were just very supportive . . . Any child needs that support, but especially if you're going through a traumatic situation. And they're not going to all talk. They're not going to say it. . . . I was used to keeping things inside. In fact, I started, really, a nervous habit: talking to myself. But I think it was a precursor to—I think I was really talking to God. And I'd be walking down the street, and there was nobody else I could talk to, and I would just talk. And some of these older women would say, "Baby, I saw you talking to yourself. I guess you just stressed. You just stressed." And . . . Mrs. Peer started taking me to church. One night my folks got in this big fight. I called her in tears, and she said, "Put 'em on the phone." So she gave them a piece of her mind, and they stopped. . . . And I had a cousin who came from Texas. I told you he sent all of these pictures out. . . . I wanted piano lessons, and in the sixth grade, I started piano lessons. And so she came, and I played the piano for her, and she said, "Baby, how're you doing?" You know, and just talked to me. And she sat with my parents and told them, "You two you need to stop this. This baby trying to do something. You don't know what kind of stuff she's going through, and you just need to quit it." And when she left they [said], "Oh she drunk." That . . . was what they said, "Oh, she drunk." . . . So people would confront them about it.

Another thing that happened—the teachers at Carver Elementary School had me come that first year and talk at the PTA meeting. It's the first time I found out I could speak before crowds, when they invited me, and they would ask me about what was going on. . . . There were parents and students there, and I really believe that was why Jeanette Abraham and Versa Williams actually started the school the next year. . . . They . . . would be really supportive. . . . People would tell me, "Baby, you're doing great, we're really proud of you," et cetera . . .

Another person in the East End—all I know is this man was called Mr. Booker—he was the plumber . . . Dad would use his services. We had the apartment complex. Mr. Booker had a nice house. And so, when my mom kind of went wild, Mr. Booker's wife confronted my mom and told her, if she didn't straighten up, she was gonna call, I guess it's human services . . . and have us taken away from her. So, that calmed her down . . .

So the community was sort of . . . policing the situation . . . They would allow a little chaos but they weren't going to let it blow up too much?

Yes, so people confronted her . . . The community stepped in. They couldn't change her behavior. But they stepped in, and they were just wonderful.

That's really awesome. . . . They didn't make a report, but they did everything they could.

They confronted her. And my family confronted her.

Which kept you all together, the family as a unit.

Yeah, kept the family together.

I don't think that I've heard anyone quite say it the way you did with regard to having experienced all of that emotional abuse . . . You said you gained some strengths that allowed you to make it through . . . East Side.

Yeah, my whole life. And I don't think that was her intent. . . . I'd ask her why she would do that, and she said, "Well you stopped me from having fun." She resented me. . . . Her family realized that too. But it had an upside to it: I had learned early on to tune it out. And I decided early on that I was not going to be like that. . . . I tried to win my mother's love by being nice. . . . She blamed me for everything. So I made sure—and that's where my perfectionism came, too—I was going to act perfect. I was going to be perfect, and then she was gonna love me. But you know it had the opposite effect. She hated me for it. . . . But I was not going to be that kind of woman. . . . I tried to be good, I tried to be pleasant. . . . I wanted to please everyone. I was a pleaser. . . . I wanted people to like me, but truth was, I really liked people; that was my personality. I think that my going to East Side was pivotal in my life. I would not change it for a minute, I developed a lot of strengths, I had strengths. There were things in me that I didn't know I had. I didn't know that . . . I could block out . . . what I saw, all of that abuse and harassment, it was like noise. So I could focus, and when I focused, that was like calm. There was a piece of me I could get to that blocked all of that out, and that has served me throughout my life . . . I hope I taught my children that. . . . I never wanted them to go through what I went through.

What recommendations would you have for parents who were thinking about placing their child in a situation where they would be a minority, whether it's race, or whether it's any other type of situation?

Sit down and be frank with the child. You know you don't have to frighten them, but tell them the truth, and tell them . . . what to expect. . . . If you don't know what to expect, do some fact finding. . . . What do parents need to do to prepare their child for any situation where they will be a minority . . . ? My answer to that is preparation. Find out as much as you can . . . and nowadays there's a lot more information—psychological, social, what to do, and especially now that they're talking about bullying. That's what happened to me, I was bullied . . . Don't be surprised that if your child does well that some people that you expect to be supportive may not be. You have to teach them how to respond to envy. Give them places where they can be a child . . . extracurricular activities. Be a family; be supportive. They may or may not want to talk about it. It may just be too painful. You don't have to talk about it. . . . One of the best supports I had was someone who couldn't talk. It was my grandmother. She was hearing impaired, but she was very loving. She loved me. She'd see that I was troubled, and, and she'd put her hands on my face, she'd kiss me; she'd hug me. I could not explain to her the pain. . . . I never really spoke about what was going on, but she could see it. . . . That nonverbal, just the concern on her face and the hugs . . . And my family, my extended family, often times they wouldn't say anything. They knew. . . . Just having someone sit with you, be kind to you . . .

I know a lot's going on these days with . . . our kids, and they're under a lot of pressure. . . . They don't know if they go out, if they're gonna come home again. They're traumatized. So what do you do? A traumatized person doesn't need a lecture. They're using every bit of energy they can to get through what they need to get through. You know, they may not do it right. . . . Things may come out that may sound inappropriate. I had . . . one cousin get upset . . . I didn't get upset that . . . something had happened to someone. But I was in survival mode. When you're in survival mode, emoting is a luxury you don't have. If you see something happening, you may feel sorry for the person, but you don't have the luxury of being hysterical or crying or, "Oh, I'm so sorry!" It's like . . . that's a luxury that you don't have. You're using every ounce of emotional strength you have just to be sane, to keep going. So don't expect them to act normal. They're in survival mode . . . and in essence, it's post-traumatic stress disorder, although you're still going through it . . . So treat it like that. They're going through; you be supportive. Don't expect them to talk about it. Maybe fifty years later they'll talk about it . . . I didn't have the vocabulary to talk about what I was feeling. I did not have the vocabulary, and so I did everything on how I felt . . . So do that, and if they're sane, and halfway talk right, just be nice to them. . . . Be nice to them. . . . But . . . just being kind and being loving goes a long way.

How do you think your desegregation of that junior high school influenced the city, the state, and even the nation?

Oh, lots of ways. . . . I'm friends with Whites on Facebook that I went to junior high school with. When I went through that situation, there were kids after I graduated, would come around, "Hey, how are you doing?" You know, would be friends. We educated them . . . probably just being ourselves.

I had one young man ask me—well, he's not young anymore . . . he wanted to know if I was traumatized at Central. I said, "No . . . Central was just the best time ever." He apologized for any abuse or anything that I suffered from their reactions. But I think we made a positive impact on the people who were around, the teachers . . . And I don't think that the school board expected us to do as well. Why would they have to change their policy? I don't think they expected a lot of people to sign up for it, so they would have an excuse not to implement the plan. And then when we signed up for it. I credit the . . . leadership of the school for bringing in that pastor. The religious leaders, people were willing to . . . talk about it. But it was our bodies on the line . . . our minds on the line. We were front line. They did support us, but when we were in there, we were really in there by ourselves.

I think it had a positive effect on the racial climate for Little Rock . . . on just the kids following along behind us. . . . It could have been much worse, or we could have decided not to go at all. I think . . . it was intimidating. That's why everybody didn't sign up for it. . . . You had to be a certain type of student. So . . . that student who would have defended himself, they didn't have that. . . . I'd like to think that we impacted, even having Obama in the office. It was like a pebble dropped in the pond, you know. It changed people from generation to generation to generation. And a lot of my White schoolmates are very liberal . . . the ones from Central and East Side . . . I think a lot of other kids realized it too, later. . . .

In high school, Mrs. Harper was the first Black teacher there, and she got a really good reception . . . at Central. She taught English. . . . A lot of good things happened for me, and I think good things happened for the community. . . . I'm really grateful that people came behind us. They just didn't let it drop. We passed the baton, they grabbed it, and they kept going. . . . It took a lot of courage for us to do that.

When my father passed away, there were people . . . who were from the East End, and they were asking if I knew someone and I said, "Oh, I don't remember." They [said], "Oh, you don't remember anyone." Well, you know I was traumatized. I said to a family member who recently married a cousin . . . "I'm lucky I know my own name." She said, "What you guys did was so important . . ." So it makes me feel good about [it], and it was a sacrifice. . . . I think we really impacted—and I may be overstating it, but it sure felt that way, you know. And . . . we weren't the only ones. There were, I liked to call them "soldiers," all over the US. You know, child in the first grade doing that. That takes a tremendous amount of courage . . . Another thing too . . . whatever their belief, they need to take the child to church. That place is where you really get the strength. You have people who will pray for you. You have people who will be nice to you. . . . I know everybody isn't a believer, but that is really what carried me over . . . It took a higher power. Nobody that I knew of had that kind of power. Nobody. . . . I believed that as a child and I thought, "Oh, they're bad; they got it going on." But when I started that school, that petrified a bunch of people, you know. So people talk; but you know . . . it really takes a lot of courage to—to act. . . . And I'm saying this for everyone, the rest of the twenty-five, you know. I am grateful that there were twenty-five. . . . Even though we may have looked passive from the outside, we were real warriors from the inside. It takes a real strength too . . . Anybody can talk. And not only that, when you are in a hostile environment—plus you still gotta study, you still gotta do your job—that takes a real strength; and I think that took God. No person has that kind of strength. And . . . you said "inherent," but . . . He placed it there. It came from someplace, but it didn't come from twelve-year-old me. I am grateful for the experience.

We . . . were young. We gave up a lot . . . We gave up the social life. Another thing too—after you've been immersed in that environment, when you go back to the Black environment, you're . . . you're at a loss . . . You haven't been—you've been socialized to survive. . . . I always have two dialogues: . . . what people say and what I interpret, and maybe everybody does that. But then you get in the Black community, and it's a different language, it's almost like you're in a foreign country. You're foreign there and you're foreign here; and the only time you're really at home are with people who've gone through your experience. . . . I don't know what parents can do there except to know that. . . . That's what a parent's job is, to interpret the world to their child. . . . To tell them how to react, what to expect . . . Just be a good parent.

Alfreda Brown

"Just passing through . . ."

[I am] Alfreda Brown. I grew up in Little Rock, Arkansas, and stayed there from birth until I came here to St. Louis in 1971. My parents were Alfred Brown—I was named after him as "Alfreda." . . . I wasn't a boy, so they just put an *a* on Alfred and made me "Alfreda." And then my mother's name was Priscilla Brown. . . . I grew up in Little Rock with three brothers and a sister. . . . The majority of my childhood was spent in an area called Granite Mountain, which was a housing project in Little Rock. . . . I discovered that has all been demolished . . . but that's where we spent most of our childhood. I . . . went to Granite Mountain Elementary School there—walked to school from . . . our apartment and just had some fond memories of growing up in the projects, even though there were challenges. We were able to, I think, have a good experience there, even with the challenges in the projects. From . . . Granite Mountain my parents purchased a home on West Twenty-Sixth Street, in Little Rock. That's where . . . most of my junior high and high school days were spent. I remember when I was at Granite Mountain Elementary School—evidently that's when they sent out notices that the junior high schools were being desegregated. . . . I'm not sure how I got the application. I think it must have been one of my teachers, maybe Ms. Chappell. I don't know if I filled it out or who—my mother, somebody, parents had to be involved. But I do remember my mother not wanting me to go. . . . She always felt that it was not necessary for people of color—African Americans, or what we were called, "Negroes," back in those days—to have to sit next to a White person in order to get a good education. She said all we needed was opportunity for employment and the same opportunities that White people had. Sitting in a classroom with them, to her, was not something that she was in favor of. . . . So it was not with her encouragement that . . . I evidently applied for and was selected to go into East Side Junior High. And in fact, she was not happy about it when I was selected.

What about your dad?

Oh, that's an interesting question. . . . Nothing registers in my mind right now in terms of his thinking behind it. I think both of them felt very strongly about education, and that . . . all five of us . . . should finish high school. And I think there was just the assumption of going on to college. My father only got as far as the tenth grade in school. . . . My mother did have a high school education. . . . She had always wanted to go to college, and was a very bright person . . . just naturally . . . gifted intellectually. . . . I'm not sure how my father felt about it, but I do remember my mother being very vocal about it not being necessary for Black people to have to go and sit next to a White person in order to advance. "Just give us the opportunities," is what she always said.

Whose decision was it for you to actually get there to East Side?

(Laughs.) Mine. And now that you ask me the question, I have no idea what prompted that. Even with my mother not encouraging it. I don't know, at that early age. . . . I'm not quite sure what was the motivating force behind it. It could have been the fact it was a selection process, and not every person in my class . . . was selected. And I think it was rather communicated to us either directly or indirectly that students who only scored a certain score . . . But it was clear that not everyone was going to be able to go. The other thing that may have prompted it subconsciously that—you are making me recall some of this; thank you very much!—you had said that this was going to happen.

I probably was still in the elementary school when this happened, but one of my cousins, Thelma Mothershead, was among the first . . . to integrate Little Rock Central High. I remember, as a child sitting in front of the television watching the National Guards and . . . Governor Faubus, watching my cousin with the other Little Rock Nine, walking into Little Rock Central High. And man that was . . . very emotional. . . . I think it probably sent a message to me that this was an important thing to do. . . . That the separation of the students was not right. And that if people, Negroes . . . were really going to advance, then the education had to be a part of it. And so even though I felt I had wonderful experiences at Granite Mountain Elementary School, and had wonderful teachers . . . we just had a wonderful time there . . . It never felt—and, of course I didn't have anything to compare it with, so I wouldn't know whether or not it was inferior or not . . . but, evidently it was okay . . .

What made those teachers and that experience wonderful . . . ?

The teachers were all very caring. . . . Back in those days there weren't really that many professions that people of color who didn't want to work at the post office . . . or do manual labor—nursing and education were probably the two professions that we could probably aspire to. So what we had, in my opinion, were probably very dedicated—mostly women, I had one man, Mr. Wood—teachers, just committed to us. . . . When I remember going to school there . . . it was challenging. We did creative things. So when you ask, "What made it so wonderful?" it's clearly the teachers and the whole building of people, adults dedicated to making sure we were safe and well educated. We . . . just had some really good experiences at school. . . . There's one class where I wish I had paid more attention to: word attack or something like that. I still have problems with that. But . . . I think . . . I did okay. I wasn't clearly the smartest kid in the class, but I wasn't the dumbest either.

What do you think your parents did to prepare you to attend a primarily all-White school . . . ?

You know, I cannot think of anything, in terms of instructions . . . like "you don't do this," or "you don't do that." . . . A lot of what I think you learned . . . came from listening . . . listening to things that were going on, like on the television. I already talked about the desegregation of Central High with the Little Rock Nine, and hearing people talk about how people talked about people of color and "Negroes" in that time. And so I think subconsciously you, sort of as a child began—and I'm sort of speculating on this—you started thinking in terms of not doing those things that they are critical of. So if "colored people" were depicted in a certain way, you tried as hard as you could not to . . . feed that . . . myth . . . in some cases, or that perception. . . . One of the things that I remembered . . . we put a lot of emphasis on was appearance.

When you say "we," who was that?

I think in terms of preparation. . . . My parents perhaps, made sure that I was dressed appropriately. . . . I never remember anybody saying this, but I'm sure that there were resources, dollars spent, for my attire, so that I didn't look like a . . . a throwaway child, and that I was probably dressed for attending the school . . . I even looked at . . . our junior high school picture and looked at all of the students of color, and couldn't help but to notice how well dressed we were . . . in those pictures. And so that just sort of fed into that idea . . . that . . . appearance was really very important. The hair, how your hair looked, how you're dressed, and that whole type of thing. . . . Your preparation and academic preparation; that was pretty much self-motivation.

Do you . . . remember attending any meetings . . . from the community or . . . other organizations . . . being involved with that preparation?

Yes, you're absolutely right. . . . I remember going to Philander Smith College, and they had discussion groups . . . I'm not sure who led those groups. . . . I grew up about maybe three blocks from Daisy Bates's house. She was . . . president of the NAACP during the time of the Little Rock desegregation. . . . She may have been involved helping to coordinate some of those support groups. And I would call them today support groups, and that would stand to reason that she . . . had some experience, and working with the kids who desegregated Little Rock Central High, and using that knowledge and experience . . . to try to prepare those of us who were beginning to go into the junior high setting. So that we would go in, hopefully, with some realistic expectations. . . . There were—thank you for reminding me of that—there were groups where we attended some meetings and they talked about certain things.

What was your experience or interaction with the White community . . . ?

For those who . . . grew up during the time when Granite Mountain existed, it was a low-income housing project, and it was all Black. There were no Whites there. . . . I can't get my directions. I think it may have been south of the central part of Little Rock, and it was south of the railroad track, and the bridge; so you had to go quite a bit of distance . . . to get to Granite Mountain. It was almost as if it was on a reservation outside of the city proper—Little Rock. . . . We were really truly isolated. . . . Everybody there, everybody, was Black. The only exposure that I had as an elementary school child was my church. I belonged to and grew up in the . . . Christian Church, Disciple of Christ. . . . My grandmother was a Disciple of Christ . . . my mother and then I joined. And they had youth programs that brought together youth from all over the state of Arkansas. . . . I served on . . . different groups, committees, panels, went to summer camp, and things, and they were all integrated. So my exposure to people who were not Negroes or African Americans or Black primarily initially came from my church experiences. . . . So that was . . . the interaction before going to East Side.

And my history of the Disciple of Christ religion is that . . . I think it was on the forefront of a very progressive, very liberal . . . My mother went to her high school days. Actually she went to Mississippi . . . I am connected to the Disciple of Christ Church through my grandmother on my mother's side. My grandmother's parents, when they died, I think they had nine children. And each child got property. Each child was willed property. Land that, unfortunately, we are in the process of selling now. And I do say unfortunately. But then when I look at this generation, and I ask, how could people who were probably only a few years outside of slavery acquire that much property, so that they could leave their children—who was my grandmother—property, and I thought to myself, what a shame that we as people of color seem to be going backwards instead of forward. And I attribute it, whatever my great-grandparents did, to their faith . . . to their faith. That gave them the discipline, to . . . that gave them whatever it takes I think, in order to move forward in life, and to be able to leave something for your offspring so, hopefully, they can leave something for their offspring. . . . I really like to attribute . . . in the faith, through a progressive religion that encouraged people to get an education, encouraged people to think for themselves, and not just be puppets of their environments . . . When I left Little Rock Central High, which is after I left . . . East Side, I went to Phillips University, which is in Enid, Oklahoma, which is part of our church.

Tell me about your experience of attending East Side Junior High. What stood out for you . . . in terms of your memories there?

One thing that I remember was . . . we had to meet with the counselor before school started to sign up for our classes. . . . I can't remember the counselor's name, but I remember going to her office, and my mother was with me. She said to me, probably a lot of things, but she did say that people like me would not do well at East Side. And I know I'm probably misquoting, but she let it be known that there were not great expectations for me to do well. I didn't interpret that at the time as a child as me as an individual but me as the group of people coming in, my classmates and all of us. That was my probably very first meeting at East Side Junior High, was the message from the counselor that I probably will not do well at East Side.

And this was before you ever attended the first day?

Yeah. This was registration. . . . I think for the most part, East Side was probably . . . I think . . . we rode the bus to school. I was still living in Granite Mountain when I started East Side, and I think soon . . . after I started East Side we moved to another location which was closer; but I think at the time I was still out at Granite Mountain. My parents—both parents—worked. . . . I remember one time . . . standing on the bus lot, and, with a group of my friends . . . Linda Brown . . . I remember Linda Brown living near Granite Mountain. She was with the group. We evidently were riding the bus back to Granite Mountain. . . . Some White boys came by. I don't remember if they were driving, although we were in junior high so they probably were not driving, but they came by and they started taunting us. They started calling us names. . . . Evidently it had been raining that day. I had an umbrella. One of them said something and I remember taking my umbrella and raising it, and stepping out from the group that was standing on the bus lot, and I think I gave him a few choice words. [I] told him what I was gonna do to him if he didn't leave us alone. That was my mother in me coming out. (Laughs.) . . . About that time, sure enough, my mother drove up and probably rescued us, and we all got in the car, and she . . . drove us home. . . . I remember not allowing myself to be intimidated, even though they were boys. I did not know that I wasn't supposed to take on boys. . . . I'm the oldest in my family and my brothers are next to me, so when I had to put them in line . . . I just figured it was another one of those opportunities. . . . That's the second memory. . . . There was another memory of . . . a little boy in class, singing the song about that blackbird to us and around us. I remember one time also, it was around Christmas time, we were baking, and I was in home economics class . . . We were learning how to bake, probably fruitcake. I remember feeling honored that our teacher had selected a group of us to bake and put together some extra fruitcakes. We were busy in the little home ec lab area putting these fruitcakes together, when I looked around, and I noticed that all of the students in the kitchen area were Black, and the teacher and the White students were back in the classroom. . . . I don't know if they were carrying on lessons or what. But there we were, the Black students, putting the fruitcakes together, while they were back in the classroom carrying on with the lesson. And that has stuck out in my mind for many years, how . . . suddenly the whole message was, "You're domestic workers. And this is your place, in the kitchen . . . and you are little girls of color, this is where you belong." The other event that stuck out in my mind was . . . my typing class. That was when . . . we learned about . . . President Kennedy being shot. I remember I was in my typing class, and the typing teacher came in and announced that he had been assassinated. . . . That happened while I was in junior high.

What stood out beyond the fact that he was assassinated . . . stood out for you about that experience?

Well, I think it was pretty universal sadness, with everybody, regardless of the color. The whole school, I think, was pretty shaken by it all. It may have been my first assassination. Little did I know that it was the beginning of . . . a new era . . . of those types of things happening . . . That was . . . pretty traumatic . . .

What was your level of participation in the extracurricular activities?

Now why did you want to go there? . . . One of the things that we realized early on—and it may have been part of the prep going into the environment or the situation—was that so much of extracurricular, especially for girls [was] based on . . . more on popularity. That is, you're selected to be on this squad or that squad, homecoming queen or princess this or princess . . . that based upon . . . your popularity. . . . Surely, those of us of color did not expect to win any popularity contests. That was not even part of [a] realm of possibility for us. So you didn't even set yourself up for that. But I can say that I think some of my colleagues did extremely well in extracurricular activities. I don't recall anything that I did, and this probably stems back to what I said earlier in terms of my intellectual abilities, natural abilities. I'm not the smartest nor the dumbest. I'm somewhere, I think, in the middle—at least that's where I like to put myself. So that meant that I probably had to spend a little bit more time [studying] than my colleagues and some of my colleagues were . . . absolutely brilliant. . . . It didn't take them as long to master certain things than perhaps it did me. And I say this also of my brother, who was maybe eighteen months behind me, and I think he also followed me for a short period of time over to East Side. His name was Layton O'Neill Brown. He is since deceased, but he was absolutely brilliant. I can recall times when he would—this was later on when we got older—would have a part-time job working at a restaurant and would come home. I would be studying all night long. . . . He'd come home, open the book, flip through the pages, go to bed. Wake up the next day and make an A (laughs). Yeah, I'm exaggerating, but that's what it looked like to me. But he was absolutely brilliant. And so I have a feeling that some of my friends who I went to East Side with were sort of in that same category. . . . That meant then that they had probably much more time that they could devote to doing extracurricular. I remember friends like Glenda Wilson . . . Equilla Banks was brilliant, as well as Glenda and Myrna. . . . All three of them were just absolutely brilliant. They did a lot of extracurricular things; but I pretty much stayed focused out of necessity, on my studies, and did not venture out too much. I don't remember anything that I did extracurricular. Maybe I was in the Beta Club or something like that, which was more of an academic type of thing.

I remember also the situation where we were in our gym class, and they were teaching us square dancing and we were told to sit in the bleachers. They didn't want the little Black girls dancing with the White boys in the gym class. . . . So we had to observe. (Laughs.) . . . We knew where we were and we knew . . . the time. . . .

You couldn't dance with each other?

No, no, no. They didn't want us touching. They didn't want us touching anybody.

So no after-school dances or any of those kinds of things?

No. And part of it, when you ask about the preparation for going . . . only a small number of students from my elementary school—I don't know how many students were selected to . . . integrate these schools. . . . I can only remember the numbers now for East Side [because] of the picture of our graduating class at least for the first group. . . . So the majority of my classmates that I went to elementary school with went on to Dunbar Junior High. Our extracurricular and social life followed them. . . . We still lived in the same neighborhoods, even though we were going to different schools. If we wanted—on the weekends—to go to a basketball game, or go to a dance, or a social, or whatever they called it back in those days, we would follow them. And we would try to stay in touch with what they were doing at the all-Black schools; that was our social outlet. But we definitely did not expect for it to be anything at the schools that we were attending. . . . So we welcomed that.

I want to ask you about any relationships that you may have formed with the White students. [Were there] any positive relationships that you had, or any interaction that you had with them that comes to mind?

Not that I can think of. . . . If any of them walked up to me today, I wouldn't know them. . . . I wouldn't know the teachers. I wouldn't know anybody from there.

Other than the home ec teacher, was there any other memory that you have about a teacher that appeared to stand out in your mind—constructive, destructive, or, in any kind of way?

I don't know why . . . and I don't have anything to compare it with, I don't know if other people my age recall. . . . After elementary school, you know, how many people they're still in touch with, how many teachers they still remember, or anything; but I don't remember any of the teachers . . . I mean, and the typing teacher only of what I told you earlier about, she being the one that walked into the room and pretty much announced what had happened to Kennedy. In terms of feeling close to her, or any of them, no, not at all; no, I don't. . . . I think some of them, maybe, tried as best as they could . . . to be impartial, and not show their . . . preferences for being in, maybe, in all-White schools or whatever; but I don't, I don't remember anybody doing anything that was just out-and-out evil, or mean or anything of that nature. It was sort of neutral.

What strengths or resources do you think helped you to get through junior high school?

Well, now that's a good question; and you know, being at that age, what are you gonna . . . you know. . . . I can only assume that it was my family, first of all, our values. . . . I think there was also in the back of my mind a sense of, a means to an end, that whatever . . . I experienced in junior high school was just, I was passing through. You know, it didn't, it was not going to define me one way or the other. It was part of the process that was necessary in order for me to get to the next level. Next level was high school, after high school it was college, after college it was graduate school. So it's part of the process.

What made you go on to Central, as opposed to Horace Mann?

That's a good question, and it's interesting. I hadn't thought about this until . . . (laughs) we started talking about . . . extracurricular activities, and the important role that my friends who did not attend East Side played in terms of providing a social outlet for us. And I do recall there was a point where many of us . . . felt like we were caught in the middle. We were not part of the White kids' social activities, and to a certain extent, we were not part of the Black kids' social experience. They were all together in school every day. They knew each other, saw each other, everything; and then here we show up on the weekend and want to be a part of that. So . . . there was a disconnect. I use that term "between," and yeah, so we were sort of "in the middle." We were not part of either group. . . . So what happened then after three years at East Side, we all bonded. We had to survive. . . . Another thing is that we ended up forming our own group in a sense, even though it was small—visiting each other's homes and becoming friends. And so by the time the third year rolled around [and] junior high school ended, we just automatically assumed that we were going to go on to Central. Well it turned out that not all of us did. And I don't know what criteria they used to determine which kids from East Side would go on to Central. But it wasn't automatic. And for some it was. And maybe again, it was based on test scores, I don't know. It seems to me that some of my friends were automatically assigned to Central. I think I was assigned to go to Horace Mann. . . . I don't know if I protested or my parents, but we had to file a formal protest in order to go, for me to continue at

Central High. . . . So at that point it was following the people that I knew and I had bonded with and that I was friends with. . . .

How did attending a primarily white junior high school, and then later high school, affect or influence your adult life, personally and professionally?

This is probably not true, but I'm gonna say it anyway. (Laughs.) I think I probably would have found a husband. I probably would have. I like to think that if I had gone to an all-Black school, I would have fallen in love with someone who was my color, and probably would have had a house full of children and been happily married by now, and, whatever. But I think . . . that social part of my development was retarded (laughs)—hindered, handicapped, whatever you want to say.

That's what I'm going to blame it on, whether or not the end results would have been the same, I don't know. . . . But I do know that one of the things that my mother in particular again—and my dad, I don't remember him weighing in . . . he worked so much, he probably didn't have time to talk very much about these types of things—but I remember my mother just saying . . . "Now you gonna be in school with these people"—and I had a cousin who married outside of our race, and she knew I idolized this cousin . . . and she was much older—and she made it very clear (laughs) to me, on many occasions, and I think I had on some black patent leather shoes at one time, getting ready to go somewhere, and she said, "You see those shoes you got on?" . . . She said (laughs), "Don't bring anybody into my house that doesn't look like those shoes." . . . And (laughs) and so those were very strong messages to me that . . . in terms of socializing, that I was to stay within those boundaries. . . . Unfortunately, many of the young people who were selected to go to these schools, especially East Side, the majority of them were girls. And I don't know if we had any young men, one or two maybe, who selected to attend East Side. . . . By the time we got to Central, of course the numbers were larger, but we girls usually outnumbered the boys. . . . Unless you were really spending an awful lot of your time at the parties on weekends or . . . socializing and stuff . . . the numbers were few to choose from.

Even at Central . . . where there were a larger number of African Americans in general—[there were] fewer males?

Right.

And then your college, was that African American, or that was interracial?

Yes, when I left Central High, I went to Phillips University in Enid, Oklahoma, which is a church-related school, and it was basically the same situation. Even though there, believe it or not, I was selected probably the first and only Black—Negro, African American—homecoming queen.

I went to Phillips two years, and that sort of . . . goes along with what I was saying earlier in elementary school in terms of knowing that even though my experiences at the schools may not have always been positive, I did have experiences in an integrated situation that were positive. That helped me to understand that people are different based upon where you find them, and their thought processes, and the role that religion plays in terms of how people treat each other, and how people see each other—I think part of that positive experience early on related to my summer camps and, you know, church camps and things of that nature. After I left . . . Central . . . going to Phillips University was part of that thinking, that even though it wasn't a predominantly Black school, that I felt, that [as] it was part of my church, I would be okay there. And I was. It was a good environment. [I] faced the same situation in terms of few number of African American, Black students there, but there was an Air Force base there . . . and there were a group of Black pilots. And of course they had graduated from school, and so they were in the Air Force learning to fly jets, supersonic jets. . . . Oh, that was lovely!

So your social development picked up there, huh?

Yes ma'am, that was, that was lovely. But I only stayed at Phillips two years. . . . My brother, the one who I told you was brilliant . . . was accepted at Fisk University. And I knew that my parents could not afford for both of us to be away for school, you know. The expense of room and board at Phillips, transportation back and forth, even though I did get, you know, financial aid and scholarships . . . to go to Phillips. So my second year, I decided to transfer back to Little Rock and enrolled at Philander Smith College, and that's where I graduated . . . a predominantly Black school. And so he went off to Fisk and I transferred to Philander Smith College. And that's where I graduated from.

What an awesome big sister to sacrifice that . . . opportunity!

Oh, you think so?

No, no, no. It's a part of the process. It's part of the process. . . . It was just . . . what was supposed to happen.

Professionally, how did that experience affect or influence your adult life, the experience of attending a junior high school?

It's . . . like, I would think almost like making a soup or a stew, you know? Each experience contributes to the finished product. So I don't know if I've ever thought about. . . . any one particular experience being more influential than any other.

That's part of the reason I use the word "influence." It's not the major thing necessarily, but a contributing factor, something that played a part in where you are today. What is it that you do at this time?

I am currently at Washington University in St. Louis. . . . I am currently a project manager for diversity and inclusion in human resources. This is what I consider to be my second tour of duty there.

Getting back to the question of East Side and influence . . . I do think that that counselor that I mentioned earlier on, and the expectation that I am a person of color, that I cannot perform, probably is one of those things that . . . stick in the back of your mind. . . . There is that need to probably demonstrate that your abilities to get the job done and to perform to a level of excellency is . . . being excellent in whatever you do, or trying to be, as close as possible. . . . And this is a motivator, but perhaps in a negative way—to prove to White people that you are capable. And so that, unfortunately, probably has been a motivator, and in some instances it probably could have been what some people may have considered positive, but I'm at a point now where I don't care what you think . . . I am done.

But . . . you also completed the work . . . finished college, and graduate school. . . . So it sounds like you—she influenced you in a way even though it wasn't the way that she expected.

Oh yes! I mean, as I was sitting there listening to her . . . I don't know what my mother was thinking, but I know what I was thinking! "I'm gonna show you!" (Laughs.) . . . So as a kid, you know—right out of elementary school, probably preteen or teenager, you know—you aren't supposed to be worried about crap like that, having to prove something to somebody. Maybe you do, I don't know. But, you know, it is what it is now, and so we can't undo any of that. . . . that was "I'm gonna show you." . . . And so it's been a driving force, and it has only been recently that I realized . . . that's something I can let go. I don't have to prove anything to anybody. I don't have to prove anything else to anybody anymore, outside of myself. . . . I am at this ripe old age and ready to retire. I'm ready to let that go . . . and just turn it over . . . to the "young'uns" as I call them, and let them do their thing. But, no, I'm tired. . . . I'm about done proving anything to anybody . . . and especially in integrated situations . . . I think I'm a little fortunate in that I've been able to be in environments of people . . . that I've not necessarily felt inferior to. We all feel less than for . . . different reasons. . . . I mean, it's clear when you're in a room with a brilliant person . . . you just, "Hey, that is just full out of my league," you know. And when you're in a room with someone who has a natural gift . . . I mean, you know your boundaries. . . . But I think for the most part, of my blend of experiences with White people—and I go back to my church experiences—that I was never quite ever convinced that all White people felt that all Black people were inferior. And I never felt that all White people were superior. . . . In some environments, that . . . has gotten me into a lot of trouble . . . that attitude. . . . But primarily in situations where I think individuals, perhaps, function better in a hierarchical situation. Sometimes I don't think I realized that that was the expectation, and of that, I think I have from time to time gotten myself into a little bit of hot water. But I can't attribute that to East Side. That was as much as my exposure and experiences outside of East Side [as] being there. But I see East Side as just a stepping stone and a part of a process . . . of where I was going and what I needed to do to get there. So I have not mentally dwelled on any of that experience one way or the other. It was just passing through . . . on my way to somewhere else.

How do you think your actions of desegregating a junior high school affected the city, the state, the community, the world . . . ?

Not, not one iota. I think something like Little Rock Central High probably did. But . . . until I guess I got an e-mail from Glenda Wilson saying that you were doing your book, I had not even thought about it. And I don't think it has, to be honest with you. I think that it was part of the progression of what was going to happen, and they experimented with Central, got that done, high schools, and then just started the process backwards. . . . I think, in hindsight, it probably would have been smarter starting with the elementary schools and rolling up the other way. . . . If you had integrated the elementary schools or the kindergartens, kids would have been accustomed to being with each other. Parents would have been accustomed to it. It would have been less of . . . the social concerns about who's gonna mix and that kind of thing, and kids would just grow up knowing each other as human beings, and by the time they would have gotten to high school, it would have been a nonissue. But in terms of—to be honest with you, I had not given one thought to any significance whatsoever of me spending my junior high school days at East Side . . . Junior High School.

Do you think that it's possible that even though you didn't think about that, that the city, the state, and the nation were affected in some way by the desegregation process?

Not really. . . . I'm not a student of desegregation . . . so I have not looked at it historically. . . . And maybe those who are scholars . . . know better. But . . . I'm sitting in St. Louis, Missouri, and shall never forget when I arrived here in the '70s, discovering desegregation like you would never imagine in the St. Louis public schools. And I recall as a graduate student sitting here thinking, "I thought we resolved all of this in Little Rock."

So you discovered segregation . . .

Here in St. Louis. The schools . . . they were segregated! And they were still going through lawsuits . . . to get the kids transferred out to county school districts. And I mean it was unbelievable. And to be honest with you, I have often felt if anything, Little Rock has not gotten the recognition, nor the state of Arkansas, that it probably deserved in being a progressive southern state. Now my brother, who still lives in Little Rock, and my . . . sister, who is a teacher in the Little Rock public schools—now a speech pathologist, Adrienne Brown—and my brother lives there. And whenever I compliment Arkansas, he can't see it. . . . Arkansas is light years ahead of Missouri . . . Compared to what I found here in 1971, when I arrived as a graduate student, and the condition that the school—segregated schools in the St. Louis area. It was unbelievable. I recall sitting here and thinking at that time, "I thought we resolved all of this . . . from where I . . . from Little Rock, we were—we had been there, done that. And they were just getting started with it here. Anyway, that was . . . of any significance, you know.

So I guess you made me answer the question. You're smart! . . . because from my perspective, it was . . . "Hey. No." But I guess when you look at it in those ways . . . But somebody probably needs to connect the dots. I certainly didn't. Somebody probably needs to get some credit. I don't know who masterminded Little Rock—who picked Little Rock, who decided that it was time to do this in Little Rock—but somebody did. I mean, it wasn't made in isolation, the decision.

You contributed to that.

Well . . . I was just trying to get my education. (Laughs.) . . . I wasn't trying to make a statement; I wasn't trying to prove anything—other than I could do the work. And as my mother said . . . I don't need to sit in the room with a person that's a different color from me, just give me the dad-gum opportunity! . . . And that's all I was after. . . . And all I knew at that time was that everybody was telling me the key to my opportunity was in that classroom. So that's where I had to go to get it.

What recommendations do you have for any parents that are considering placing their child in a situation, an educational situation . . . where they may be the minority—not necessarily ethnic or racial, but just a minority in any kind of way?

The first thought that came to my mind was . . . my colleagues, my friends, people that I know—in most cases, they are already in environments. Many of them can orchestrate whether or not the percentage of kids who are African American or not . . . they have the resources too. In most cases, unfortunately, it's about residential areas where you, you know, decided by house versus living in the housing project. But that brings home my point, and I think it's one that . . . I discuss with friends of mine. And the question today is, "Are we segregated more based upon race / ethnicity than on economic status?" And I'm beginning to wonder if the thing that is bridging us . . . is the gap between the haves and the have-nots. . . . And that's regardless of what color you are. If you do not have the resources, I don't care what color you are, you will not have access to certain things: healthcare, decent education, quality of life. All of that is impacted by your economic status in this country now. If you are a person of color, and you have the resources, you are more likely to be able to make the decisions about when and where you want to enter into an integrated situation or not. It's optional now. Those are the opportunities that my mother was talking about.

What should they do to prepare that child, beyond to live perhaps, in a different residential section that would allow them to be surrounded by people that are equally like them?

In my old age, I think that one of the things that I've come to understand and appreciate is the individual who knows him or herself, and [is] comfortable with who they are. . . . If I were blessed with a child, and I was trying to get that child prepared for the world, I would focus on that child understanding who he or she is as a person and being comfortable with that. So much of where a person goes in life is so unpredictable; and wherever they go, they have to have . . . self-confidence. I think with that self-confidence that they can probably do okay wherever they find themselves. . . . Some of the stuff we can prepare kids for, and some of it we can't. But I would want a kid to be okay failing and knowing that there's something to learn from failing, and being able to get up and try again. I would want a kid to understand that people hurt other people [because] usually they are hurting, and it sometimes has absolutely nothing to do with you. So don't self-internalize that. Know what role you play in whatever situation it is. Accept your responsibility for it, and move on. . . . I know that a lot of parents today, from what I observe from a distance . . . talk about kids being popular and friends and socialite and stuff of that nature, and that's important. But I think . . . in time—and it doesn't come overnight—a kid . . . should be moving toward being comfortable with who he or she is. I see that so much in our college kids when I was working . . . in the career center. . . . Many of them would come into the career center confused about what it is they . . . should do. They . . . relied so much on what others thought about them . . . and pleasing other people, that, when you stop to ask them, "What do you want? What makes you happy? What are you willing to strive toward? What's important to you, based upon who you are as a person? Who [do] you want to become . . . ?" Those are the kinds of things that I think, will help a person get through whatever situation they may find themselves in. And of course, that's age-appropriate . . .

It seems as though your parents actually had done well enough by the time you met that counselor that, whatever she said, you did not internalize.

I can only give my mother credit for that. That . . . was amazing— the strength that she had—just so insightful . . . about a lot of things, and I'm very privileged to have had her. And, you know, my daddy was there as a support too. But I just have to . . . give that to her . . . for what it's worth. So it's been a process.

[Do] you have any other comments or recommendations that you would like to make . . . ?

I'm at a point in life where I think none of us want to leave here not feeling that we've made a contribution in one way or the other, small or large. . . . I'm not quite sure how it will influence where we're going. The world is so different from . . . what we experienced as children. But I certainly hope that it will be a much more positive world than what I'm currently observing in Ferguson, Missouri . . . very disappointing— thinking that the racial relationships had moved far beyond what, unfortunately, we have witnessed here in St. Louis in 2014, with the killing of Michael Brown, an eighteen-year-old teenager in the streets of Ferguson, Missouri. So that just says to me that there's still a lot of work to do, and it also says to me that this is not about Little Rock, but it is about St. Louis and the state of Missouri. As I said before, Arkansas probably needs to give itself a lot more credit in terms of racial relationships than it probably has received. . . . As I sit in the city of St. Louis, in Missouri, there are a lot of lessons that probably could be learned from this . . .

Myrna Davis Washington

"I always had a strong sense of who I was."

Tell us about where you were born [and] about your family.

My family's—I guess you'd say my mother—was born in . . . old Little Rock. My grandmother . . . her mother, came from Morrilton in Conway and the school system there was named for her. It was the Sarah E. Clark Unified School District. . . . I think it's a building now or something. We've looked into it a little bit, but my grandmother—my great-grandmother—was an educator. My grandmother lived up the street from us. We lived on 2420 Center. . . . Center ran into the governor's mansion on Seventeenth Street. So very often Blacks and Whites prior to desegregation or integration really did mingle. We knew each other. We . . . lived around each other. I had a White girlfriend that I grew up with and the lady behind me kept her. We didn't go to school together until East Side, but the day that we went to East Side together we—[because] of peer pressure—were no longer friends. We grew up together.

There were so many different things that were going on, so many personal relationships. The way Little Rock is structured, Twenty-Third Street was sort of like the cutoff. . . . There were no trolley cars when I came along, but you could still see the trolley car lines and then the bus line then ran down Twenty-Third Street and went up to, I think it was Ringo, and cut over. It went up to like Thirty-First and had this route. And then it went downtown. . . . I think it's north of Twenty-Third was all White. It was the cutoff line. South of Twenty-Third was . . . they called it "Niggerville." And they would say it. My mother had this cloak—she would be walking from church and she said there was a little girl who would sit on the porch and ask her if she lived down in . . . So I'm remembering this but I'm also remembering that we had Ys, South End clubs and we had churches, a whole network of churches . . . a sense of community that was totally separate—separate but equal from the White world. I lived down the street from East Side and it would have been a shame for me to go to school at Dunbar when Dunbar was so far away from me . . .

How old [were you] when you went to East Side?

Eleven. . . . What I brought to that experience was the summer before East Side . . . the summer before the sixth grade before I got chosen, our house had burned down. The little boy next door had set it on fire. So when you think of all the traumatic experiences you could bring to an experience like this, this was nothing compared to what I had gone through. . . . The day that it burned down, my aunt in California had killed her husband by accident. My mother was at the airport leaving for California to go to her sister when the little boy next door got into the back of the house and set it on fire. We were at Bible School. . . . I got home—you know how little kids are walking down the street when we saw smoke coming out. "Oh, let's go see the fire," and when we got down there it was our house. So there were memories. There were things that just left us. I don't have very many pictures before East Side. I don't have very many pictures of my childhood. They saved the little boy, but they didn't save much else. When East Side hit, you compound that with several—each one of us had some, not so much trauma, but childhood traumas. Black life in America's full of it. That's the way it was designed. We brought that to the table. When I . . . went to East Side, I think the biggest thing for me was rejection. I had been a model student. Each of us that were chosen to go to those schools—they didn't do that so much with the Little Rock Nine but with us it was a grade point thing . . . These were all the smart kids, you know. They were the top students. . . . Glenda and I were the top students where we went to school. Equilla was the same way, and Alfreda was, too.

Did you all go to school [together] . . . elementary school?

We all went to East Side. No, we didn't know each other prior to this. I knew Glenda. . . . I don't even remember when I met Glenda. Her mother and my mother are both from Morrilton, and so the way we met was my mother—they were very civic-minded—and so my mother didn't drive and her mother did. . . . They went to . . . PTA meetings together, a lot of the civic things together . . .

How did you learn you were going to East Side?

You know, I don't remember. I'm trying to remember if it was the article or if they told us at school. I'm not sure . . . I'm trying to remember if it was . . .

You're referring . . . to a May 25, 1960, article in the Arkansas . . . Democrat. . . . So you think that you saw that article years ago?

I read the newspaper. . . . I don't know if I learned it [t]here or if they told us at school. . . . I don't remember that one.

But you also remembered the issue about grade point and being chosen?

I do. . . . I remember them sending a paper home . . . It was . . . a big issue. My mother was not as impressed as she didn't want us to go there. She wanted us—our separate but equal—but she didn't think it was a step up for us to go to White schools. . . . For instance, my older sister was supposed to go to school . . . as one of the Little Rock Nine, but she had a hot temper for one. She was a teacher for years (laughs) and she's now a minister. But my mother just felt like she wouldn't do well. I was so soft-spoken until my mother didn't want me to go to East Side. She didn't feel like it would have been the best experience for me. I wanted to go. I wanted to go to Bryn Mawr College. I'd read about it and I wanted to travel, and I told her I was going to leave. I was kind of precocious. . . . after East Side, I was gonna leave and never come home. . . . That was what East Side did for me

Did . . . your parents do any preparation for you . . . to move towards that school process . . . ?

Well, they did it all along. I was very . . . very self-confident. Like I said, I was one of the top students and if I was not *the* top student I was one of the top students at my elementary school . . . Booker T. Washington. . . . We went to church. We were very strong in the church community. The church community supported us. We were members of the YWCA. I was a Girl Scout from first grade through twelfth. I was very active in the Scouts.

Even when I went to East Side, the kids at East Side will tell you they knew me as someone that color was not something that defined me. I never wanted to be reminded that—I don't know if I knew I was Black. You know, I just didn't want to be reminded. I didn't want anyone treating me differently [because] of my color.

You didn't want to be reminded that you were Black?

No. I didn't even think about it. Who wants to think about being different? I didn't see myself as different. They saw me as different. I had a strong sense of self. I always have. My initials were M. E., and they always teased me . . . A lot of us have not sat down and thought about that time. For me it was very, very hurtful. But it was hurtful on a personal level that had nothing to do with—in the beginning with East Side, it was my friend that I lost, my lifelong friend that I lost to integration. I played with Linda every day. . . . the little White girl. . . . They lived on Twenty-Third and her house . . . was a stark change from Black to White. Twenty-Third was White and from there on, you came down that hill—if you were Black and you had to catch the bus down there—you got off on Twenty-Third and you walked down the hill. My grandparents lived 2308, so they lived right off the bus line. Linda's family lived in some homes that were on Twenty-Third. Her mother worked. She was a single mom and her brother was best friends with my older brother. They joined the Navy together and they played together. This is the kind of friendships that went on, on a personal level that they don't even bring up when they talk about integration. We were already integrated on a personal level. . . . The lady that lived behind us watched Linda during the day, and our backyards connected. So all day long we played out back for years. We knew each other very personally. We played. We talked. And the night before we went to school, she and I get to go to school together. "We're finally in school together . . ." We were talking. We were both excited. I remember sitting on the front porch and my mother . . . was making me come in to get ready and Linda had to go home. . . . It was, "Okay, I'll see you tomorrow." . . . I never saw her again. When I was walking in the school and my daddy dropped us off that morning and there were just all these people in the front of the school—I remember . . . it might have been more, might have been less than what I thought, but I just remember to me it looked like thousands of people, I was just a child—but as he let us out and we had to go through, the police walked us in and out of all those voices, I heard her. And it was—I still do this now. It would be, "Two, four, six, eight, we don't want to integrate." "Nigger, go home." All the little chants that they could chant. They were out there chanting these racist slurs as we were walking into the school. And it was Linda's voice that I heard that hurt me so much . . . I saw her on the line, and it hurt me and I still cry about that. That was my friend. . . . That was an emotional tie, so it was deeper than just the integration thing. She was my friend, you know. All of a sudden it turned her against . . . I had one other friend and we've since gotten together on Facebook. I won't mention her name, but . . . when I was going to school I thought she was a little Mexican girl, but she wasn't. She just had the darker hair. But for some reason we just loved each other and we played on the school ground. And there was a lot of peer pressure not to be friends with . . . Whites couldn't be friends with Blacks. They called them "Nigger lovers." And they beat them up. And they beat this little girl up and she wasn't our friend anymore. She'd still hang around, you know, at lunchtime, at breaks . . . she was just a sweet little girl. Children don't see those, but the peer pressure of some of those who did was astounding.

So the first day of school was like that—the "Two, four, six, eight?" . . . Now, were there other days of school that you heard those people chanting?

You know, it got kind of quiet after the first few days. . . . I seem to remember police presence quite a bit. One incident that stuck out in my head—my father was a tailor. He worked downtown Little Rock and my mother; we had a cleaners. My mother sewed. I could make my own clothes by the time I was ten years old. I could make them as good as anybody that was older. . . . My parents gave us a lot of skills. So for East Side, she let me make my outfit for the seventh grade. She never let me wear anything that I made out before, but for this one . . . they took the skirt. My daddy took it in. It had box pleats in it and I made the blouse. You never would have known that I made it. That was what I wore the first day of school. I was so proud. . . . We had some cards. You know those cards you get signed when you go from class to class? I had left mine in the class before and they had told us not to be in the hallway without our police escorts. I guess the teacher forgot and I forgot. I just asked if I could go back and get my card, and she said yes. I ran down the hallways—and I remember them being bigger than they are now, but they were, and I remember thinking how big the White kids were in comparison. . . . This is the incident that happened; it is one of my most traumatic events: As I was coming up the steps, about ten or eleven huge white boys surrounded me and spit all over me. It wasn't so much the spit that hurt, but remember I told you I made that skirt? Well it was dry-clean only, and those marks could never come out of that skirt, so I got to wear it once, and they destroyed it. But more something I had done, something I had worked so hard for, and they just didn't care. . . . When my mother went to the principal, they didn't do anything about it. . . . I think she wasn't as vocal at East Side as she was at the other high schools. I had watched her at the PTA at Horace Mann and Dunbar, and at East Side she let them intimidate her to where she didn't back me up the way I'd felt I should have been backed up at East Side. And so I, I think I retreated more . . .

They destroyed the skirt, but they destroyed a part of you, as well.

That hurt. It just hurt to the core. . . . That's the only way I can describe it. It hurt. So I went into my books. I studied. I read everything. I had another incident that had happened. It was on a personal level, but it had happened years before, so you had this little girl who had been damaged psychologically. I'd retreated to books then. That is why I read all the time. I didn't have anyone that defended me there, so I already knew that. Then I had my Christian upbringing said, "Turn the other cheek." That's what you're supposed to do when that happens.

After they did it, they left. . . . No one was in the hallway, and when I went and told the teacher . . . she took me down to the principal. The principal—I can't remember what they did but I remember my mother was mad. So my mother took me back up to the school. I don't remember what happened. . . . I left her talking in the office. But

I just remember feeling like they didn't do anything to those kids. . . . It seemed like that was always the case that—I remember several other little kids that got into fights, that got beat up. . . . Even if the little Black kid got beat up, he got punished—they never punished the White kids.

You know what I found? What I found out was if you were smart, they respected you. . . . They graded on the curve back then, so I learned to make the best grades, set the curve, and when you're smart they respect you. . . . They might have . . . used the N-word here. It's used a lot. But they might have called me a "Nigger," but they called me a "smart Nigger," and it makes a difference. . . . I was—I don't know if I was cocky in who I am. I've always had a strong sense of self, but they didn't get to get to that. . . . I don't know if it was the Girl Scouts [where] we learned "This Little Light of Mine." . . . We learned to be prepared. I don't know if it was church . . . Certainly, my mother gave me a strong sense of God. . . . I asked her what she felt was her main mission in raising us, and she was a hands-on parent all the way. She said, "I wanted to make sure I gave each of you a view of God, your own view of God." And she did.

Do you remember any other people who actually were positive in your life? Any of the fellow students who were Caucasian . . . ?

Oh yes . . . I'll tell you what I remember. My cousin lived on Twenty-Sixth and Ringo, and that had been a White neighborhood, an upscale White neighborhood that had become Black. I remember Mr. Adams lived across—he was the band director at Horace Mann. But catty-corner from her was the Glasscocks. . . . He was the chief of police, and he had a set of twins that were our age, June and Jean. . . . I spent the night at their house several times. June and Jean were really pretty, popular girls at East Side. One was a little conservative. They were cheerleaders. . . . The other one was really smart, and like I said they were really pretty girls. They were the type of children who, [because] of their background, weren't afraid to befriend us. I had one other girl, I can't remember her last name, but Karen and I were Girl Scouts together. . . . She lived way out, and I just remember when I would stay at her house. I told you I came from a family of ten and I was number seven. We had two bedrooms. We lived in a house. Our house on Center Street didn't have any paint. The yard was dirt, but we swept it up. The floor was clean. There were curtains up to the window. Linoleum on the floor, bedspread—my mother was good about keeping the house. She was a firm believer in being a good steward over what God gave you . . . My father . . . worked downtown. . . . He also was a maître d' at this posh restaurant called—he had two jobs always—called Old King Cole on Broadway. It was where the rich, the elite Whites that lived over on Broadway [frequented] . . . my father worked there and then he was the tailor at Steins Clothing, which was an upscale men's store. . . . When Ninth Street was all Black—it was the Black business area for downtown—my family had a cleaners like right there. I was young, but . . . I remember the area. I remember going to the store, and I remember that the freeway came through and they tore all of that down.

When you were in junior high school, were there any teachers that stood out for you, positive or negative?

You know, I'm not remembering names, and I probably should, but I have one . . . I don't remember any of my teachers ever not being a positive. They were the ones who made me feel like I was a good student. . . . They weren't prejudiced. It was like, "Why aren't you more like Myrna?" I set the curve. The kids didn't like me. They called me "egghead." They called me names. And it wasn't a color thing. It was what you did to the smart kid, you know. If there was any prejudice, I remember one little boy and . . . he was a particular bully . . . but he was cute. If you look back he was cute. We would have words in class, and he was the one that called me a smart Nigger, and I said, "At least I'm smart." My mother told me, "They can't take away what's in there. . . . You get education; you put something in your head, not on it, and they can't take that away from you." I always had a strong sense of who I was. I came from a long line of educated people. I just wanted the opportunity to go outside of what they were offering us. . . . At the time everybody . . . went to normal colleges. . . . Blacks had a network of Black schools. . . . People don't realize this even now, but this started after slavery, and it started in particular in the South. But we have a network of a hundred different Black schools. Back then it was fifty something. Black-owned universities. Nobody else has done this. . . . They were mostly normal schools—agricultural, mechanical and normal. That's what AM&N was. My whole family went to AM&N—my older sisters. If I had not been exposed to East Side and Central, I was going to go to Baptist, Philander and AM&N, too. I wanted something else. That was what I wanted. I'd read, and I knew there was a world outside of this. I wanted something else, even from that age. Going to East Side meant, regardless, that not only was I going to have something else but I remember thinking that . . . I was sacrificing so that my children would not have to go through this. . . . I thought about that even then. I thought I was sacrificing for them.

Remember I told you it was turn the other cheek . . . I grew up in the church. It was, "What would Christ do?" That's what I took to school with me. So I remember turning the cheek—literally, turning the cheek. I've got another one. . . . I'm a poet. I've been writing since I was five. I've been published since I was five, and I have a poem from back then that says, "Hit me, I can take it. . . . There's nothing you can do to me. The shield that I have around me that God put around me, you can't touch it . . ." When I see these people coming to that realization now, that's a beautiful realization to come to, but East Side and the experience I had just prior to that—psychologists call that, not a rude awakening, but it is awakening. A lot of people have it when they go through traumatic experiences. . . . It's almost like when you've hit something like this and a lot of information is thrust at your brain at one time. For me the first one was I was molested as a child, as a five-year-old child. I woke up. I woke up to the light, I woke up to God, and I remember it. I remembered it such that when I became baptized, the experience of being baptized was—I was called when I was five years old. I remember the light. When I went to East Side, that was another experience that called the light out, and I've been called since I was a little girl. Those are awakening moments that you can either use to define you positively or negatively. I used it to fill me positively, too. There was nothing they could do. They could not—the worst thing they could have done was to assume that I adopted their opinion of me. And it wasn't. It didn't mean anything.

Did they allow you to participate in extracurricular activities?

Not the social-based ones. If it was academic and I earned it—the Beta Club, the National Honor Society, the Honor Roll, any of the awards that went . . . I always got the awards. . . . Alfreda and I danced . . . I have a strong dance background. . . . We were doing modern dance . . . I'm guessing that's eighth grade—seventh or eighth. We were in the talent show. I was always in a talent. I did a talent show at

Central. . . . I took piano all the way through the twelfth grade. . . . I had dance. . . . I went to . . . Dunbar Community Center . . . every summer for all the classes. . . . I always felt like my sense of self-efficacy is, if it could be done, I could do it. . . . I also . . . worked on the school paper. I didn't want to do it. I got discouraged. [I] had an incident with a fellow student. . . . It taught me . . . racism was replaced by colorism. It was the first instance that I had.

Being the seventh child, for one—that's a very special place to be among ten children. I could see; I've been able to read people. I noticed that the Whites tended to judge us by color. The lighter you were, the better they treated you. The darker you were—and even at eleven years old I could see this. I wasn't very aware of my color. . . . One of our people called my attention to the fact that I was darker, but I was not aware of that until that moment. But I did notice that the Whites treated us better. And with this person, when she stole my poetry and turned it in as hers—and I remember the whole incident—and I told the teacher what happened, she said, "No, she wouldn't do that. She looks . . ."—she said—"She's too . . ." something. "She wouldn't do that." . . . Whatever she said, I got the impression that she was saying that [because] she was lighter in color, that . . . she couldn't do it. I did it. And it was mine. Then I got in trouble with my mother for letting someone see my stuff before I turned it in . . . I was in the speech club. . . . I did do well in speech. . . . I loved home ec, and I only took that in junior high school.

And it was, I think, the Home Ec Department where I heard about John F. Kennedy. I was at East Side when that happened, and that brutally flavored my tenure there . . . Actually I was cutting through the Home Ec Department. My . . . teacher had told me to go pick up something. . . . It was on the other side of the school, but the Home Ec Department and the kitchen and the lab was sort of in the center of the building. If you cut through there, you could cut through the back of the classroom and you'd be on the other side like that quick. And so I would do that from time to time. [The home ec teacher] liked me. I was cutting through the home ec lab, and she had left the TV on. There were no students in there. As I passed through there they were, announcing that John F. Kennedy had been shot . . . The whole thing was on the TV, and so I stood there by myself. I heard it and I remember falling to my knees. I remember it was—there was a darkness that came over, and I ran back to the classroom and I threw the door open and I said, "The president's been shot. The president's been killed." And it was—I remember the teacher saying, "No, Myrna, don't, don't play with us like that." And she ran across the room and ran into the—the television was on and she saw it. And I think the school nearly broke into a riot, right then and there. Just the way that reached into and bonded us as a group. Everybody loved him. . . . We were crying. We were upset. . . . It was like—I remember it rained and it got dark, you know, to me, like as a child . . . and it was November. And I remember that there was an overcast, a darkness that came over and everybody was very distraught over losing the president, you know. And it . . . was all over the whole school . . .

So you completed the ninth grade at East Side?
Yes.

What made you decide to go on to Central . . . ?
I thought it was just a natural. . . . I don't remember thinking about it. We moved that year, my ninth grade year, and Central was my high school. . . . I moved over by Central and . . . if it weren't about color or anything, Central was my high school . . .

So there was no thought in mind about the possibility of going to Horace Mann at that time?
No . . . Horace Mann would have been way back the other way . . . and we were now in Central's district . . . If I'd still been living over there in Horace Mann, I might have thought about it. I knew the teachers. . . . My family taught school. I knew the neighborhood. All my sisters and brothers went to Horace Mann. In fact . . . I chose Howard [University because] I felt like Central . . . I didn't get to do anything. We didn't integrate socially at Central. If I didn't earn it, I didn't get it. . . . Until the year after I left, there were no black cheerleaders. . . . I remember working on the prom committee and not enjoying the prom. Not liking it. It was still very, very Caucasian. It wasn't what we liked . . . so it wasn't fun for us. The music wasn't our music, and we decorated—we did what they wanted. I remember we didn't go to games that much . . .

I remember my senior year they wanted to change from "Pomp and Circumstance" and "War March of the Priests" to something stupid, and I don't even remember what they wanted to change it to, but one was a deviation from tradition, and I had watched all my brothers and sisters graduate, march to that. Every place I looked that was everything you heard and you still do. I led a campaign to keep it in—I think it was in the paper—but we won. We got to keep "War March of the Priests." . . . I actually remember being very outspoken and very passionate about whatever it was that I believed in. . . . Central was just someplace I had to go through to get to wherever I was going.

That's a powerful statement. So you said that it robbed you. So it robbed you in different ways.

The fun . . . the social aspect. . . . High school and college are fifty percent social. . . . We need to learn those social skills. As I get more and more into online education and looking into that as a form of delivery for education, I see a need—and it personalizes education. We're all different types of learners. But social skills are missing in these kids now. They're not growing up with any life skills. They're coming out of high school not knowing how to take care of themselves. These are very practical, logistical skills they used to give us. They used to teach us how to take care of ourselves, how to manage books. You give those two skills in some of the life skill classes now, but it's not emphasized as much. The physical aspect—the activity aspect—and the social aspect now are being neglected. . . . We're coming up with some children who are almost emotionally retarded. . . . We've got to go back and give them those skills. You can't abandon that with the children . . .

How do you think attending East Side and Central influenced your life?

I've reconnected with all these people on Facebook . . . Reflection is so important when you're healing, and I think what it did with me was it propelled me out into the world. You can use something to hold you back; you can either let it hold you down or you can let it propel you out. What it did was it shot me out there. I left Little Rock . . . at sixteen. . . . I promised myself that. . . . "I'm leaving and I'm never coming back." So the first opportunity I got to get away from there, I latched on to everything that I could to make my stay away from Little Rock permanent. And I spent years away. I didn't want to go back . . . I've been very much a loner. I went . . . to Howard. What I found at Howard from East Side . . . this is how I felt about Howard. They were doing the same things to themselves. They were perpetuating what the Whites did to us in Little Rock but they were doing it to themselves.

Discrimination. . . . I had seen the fact that they judged us by color.

Those who were more Europeanized in their features . . . they thought were more intelligent. Those who were darker had to fight to . . . be perceived as intelligent. I noticed that at East Side. When I went to Howard I saw it and I saw that . . . Blacks did it amongst themselves . . .

How do you think attending a primarily White junior high and high school affected the community of Little Rock, the state, and even the nation?

You know, there's something my sister told me. She went to Horace Mann. My older sisters and brothers . . . were teachers, and my cousins were teachers, and they were all in the Black community. [She told me] that Black leaders come from the Black community. So when those of us went to East Side, they took the top students and they put them through an integrated experience, and most of us left the Black community. We're not there. . . . I don't know how many have fed back into the community. I am feeling a sense and the need to feed back into the community now. . . .

I think it destroyed the Black community. I remember after East Side, I remember walking through the Y when they were tearing it down and feeling sad and crying. We'd gone there for meetings; we'd had teas, plays, and we learned things at the Y. I remember walking through there and they tore it down. . . . My folks owned the cleaners on Ninth Street. . . . They tore the movie theater down. They tore everything we had down. For us integration meant that we lost everything we had and we went to the White schools as second-class citizens. . . . Everywhere I went I remember them telling me I had to be ten times better than my competitors just to be considered for the game. So when I went out into the world, I really did have some very good jobs. . . . When I went to Howard I always worked for the Small Business Administration, for the American Medical Association—these were just jobs that even now I see people trying to get jobs in there. . . . When I worked at San Diego Unified School District, I ended up modeling for the school district for ads . . . somebody at the School of Modeling at John Robert Powers saw my picture and wanted to put it in a contest for Kodak. And they asked me to pose for their Kodak pictures and my pictures won and—I thought they were ugly but they won. I ended up moving to LA. . . . I was traipsing through Hollywood when nobody was there. I remember meeting Johnny Carson and going through all the studios when none of this was in the media. When . . . I would be like the only Black there, and moved to North Hollywood. . . . We were the only Blacks there. It set me up to be in situations where I would be the only Black at my job, where I worked for Xerox as a customer rep. . . . I got a job through one of the—one of my sister's friend's husband somebody—they needed to hire somebody Black. It was . . . affirmative action. . . . But I'd had a strong background at East Side and Central . . . I felt like I got a better education . . . than . . . Horace Mann or Dunbar. . . . I felt like I got exposed to more. I don't know if that was true, but I felt like I did. I felt it when I went out in the world. I had that sense of confidence with me, and I was always amongst the only Blacks that were there. I wasn't intimidated when I went on the job interview. . . . With . . . the job through Central Casting, I had a contract at NBC during the time when nobody was writing that kind of stuff up and I had fun. . . . I owned gyms in LA, when they weren't even talking about Blacks doing those kind of things. It meant I had those kinds of experiences before people went through them. East Side gave me a rich life. It did. You had to go through it. I had to go through it to get to where I am today. It was very painful, but it was an awakening that awakened me to something inside of myself. That was where I retreated . . . in here, and everything that I'm studying right now in psychology wants you to retreat to that internal locus of control, they call it. In religion we call it God, you know, but it's your internal locus of control. And those people who have an internal locus of control will fare better. That's why I was able to overcome on such a profound level, on such a deep level to have such—I mean, I have—my biggest sense is family. I have beautiful grandkids. I have beautiful children. I have such a rich life, and East Side prepared me for that. You know it.

What recommendations you would have for any parent who is considering placing their child, now at this time, into a situation that is a—going to be a majority/minority situation where they are in the minority?

There's so much I would say. The biggest thing I would have to say to any parent, I don't care what—Black, White—with this education the way it is today, don't send your children to school; take them to school. And it makes a big difference. You need to be in there and be active with them. Be active with them with their homework. Go talk to the teacher. Let the teacher know that that child has a home, that they're coming from a home. When I send my child to school to get educated—and I have to; I would prefer to educate them myself, but if I have to send them to school to get the social experience—then I will coeducate them. I'll come with my children. . . . My mother would tell me, "They can put more dirt in your child's eye in one second than you can take out in a lifetime." You need to be there. You need to be present in your children's lives. Don't send your children to school thinking the teacher can be a babysitter. She's got enough paperwork going. Now it's all about the accountability . . . These—the teachers have so much to do right now. They have to spend money out of their own pocket. I've watched them. I grew up with them. They need to know when the child comes into that classroom that the parent is helping her. But the parent also needs to know that the teacher's supporting what they're saying as well. So it's . . . a job that needs to be done together, but I would say don't send your children to school. . . . When you let them know that we can do this together. "I have to send my child here to be with you for six hours today. I need to trust you when you do this." I watched my sisters make a difference in children's lives. . . . Don't send your kids to school. Get back out there and be active and supportive of your children while they're away from home and it'll make a difference. If my mother had been able to come up there and fight for me the way she did for my sisters, I think it would have made that difference for me, but I overcame anyway, you know. It's going to work out in the end anyway. Our track records says we're survivors and that's what we are. We are the strongest of the strong, you know, so—that would be all I would have to say to any parent: just go to school with your kids. Be active . . . Volunteer in the classroom. When my granddaughter goes to school, I'm going to be a grandmother—they go up and read to the kids. . . . If a parent is going to school and working and taking care of children, it's the grandparents that have to step in and be active now. And I'm even calling, as I get more into education, calling for grandparents, not for just their own good, to stay active and to keep that neuroplasticity strong, but we're having to step in and to extend that family just more. Don't let go of family. Don't give that responsibility to the teacher.

Is there anything that . . . you would like to add pertaining to your memories or experiences that you had or where you are at this point?

Where I am right now is such a beautiful place. I'm at a place—when you get healed, to go out and help heal. I'm about healing, and that is what my whole life is about. It's about overcoming this and over-coming the scars that come upon us. As a nation we are plagued by non-communicable diseases. Those are things you have some control over. Those are diseases like heart disease and diabetes and hypertension. As a race we are particularly plagued by these, and I could spend a whole day telling you how what we went through contributes to our health situation—that the mind and body are not separate, that they are one. So from this situation I can say thank you, for without it—I think that the type of person I was, my husband has a word for it—and I would have been a snot. I would . . . not have been centered. I would have been very pretentious. . . . There are so many things that this situation saved me from; it made me turn to myself. It made me turn back. So I have to say thank you for everything that has happened to me—whether I perceived it as good or bad; whether it was painful or not at the time—I have overcome it. . . . There are no mistakes. This didn't happen—there are only lessons learned. So for this situation I had to look at the lessons that came from this. . . .

I have two or three books of poetry that I've written. . . . I've been so busy with education I haven't had a chance to get to publish them. But I have a poem I'm working on as a book, a child's book for my daughter, and it will come out about the time this comes out. But it's about that little girl who went out there and had to go in. When I went in what I did was I read. I called "seeking the light," but the light has to do with knowledge and the acquisition of information and learning. I went in and I just started to learn and to study. It gives you such a profound sense. That is the knowledge . . . Our new gun is the book. You know, pick up a book. Go back to school. Get some brainpower.

The brain of an educated person is bigger and weighs more than the brain of a person who's not. When you talk about morphology and the actual way the brain is built, that leads to function. It'll function better if you do it. There are things that we have to go back and do. . . . So as we go toward 2030 . . . 2050, there's going to be as many older people in the world—you and I are going to live longer hopefully, so we're really entering the third chapter of our lives. We have to do things, and we have a lot to offer these young children. We need to go back and connect, reconnect and contribute what we have learned. There's no reason for us to have to repeat the lessons we've already learned.

Children don't want to listen. There's a chance for us to all reconnect and to all get back in there. I'm just grateful for the whole experience. Without it I wouldn't be where I am today. I wouldn't be at this point looking out at the world with some clarity. Everything's happened the way that it's supposed to happen. I had to go to East Side. I was too timid . . . for Horace Mann. I think they would have squashed me. . . . I hear a lot of parents say they were straight-A students until the eighth grade. . . . I think that would have happened at Dunbar for me. East Side gave me a chance to get away from that.

Shirley Hickman

"If you do something to me, I will defend myself."

[I am Shirley Hickman.]

You were actually in the first class to desegregate which school?

East Side Junior High.

East Side in 1961 . . . You were in the seventh grade at that time?

Yes.

Do you remember the approximate number of students that entered with you?

There were two boys: Jessie Walker and Larry Davis, I think was his last name. And then from Granite Mountain it was Alfreda Brown, me, Sara Jordan, Linda Brown. And then . . . there was Glenda Wilson, Myrna Davis—that's all I can think of now. . . . Oh, Equilla Banks. . . . How could I forget her? It was her father that picked us up after classes for the first few months or so.

You said for the first few months Mr. Banks picked you up?

Yes.

Did you finish East Side?

Yes, I did.

How did you learn that you were going to attend a majority-White junior high school?

If I remember, they told us in a sixth grade class and then my mother getting notification of it. And then when my grandmother found out about it, that was the biggest hurdle for me . . . I had to promise her that I would not fight.

What made her think that you would fight?

I would fight . . . If you do something to me, I will defend myself. That was the way that it was . . . And the very first day of school . . . oh, this White guy slammed his locker onto me and I slammed it right back, and stood up, and looked him in the face—ready. "If you want to hit me, hit me. The fight will be on . . ."

Oh, and what happened after that?

Nothing. He did not slam the locker anymore. He left me alone.

So once you took your stand with him at least, you didn't have to do anything else?

No . . .

But your grandmother knew . . . that you would defend yourself?

I would fight. Yes.

You said that you learned that you were going to attend in a meeting in school. Was the entire student body in this meeting, or the entire sixth grade class?

I don't remember that. I don't remember . . . if it was the entire sixth grade. That's going back a long way.

Do you think your parents knew before this meeting or had they already planned for you to go?

If it came in the mail the same day, then they probably wouldn't have known until after I did. It would have been later once they got off from work and everything and opened the mail.

So you don't remember whether you had a special selection or whether you indicated that you wanted to go to East Side?

I do remember a decision to be a part of the class that would integrate on the junior-high level.

You made that decision?

Yes.

And your parents supported you in that decision?

Yes.

Did they prepare you in any kind of way to enter the school—your parents or anyone else?

We had a committee . . . formed that dealt with us. . . . There would be meetings and everything like that about conduct and what to do if something happened to you. [If] you got hit or something, report it to the principal, and that's what I did. But the principal's thing was to call in the person who offended you and ask them if they did it, and if they said no, then that was the end of it.

It seems as though you were the defendant and the other person would always be right?

Yep. That person never did it. They'd say, "No, I didn't," and that was good enough for the principal . . . The biggest thing was a boy spit on me one time and I followed the rules—went and told the principal. He called him in and asked him. He said no, he did not, and that was the end of it. . . . For him and the principal . . . but not for me. I was going to get him back some sort of way. Then I noticed that whenever we had to go to the auditorium—it was like a breezeway to get from the school to the auditorium, and it would always be lots of kids there and everything—and I noticed him ahead of me one time. Then I formulated a plan, and what I ended up doing was getting up close enough to him to stick him in the back with a thumbtack. Then I stopped immediately in my tracks to let the other kids moving around and everything. And when that boy looked around and he saw me, I was giving him an evil look, but I had started to walking forward then, putting students between us . . . I think he realized that, hey, it could just have easily been a knife. Nothing came of it. Well, [we] went to the principal's office, but I said I didn't do it.

Nothing happened?

Nothing happened. . . . So, hey, if that was the way he was going to do business, then that was the way that he was going to do.

What kind of experiences did you have involving the White community before you attended that school?

Basically none. I remember being downtown with my grandmother one day and this White lady came up to her and she knew her. . . . The lady had some candy and she offered me some. I said, "No, thank you." I did not want it. She was grumpy; her fingernails were dirty and everything, and so I said no. Once she had left, my grandmother told me, "Sweetheart, whenever a White person offers you anything, you take it. Once they're out of sight you can throw it away." And . . . for the longest I thought my granddaddy was White. He was very light skinned, the straight hair and everything like that. Then he had a brother . . . with . . . red hair and the freckles. So I thought Daddy Henry was White for the longest.

Did that shade, color, or influence . . . your thoughts about White people when you thought your granddad was White?

Yes. It would have influenced the way that I acted around them and everything. I'm used to him . . . being friendly. . . . So it was easy. . . . It surprised me that there weren't as many vicious students there as you would have thought that there would have been. Friends were formed, and one White girl even asked, "Can I use your comb?" to comb her hair. . . . I gave it to her and she did . . . Her name was Barbara. . . . One of my first two close friends was Barbara and a girl named Camilla. So it was easy. . . . Basically my thing was to get around my grandmother's promise not to fight. I assumed she meant in school, and so after Mr. Banks stopped picking us up and we would catch the bus home in the evening, if I got into a confrontation with someone at school, I always let them know where I would be after school. And if they wanted to come, they could come.

Did you ever have to fight during that time?

No . . . I was basically a tomboy. I was . . . we had two bad teachers there that I remember, one of them being a gym teacher, and we had just gotten through doing something and my legs were killing me. It turned out shin splints is what it was. I was sitting down and she told me to stand up, and I told her I couldn't. My legs were killing me . . . And she came walking back with a paddle in her hand. And I just looked up and said, "If you hit me with that paddle . . . ," then I just told her what I would do to her. . . . She turned around and she left me alone.

She didn't send you to the principal or anything?

Nope. She left me alone. No sending to the principal or anything. Then the next time we got into it was we were outside and she was timing how fast we could run, and I ran this distance and she goes, "Wow." And she thinks something's wrong with her clock, and she wanted me to run it again. And I ran it again for her and it was still the same, you know. So the next thing was after class she asked me about being on the track team . . . My response was, "When a Black can become a cheerleader or be on your pep squad, then I would be willing to run on the track team. Until then, no."

You had . . . quite a bit of insight about the situation at the school. But you had quite a bit of courage, too.

Yes, that's me. I'm known for courage, standing up. . . . But as long as . . . they didn't feel we were qualified to be a cheerleader or in the pep squad, then no, I would not run track for you.

Were there other extracurricular things that you recall you all could not participate in?

Everything, we could not participate in, with the exception—I don't know about band.

Do you recall other memories, positive or negative, about your experience there?

[There was one teacher.] I believe he was at East Side. He would have been a health teacher and he had this habit—although we were integrating the schools, there was never a Black student alone in a class, at least two or three. We sort of segregated ourselves within the class by sitting next to each other and everything. He was [the] seventh grade health teacher, and he had a habit of assigning a writing test during the class, and then he would go to a certain spot where he could look at the Black students. He would just stare at us. It was an eerie feeling—creepy. I reported it to the committee, and they were supposed to take care of it and nothing changed with him . . . until the day . . . that I decided I had enough. He gave his writing assignment . . . and he selected his place. I . . . turned in my seat and I stared him down. I stared and I stared and finally other students . . . caught on to what was going on and he finally moved and went back up to his desk. But his revenge for me was we had to do a weekly health report and he gave me a D. . . . I promptly went to the counselor. Now they were involved in it and everything. They found out how he had been treating the Black females and everything, so he had to change my grade and he gave me a B. And I said, "Okay, satisfied with that." This would be the end of it. That was the end of it . . . until I met him again when I was in high school.

I had a part-time job at Tommy's Men's Store. I ran the elevator on Monday nights and Friday nights. And he came in one of those nights. He got on the elevator. I took him up to the floor he wanted to go up to, and on the way back down he had the nerve to ask me if I wanted to go on a date with him . . . I had the nerve to tell him which part of my anatomy to kiss. He got off the elevator and he went over to where the White salesmen and the men were standing, and he reported me. One of the men that was there was Tommy Karam, the owner of the store. He came to me and he asked me did I say to him what I did. I said, "Yes, I did." He said, "Okay, close the elevator. Let's go up to the second floor." He asked me why, and I gave him the story going all the way back. And he said, "Okay." When we went back down to the first floor, his thing was to ask [that teacher] not to enter his store again. Tommy Karam was one of the nicest White men I ever met. . . . He was way ahead of his time, too. That's how as a teenager I had a checking and savings account; he took me around to Worthen Bank Building to open it up. He was ahead of his time in that he was not going to be passing out the paper checks anymore. It was going to be direct deposit into your checking account. . . . He asked me if I had done it. I said, "No." He got somebody else to run the elevator. He took me around to Worthen Bank and he had a girl to help me with filling out the papers, to show me how to write a check out and everything.

He stood up for you . . . When the principal wouldn't do it.

Yep, it was. . . . Basically I think East Side was okay after that, if I got everybody that was . . .

It was someone else that you thought or some . . .

The principal and the librarian. I turned in a book; they said I didn't. [They] called me out of class, opened my locker searching for the book. I assured them that I had . . . turned the book in and they were saying that I didn't. And the principal was telling me I was going to have to pay for the book, and I'm telling him I turned it in and I'm not going to pay for it . . . Eventually they found the book. It had been turned in. So nothing came of that.

The assumption was always that you were in the wrong?

Yep, it was. And then on the last day of school there—that would have been ninth grade and we all had put in to go to Central High—we go to his office and we find out we've been assigned to Horace Mann. He says that we did not fill out the papers for Central and I just told him he was a liar.

What happened as a result?

Nothing. There was nothing he could do. But we did make it to Central.

Did you appeal?

I don't know what steps they took to . . . do that. The committee did it and everything but we . . . got in

What committee is that?

It was made up of parents that were supposed to help us when we had problems and things like that, so . . .

Parents of all of the . . . nine students?

And then some outside help. Sometimes Daisy Bates would be at a meeting or something like that.

I don't remember when we started to meeting and everything. Probably did start meeting before we went to the school to tell us how . . . we should act in school and everything.

How did you all get to school?

Somebody would drop us off at school . . . We did not take the city bus for a while. Then we got to the point where we rode the buses, so I don't remember who dropped us off. It may have been various parents. It may have been . . . Alfreda Brown's daddy bringing us to school.

It sounds like . . . there was always at least one other person in the class with you and you had people early on taking you to school, picking you up. You never felt alone during that time?

Right. We pretty much segregated with them. But that is how I was, and that is how I operated, and push came to shove, I was ready to push and shove with you. . . . And we did . . .

What made you decide "I must go to Central?"

Central was Central. It had been in the news, national news and everything, and we wanted to be participants of it and everything . . . Central was *the* school to go to in Little Rock. . . . So that was . . . why we wanted to go.

What strengths and resources did you have either within you or outside?

I think my willingness to stand up for myself, and I've been known to stand up for the underdog and everything, and that's something that I passed down to my son. He hadn't come in from school one evening, and I looked out to see where he was, and there he was sitting in the backyard with a guy and talking to him and everything. When he finally came in, I asked him what was going on—and this was the child that everybody picked on. And so he had a compassionate bone in him just like me. I sort of always believed in standing up for myself, and I always did it. I remember the time my mother sent me to the grocery store to get some pressed ham. She asked that it be sliced thinly, and when I got it back home it was so thinly it was mush. I told her that I would take it back to the store. She said, "No, that's okay. This is fine. I'll use it like it is." But I knew that a wrong had been done. She put it in the refrigerator. She left the room. I got it out of the refrigerator, and I flew back down to that store, and I slammed that meat up on top of that counter, and I told him, "You sliced it until it's nothing but mush. I want another half a pound of pressed ham and I want it sliced right." The owners were there and they saw what it was, and they made him slice it right and give it to me. Then they also gave me . . . the mushy part, too . . . It's having nerves, I guess, when other people don't. . . . I was basically a tomboy and . . . I've always been like that. I was the type that parachuted off the top of the house with an umbrella . . . So rough and tough . . . did not bother me in the least. So I think that was a part of it. For the most part students, after a while, left you alone, except for one guy, music class. I'd be going in and seemed like he'd always be coming out, and he [would] get way over on the other side of the stairwell like I am contaminated . . . And he did it every day. One day, enough was enough. So when he did it I moved closer to him, and I kept moving closer to him, and I kept moving closer to him until he was bent over the stair rail backwards. But I was at least a foot and a half away from him and everything, but that was not enough space. And I don't know what would have happened to him if the music teacher hadn't come out and saved him.

Did other students happen to see situations like that happen?

The other students with the health teacher—yes, they saw that and everything.

What did they do when they realized what he was doing?

Well, there was snickering, with me staring him down and him finally moving back to his desk. There was snickering. But, I think, basically from us it was a sigh of relief. Maybe he would not do it to us again.

You went on to Central . . . What was that experience like?

We were pretty much used to being around the White students and everything, so it wasn't really no problem as far as I was concerned . . . I didn't get into any fights or anything like that. Moved through classes easily and everything . . . I remember two things at Central. There was this coach, I don't remember his name, but in the cafeteria when you put your trays up there were a basketball player, football—they were athletes—behind the table to make sure everything was okay. A White student ahead of me, a napkin fell off their tray onto the floor. I put my tray up there, threw my napkin in the trash can, and I was ordered to pick up the napkin that the White student had dropped on the floor. My response was, "I did not drop it and I will not pick it up." "You pick that napkin up!" "I did not drop it and I will not pick it up." "Coach! Coach!" I don't remember the coach's name, but at any rate I called him the meanest coach at Central. Here he comes over. He asked them what was going on, and they told him, and he did not ask me anything. He turned around and told me to pick up the napkin. I told him that I did not drop the napkin on the floor and that I would not pick it up. "I said for you to pick that napkin up!" "I did not drop the napkin and I will not pick it up." He said it again. And my response was, "You can't make me pick up that napkin. [The principal] cannot make me pick up that napkin." I went on with the governor, whoever was the governor at that time—they couldn't make me pick it up. It ended with the president of the United States not being able to . . . make me pick that napkin up. By that time, everybody that was in the cafeteria at that time, they were listening. So he ordered me to Ms. Huckabee's office. And I get to Ms. Huckabee's office, and she's got the phone way out here from her ear. He is so mad, but she's also laughing. So when I get in she says, "Shirley, what did you do?" And I told her. Well, I'd been to her office once before, and I told her what I did . . . We sat down and we talked and she laughed and everything. She said, "Sit there for a few minutes, and then I'm going to send you to class. Not going to write up anything." And that's what I did. I went to my class and when I got to my class it surprised me. A White guy, his name was Don, he started clapping for me, and everybody in the class clapped. Just about everybody that I saw and everything . . . So I sort of developed a mouth to replace the fist. And if you left me alone, we got along perfectly. But if you tried to embarrass me or harm me any way, it was not that easy.

There was the homeroom teacher, [the principal] was retiring. The decision was that if everyone in the school gave a quarter towards his retirement, they could buy him a color console TV and a set of golf clubs. [He] was racist in my book, and he was not going to get any of my money. So they passed the envelope around in homeroom each morning, and it kept going. I'd pass it . . . to the next student. There was one other girl in the class with me, Black female, Tony, and she said she wasn't and it turns out she did cave in. And then came that day. The teacher came to me and she goes in a loud voice, "Everyone in the class has given their quarter towards [the principal's] retirement except for you." Why'd she do that? I reached down. I picked up my purse. I went in my coin purse. I pulled out a penny and then I asked her, "Do you have change for a penny?" And everybody started laughing, and she took her red-faced butt back to her desk. That was just me.

Did you ever get nervous or anxious when you made those statements?

No. Not in the least little bit. One day I ended up missing the bus, and so when the next city bus came along, I got on and I put my money in the little thing they had for you to drop your money in and I asked for a transfer. He said it was after hours. I could not get a transfer. I had to pay full fare. I showed him my student card and everything and that it was not after hours. He ordered me off the bus. I . . . grabbed me a transfer and I went and I sat down. He pulled the bus over to . . . a public phone, and he called the police. All of these Black women that were on the bus were begging me to get off the bus before the police came. "Please, honey, get off of the bus before they come." And I refused. "No. I'm not going to get off. I have a right to be here and I have a right to pay the student fare and to get my transfer." Policeman came. He listened to the bus driver and then he came to me and he asked to see my student card. He looked at it and he looked it over, and he went back to the bus driver and said, "She's doing nothing wrong. She has a right to be on the bus." So I stayed on the bus and went on home . . . That was me. . . . He was determined that I was going to pay full fare and he wasn't going to give me a transfer. So I just got my own transfer and went and sat down. And the way those ladies were, they were really begging me to get off that bus.

They were really frightened for you.

Yeah, but I wasn't. I was not.

What do you think it was that helped to build that internal strength?

Persistence. I think that it what it was. We used to go down to my grandparents' . . . They had a horse. I decided I wanted to ride the horse, so I'm out back where the horse is in a pen and trying to get the horse to come over to me, and the horse wouldn't come over to me, so I get in the pen to go to the horse. I'm going to ride this horse and everything. I didn't even stop when the horse started to rearing up on its back legs and giving its whinny and everything. But it did bring my granddaddy out . . . He swatted my bottom, but then we had a practice . . . Every time I was down there, me and Daddy Henry rode that horse. I don't know where it came from . . . but it's just always been a part of my life—a part of my life.

How do you think that attending a White school—the junior high school first and then the high school—influenced your life as an adult, personally and professionally?

It made me feel that I was on equal ground with them. And that's the way that I felt. They were no better than me. I was no better than them. We were on equal ground. . . . And it sort of went on over to when I got hired at the phone company. When I stepped off in there, I was someone they did not expect. "I've had six years of school with y'all." . . . So the things that they were able to do to other Blacks, they could not do it to me . . .

I would speak up. There was one case where there was a chief operator and she was having a meeting . . . it was a one-on-one meeting, and the Blacks that were coming out of the meeting were saying that she was using the term "Nigra," and they were complaining about it. I said, "Well, instead of complaining about it, file a grievance against her." There was a union. We're part of the union—paying it . . . "Read your union book and you'll see your rights . . ." Nobody did it. So then came my turn. Then came that word, "Nigra." I pounded my hand on that table and asked her who she thought she was calling a "Nigra" and that I was going to file a grievance . . . against her right away. She was gone within a day or two. They sent her to St. Louis. That's where the Bell's Company office was . . . I guess they gave her some more training and everything. But here in Arkansas, as far as being a chief operator here in Little Rock, you were the head as far as it went and everything. They sent her to some little podunk town in Arkansas. But here's the funniest part about it. Whenever she came to Little Rock, she always made it her business to locate me at Southwestern Bell and come by and say hi.

That's one thing I learned. A lot of them became your friends after you've had a confrontation and everything. Well, they appeared friendly and everything, so I just basically stood my ground . . .

You were with the phone company for how long?

About eighteen years until they did the divesture . . . And they gave us a chance to be hired back, but I sort of knew I wasn't going to be hired back. We had to go up to the office and sign some papers. At that time I was in the field selling the Merlin Phone System, a new one that they had out. And we had to sign some papers. And this was the amount of money that they were going to give us when we left and everything. So I go up there and I get the paper, and I reads it over and everything, and I look at the amount and I refused to sign it. And the girl says, "Why?" I said, "Are you a member of the union?" She said, "Yes." I said, "Have you not read your union book about termination when something like this comes along?" "No." I said, "Well you need to read it. Looking at this they're offering me three thousand dollars. The amount should be nineteen thousand dollars."

So I didn't sign it. Everybody else went and got their papers back. The word got around in the office . . . that they were being cheated and everything. So even when I went back for the interview and everything, I knew that they . . . weren't going to hire me back. I cost them some money.

I heard you say that . . . your belief is that everybody . . . should be treated equally. Any other way that [desegregating a junior high school] personally influenced who you are?

Yes. It just went on like that. The next place that I ended up was at the state. And at that time they were getting rid of Southwestern Bell and going to have their own phone system. So my skills were needed and . . . I don't think they were quite ready for me.

Now you're talking about somebody behind in the times, they really were. A White girl once told me—her name was Tammy—she said, "Shirley, the things that you have told them, anybody else would have been fired. How is it that you can still keep your job?" I said, " I know my rights. I know when they're in the wrong." And so I exercised my rights. Learn your rights. And that's what I did. I'm pretty much . . . outspoken.

I did that for my kids and everything . . . And I did what was considered to be the impossible in that I got a teacher fired from the Little Rock—well, from—Baseline? I don't think they were a part of Little Rock School District then. . . . I complained about this teacher. Well, I knew from parents' night that there was a problem with her. Her clothes looked like she had . . . gotten them out of the dirty clothes hamper or off the floor and put them on. She had on some white shoes that were the type that you see the women wear when they're doing square dancing, but they were filthy and everything. And I knew that she'd had a baby. A lady that stayed across the street from me was babysitting for her. But when . . . my son started coming home never with any homework assignment or anything like that, I started to going up to the school and complaining and everything. And one of the things that I told the principal was, "I think she has depression, postpartum depression, and y'all should work on getting her on medical leave." But I guess that didn't go anywhere, and I go up there one time for parent-teacher. She's going to tell me, "Charles is teaching the computer class. He does a great job." . . . I'm like, "That's your job. That's what you're getting paid for." So I go to Bob and I complain . . . again. Then she made the ultimate mistake: not only was I complaining at Bob, I was down at district office complaining about her. I go up there and actually it was on another issue . . . and I mentioned, "Oh, and by the way, Bob. Kim bought her report card home last night. Charles didn't. Can you find out for me why he didn't?" And he said, "Thank you." I said, "For what?" He said, "Now I can finally get rid of her. We can fire her." I said, "Geez, I really didn't want her fired. I think she needs medical help." . . .

But persistence and, and not backing down . . . I took them on at the schools on behalf of my kids.

How do you think your act of desegregating, beginning at East Side on up, influenced the community and the state and the nation?

I think it was a good thing. . . . Desegregation, the second time around, was much smoother, much easier. There was not as much press and everything . . .

When you say second time around, you're talking about Central?

Yes . . . when they closed it and everything and . . . started over again. It was just so much. I would be glued to the TV watching that stuff and asking my mama, "Can I go sit in with them at the lunch counter?"

And her answer was, "No." That's the way that I was in our house. We got two daily newspapers, the *Gazette* and the *Democrat*. I read both papers and everything. . . . The Black newspaper came once a week. I read—I was a prolific reader—and I would watch stuff like that on TV. It mesmerized me . . .

So you think that your act of desegregating and everybody else's act was an important thing?

Yeah, it was . . . It got everything started, so that opened up more desegregation in a lot of places—jobs and things where Blacks had not been hired before. You started to see them showing up in the banks and not just being the janitors in the department stores and things like that. So it helped a lot.

What recommendation would you have for parents who are contemplating placing their child in a school or a setting where they would be the minorities?

Nowadays, it's really not like that. It's more or less somehow going back to a segregated situation. The charter schools that are being opened up and everything. Some of them are not integrated at all. . . . It's like we're going in reverse now . . . I think that's a question that the Mexicans need to be asked, but not for the Blacks. I don't think so. We've pretty much become used to it.

There could be other situations beyond race or ethnicity. . . . What would you suggest that the parents do to prepare them for something like that?

Let them know the ins and outs—the things that could happen, you know. If you're a female in all-male, you know. If everybody starts hitting on you, you don't have to say yes. You can say no. You can keep boundaries; set your boundaries and, and go on from there. . . . Learn from what knowledge they have that you don't have and vice versa.

Is there anything else that you think would be important for the world to hear about your experience . . . ?

Well, it was a good experience. It gave me an opportunity to participate in an area of which I wanted to participate. . . . It was not as bad as it was for the junior-high level as it had been for those kids that first integrated Central and everything. The surprising thing to me was that a lot of them that maybe you had confrontation with . . . they would turn out to be your friends. . . . It wasn't nearly as bad. Not the fights that you expected or anything like that.

Sarah Jordan Talley

"At the time we just did what we were instructed to do."

My name is Sarah Ellen Jordan Talley. I now live in the Atlanta area and have been here for the last three and a half years. Prior to that

I lived in Baltimore where I was working for the federal government between Baltimore and Washington, D.C. I retired in December 2010 and relocated to the Atlanta area. . . . I lived in Little Rock, Arkansas, on Izard Street—1911 Izard Street . . . I don't think the house is there anymore, but that's where I was residing when entering the junior high school. . . . Actually I was born in Hammond, Indiana. . . . My grandfather, my mother's father, lived in Indiana. My mom was there [with] her parents before they [all] came to the other grandparents in Little Rock, Arkansas. . . . Once I was born they moved . . . to Little Rock, Arkansas, and remained there until the summer prior to my senior year in high school there at Central.

What elementary school did you attend?

Oh, wow! Granite Mountain Elementary . . . [That] took me all the way back. We lived out there in those projects . . . at that time, and that's where I attended school . . .

What junior high school did you attend?

East Side Junior High School is where I attended my junior high period. . . . I believe . . . it was in the seventh, eighth, and ninth grade. . . . I completed the entire time there at East Side.

Do you remember how many other African American students went with you to East Side?

Seven, I think, was the number of us . . . that started at East Side together.

Do you remember whether you knew some of them before you entered that school?

I did know a couple. I knew Equilla and I think Myrna. . . . I think we were all in the same general area in terms of residences—and I think Kenneth perhaps . . .

How did you learn about the fact that you were going to attend a majority-White school?

Well . . . during those times you didn't have anything to say about anything, so I was told . . . by my parents and grandmother that's where I would be attending. I think my grandmother was super-duper—who was actually my great-grandmother—was super excited that I would be attending that particular school. I think in her heart . . . that's who I'm named after actually, her name was Sarah Whitaker . . . she knew the quality of the school that they had—"they" being the Caucasian people—had, versus our schools' quality . . .

Did she talk with you about what those differences might be in terms of the quality of the schools for the Caucasians as opposed to the African Americans?

I think in her limited world view she, perhaps, felt that if we were now going to go into those schools, things—the materials, the resources, the things that would be at our disposal—would be, perhaps in her mind, a lot better or much more accessible than what we could have gotten at the other predominantly Black schools during that time.

This was your great . . .

My great-grandmother, who, at that time, was doing what they call "day work" for a White family, the Fields family. I remember clearly her walking—we'd go meet her—walking home from a day's work loaded down with goodies and things. . . . She was born December 12 [1894]. She was a twin. Her twin was Katie. My youngest sister is named after that twin. Katie, or Mary Katherine, but we called her Katie. . . . Children at that time were literally seen and not voicing their thoughts on anything. I didn't know enough to say what I felt or thought about it . . .

So you had no choice about it. You just were told . . . this is where you're going?

I was told.

Do you know how they learned about the desegregation process?

Our family did a lot of work with Mrs. Daisy Bates and the NAACP, and I'm reasonably now believing that's how information was relayed to us . . . I think they may have selected a few kids just as Mrs. Bates and the organization would have us out at ages twelve, thirteen, and fourteen going door to door to register older Black people to vote. . . . I'll never forget them telling us that we could read and write and explain it to the other older folks what voting and everything was about.

Do you think that Mrs. Bates helped to make this selection?

Oh, I don't know if she helped make the selection only, but I think she may have had some input. . . . As I think back, I'm pretty sure she may have had something to do with it. . . . We were . . . at Granite Mountain, at the elementary school; and then we must have . . . moved to the other area in Little Rock to . . . even [be] eligible for that school district . . .

What experiences did you have with the White community prior to attending this junior high school?

Personally, I did not have a lot of interaction with the White community aside from maybe store owners, shop keepers, shopping downtown and seeing them operating in—as clerks and cashiers or what have you. . . . The most up close and personal interaction was my grandmother working for that family every day. And sometimes . . . the elder White gentleman would drop her home in his car. . . . The elder Mr. Field would drop her right at the house.

Tell me some of your experiences, positive or negative, about the time that you were in junior high school.

Well, a couple of things. One, I was just overwhelmed as to the size of the school. I can remember going up and down the stairs and saying, "Wow, this is a big school." . . . I didn't have real incidents, especially negative incidents, except for I brought a little transistor radio to class. . . . The teacher must have heard it or maybe somebody told it. So they took my transistor radio. It fit right in the palm of my hand. They took it—the teacher took it . . . to the principal's office, and it stayed there until the end of school year. Not just that day, but they kept it and didn't give it back to me until school was out. I also clearly remember the day that President Kennedy was assassinated. We were in class and I remember the teacher—either we were doing nap with our heads down on the desks, but I remember the room getting dark. She either pulled the shades or turned out the lights or something and said that—and made the announcement that the president had been shot and that we needed to be quiet. But other than that, I don't have any negative memories about my days at the middle school.

How would you describe your experiences there?

I think they were good. I think they were good in terms of the education that I did receive that enabled me to go on into Central High School and be able to maintain and keep up with the other students there from the other ethnicity—predominate group. . . . It was [an] . . . excellent education. The teachers didn't single me out or give me any hassle or, or anything. . . . I remember cutting my hair into a Beatles haircut with the bangs and wearing a Beatles T-shirt to school one day. . . . That's why I had the transistor radio. I'm trying to hear the Beatles. And I had my haircut and my T-shirt on. But they just took the radio. That was it. See the more I talk, it's coming back to me. Oh boy, that's over fifty years ago!

Tell me about your relationships with the other students there.

We were all relatively close. Not just for the fact of attending school, but we would do some things afterwards together. Like I said Equilla—I would consider her my best buddy at that time—we would go to each other's house. I was generally down to her house. . . . I'm the oldest of eight, so any escape for me was good. . . . Equilla just had her brother. I would go down there and visit with her and her mom and dad . . . just do some social things.

When I said the other students, I also meant the White students . . .

Oh . . . I didn't have any. . . . I was a shy student so—not that I necessarily faded into the woodwork; I did participate in class . . . raising my hand and getting acknowledged—but I don't remember any oversights or comments made to me from anybody that I can recall.

Do you recall having friendships with them?

Other than maybe interacting during class. . . . But nothing, certainly nothing after class . . .

Would you describe the interaction, the quality of the interaction you had with the teachers or administrative staff?

I think the teachers were . . . good. . . . I didn't experience . . . anything negative from the teachers. So I think they were equally teaching me along with the others, and I don't know if that's [because] they realized that I was keeping up. I did know the answers and had good grades and that sort of thing, and it possibly helped them to not give me a hard time . . . with them during class.

You were actually a year ahead?

Right. I actually started out in school early . . . at age five, I think, instead of age six. . . . I was able to keep up and maintain the grades enough to stay right in line with them. . . . My parents had put the fear of God in me. . . . Back then, if they told you not to embarrass the family, you didn't. You dare not . . . ! . . . I was the oldest of eight, and we were all like stair steps. It would not have been a good look for me to be disobedient or getting bad reports. . . . They [had] to come along behind me . . . with the same teachers or same atmosphere that I was in. . . . I didn't talk back. I didn't question. I don't think my grandmother—maybe my mother did, but she wouldn't say anything out of fear from the grandparents—again to embarrass the family. Like, "Why does she have to go there?" or, "I don't want her going there." None of that would have gone on in the household. Nothing. . . . My grandmother, as limited as her education was, could have, or would have understood the implications and the good that could come out of me going to that school.

When you're saying grandmother, you're still referring to . . .

I mean great-grandmother . . .

Did she take on . . . that matriarchal [role] of the family?

She did. . . . There were three generations in the house and the twin sister, my Aunt Katie . . . they were the matriarchs. No questions. No if, ands, and buts about it. My mother even knew that. My father knew that. Everybody knew that. So it was a certain . . . respect that everybody had to be given or you would get out, literally . . .

Did you participate in any extracurricular activities?

No, I didn't. . . . Being the oldest of eight, I still had to help with my siblings, and I didn't do any cheerleading. I did run track . . .

What strengths, internal or external, do you think you possessed at that time to complete your junior-high level?

Oh . . . again, I defer everything back to my great-grandmother and my great-aunt. They were so strong themselves. . . . You were in church all the time, Sundays and whenever. They were mothers of the church. . . . I can clearly remember them actually making the communion bread at home. I had to flat iron it with an old dry iron and help them get the wine—grape juice, actually—together. They would . . . put their little bonnets on and take it to church on Sunday mornings. All of us had to go to church. If you didn't go to church, you got locked out and you better not come in the house while . . . we were all away at church. That was really for my brothers, you know. They were kind of difficult sometimes. But you had to go to church. I'm pretty sure that's where a lot of my strength, even now, comes from those two. I find myself even quoting them a lot, talking to my grandchildren and other relatives. It's just amazing some of the things you say. . . . You're repeating things that they said. . . . You didn't know that's what it was, but it was, again, just obedience and respect for your elders—not just those in your house, but outside your home that you were drawing your strengths from. I think I did. . . . And then working with Mrs. Bates, and the NAACP and Mr. L. C. Bates . . . Mrs. Daisy Bates . . . was really a strong lady. . . . You don't know at the time the impact and the significance . . . Just to . . . know that I was right there with them is just amazing. . . . I was right there in the middle of all of that and trying to help people have a better life through voting. I think that's where my strengths came from . . . the ability to speak up and out now.

You were pretty timid?

Very shy.

How did you move past that? Did you do that in your junior-high level . . . ?

I think it may have started then; and even with me being able, or beginning to express myself, I still could only go so far. You still were under the rule of the household. . . . I think I started to open up or show signs of opening up and becoming more vocal as the quasi-parent. When my parents were at work, everybody knew I was in charge. . . . It didn't matter; they still tried to do what they wanted to do, even though they knew it was going to be me in trouble. . . . It's a wonder I still speak to them! . . . I think that those experiences—and there's a song that says that—built my muscle, that helped me to get stronger and to be able to endure and, along with the good Lord, go through some things and come out okay. You know? So . . . yeah, I think it started back then.

What made you decide, if that's the correct term, to go to Central?

I think it was a natural progression, having attended East Side, a predominantly White school, and now here's Central, still a predominantly White school. . . . My grandmother was still in the home, and she may have had a conversation. I'm not sure. But I knew . . . that's where I was sent or that's where I went. Either way, I didn't have input. I think the only other option at that time was Horace Mann High School . . . That's how I got sent. . . . Natural progression.

How did attending a primarily . . . White school—junior high and high school—affect your adult life? . . . Think about it from personal as well as a professional standpoint.

Personally, you know, Little Rock wasn't that large of a city. . . . Even though I was at Central High School, I didn't get to finish . . . to graduate. My family moved to Detroit for jobs on the assembly line back in the early '60s. . . . In fact, they moved us there the summer prior to my senior year starting . . . the summer of '66.

How did you find out about that move?

(Laughs). They just packed up . . . the cars and we drove up.

Did you know when you were finishing school . . . you wouldn't see these students . . . anymore?

No. You know, they didn't tell kids anything. . . . You were told. You were dictated to. You . . . weren't asked. You weren't asked about leaving your friends. You weren't asked . . . a whole lot about anything. So I just remember—even my aunt moved too . . . They were going up there to get better jobs in Detroit—"making cars," I think is how they put it . . . So having attended those schools, when I got to Detroit . . . it wasn't an obvious racial imbalance up north . . . Everything was equal. So although there were pockets where we were—"we" being Black folks— lived, you didn't notice a stark difference. You were free to come and go anywhere you wanted to. You could shop anywhere. Go to the movies, theaters, all of that, anywhere with, with the other races without any real incidents or anything . . .

When you made that statement, it made me wonder whether you noticed those differences in Little Rock.

I just knew that there was just a handful of us Black kids at East Side, and then I don't think it was that many more, three or four years later, going into Central High School. . . . I can clearly remember even in 1957, I'm only seven years old at that time, but I remember the troops or seeing it on TV—the governor standing there rebelling and not letting the kids into the schools. . . . Then here I come along . . . about nine years later or so, and here I am at the same school. . . . Things hadn't really changed a whole lot. But . . . you would know when you were the little fish in a big pond. Just common sense was telling you that . . . And you're hearing your family in your ear about obeying, "Don't cause any trouble," that sort of thing. So that's what I meant about I didn't have any problems. Not that I was just shucking and jiving, but you know, I just didn't have any issues when it came to school.

You lived in a household that was authoritarian . . . and you obeyed, you complied, and when you went to the schools you did the same thing?

Yes . . . And that's what was expected . . . Not to go there to cause any trouble or make any waves . . . I still had a good time. . . . Like, I had the nerve to bring a transistor radio to school thinking I'm going to sit there and listen to the Beatles and not get caught.

So when you went to Detroit . . . you noticed that there was a difference?

Yeah, there was a difference, and there were good numbers of both races at the schools up there. Even if you had to ride the bus, you could see the buses were integrated. I don't remember any ugly names. Although I didn't hear any, personally, down there in Little Rock, either. But I think it was an easy transition. I was being conditioned for the big numbers of Caucasians when I did go up north. So it wasn't like I was afraid of them or anything. I had been assimilating with them for a couple of years or so already.

How did attending those schools influence or affect your life?

Educationally it helped a whole lot when I did go to Detroit. . . . Having attended East Side and Central High School, when I got to Detroit [for] senior year, I only needed [to take] senior English. . . . I was out of school by ten o'clock. . . . I had enough credits almost to graduate except for senior English. . . . So the education . . . was one of the best. . . . That carried me quite a way. I didn't go right into college after graduating high school.

It influenced it quite a bit. . . . I only had to go . . . to that particular one class for my whole senior year. . . . I was able to get a job, full-time job in high school. . . . Once I graduated high school, I went to work for the telephone company, Michigan Bell at that time . . . I would have to be at work at ten in the morning, get off at two in the afternoon, then go home, come back by six to ten at night. So one time between that two o'clock and that six o'clock, I walked over to the federal building and put in an application and they called me. . . . I stayed with the government almost forty years . . . I had to work my way up. . . . That foundation did it for me. . . . So I'm still grateful for that.

You said that you didn't go immediately into college?

To this day I haven't finished, but I went to . . . Wayne County, Wayne State, University of Detroit—just different schools in between the jobs . . . trying to work. . . . As far as I'm concerned I do have my degree. Life will do that to you if nothing else . . . Good education is priceless.

And then to work over—you said forty years at that one job?

At that agency. [I] worked up to the point where I had radio shows, TV shows, [and] newspaper columns in the position that I was in with the federal government—public education regarding our benefits . . . I still say "our," even though I've been retired now almost five years . . .

How do you think your actions of desegregating a Little Rock public junior high school influenced the city, the community, the state, the nation?

I think it's had a tremendous influence throughout my lifetime. There have been situations that have arisen either socially or personally where I've had to let people know about the school I attended—primarily Central High School and the history behind that. A lot of them, my peers, know that name. I told them, "Oh yeah. That's where I went to school." [They] say, "You did?" . . . Then that little pride comes up and I said, "I wasn't there in '57, but I was definitely there in the '60s . . . shortly thereafter." . . . That has been a wonderful thing to recall and brag about and just remind myself as to how far I have come from that experience there at Central High School. So it's been good . . .

You mentioned that your junior high school days went very well for you. Did the same thing happen at Central?

It did. Central, I think, I was getting more acclimated to the physical size of the school. . . . Central was huge; but then when I started the high school period, more African American students were there . . . I guess coming from the other feeder junior high schools. So I was getting more comfortable being in that environment. I don't know if it was a "safety in numbers" point of view, but it was . . . I wouldn't say stress. I didn't have any stress. But I was more relaxed with the more people there. We would walk home together from school; just little things like that made it a lot easier. . . . Maybe by that time they figured we weren't going anywhere. . . . They kind of backed off or slowed down . . . from the other races.

What recommendation would you have for parents who are contemplating placing their child in an environment where that child might be a minority . . . based on ethnicity, or gender, or something else?

Well, the first thing I would tell them is to make sure before that child leaves them that the child is rooted and grounded in themselves and they know who they are. They have good self-esteem and biblical knowledge is in there—that's really the foundation they need to be able to draw upon at any time. And also to remind them that everybody is not in love with you . . . Not everybody. They may grin and talk . . . I tell some of my family members and other people who like to be in that environment where they're the only one, or maybe the only one that they want in that environment, I tell them "Okay, when the revolution comes, see what side of the street they're going to be on, versus where you are," you know. "I know they're cool. You think they're cool and they may be," I say, "but don't believe all of that . . ." There are some things that are innate, that they have been taught from their homes about us—not that we did a lot of teaching about them to our kids. . . . I would certainly caution any parent who's about to put their child in that situation. Children nowadays don't get what it has taken for them to be where they are, even though there are still barriers that have to be knocked down. They can't go trying to knock the barrier down believing that these people love them . . . that everybody loves them and wants them to be there. They don't. So I would let them know in no uncertain terms, "Just be prepared. Be overprepared. They're going to throw some curves at you; so you have to be able to stand through all of that." But I think if they have that good foundation and the parents let them know that they love them, they'll be with them to support them—but also if the parents are confident that the child can withstand those sorts of slings and arrows, then let them go. But if you already know little Johnny is [a] hothead, little Johnny can't do his or her work, don't send them over there. You're setting them up to fail.

You took me back to a question I might have overlooked. Who prepared you to go into East Side?

I think my household did. . . . I'm the first born . . . so there were always responsibilities for me to make sure they were taken care of before I did anything socially . . . I don't know if at that time I can say back then that I was ready for it or not; but the preparedness was from home . . . with my great-grandmother and great-aunt and my parents . . .

Did some of the community organizations also help you with preparation . . . ?

NAACP. That's the only one that comes to mind for me . . . is the NAACP and how they would get us young people to . . . help them canvass the community.

But not necessarily to talk about the school desegregation with you all?

No . . . That was my family's, as far as I know, unless Mrs. Bates mentioned it during some of our meetings. We actually went to meetings with them . . .

Do you have any other comments that you would like to make with regard to your experience?

To even think that I was a part of some history that people want to hear about when I was just a little girl with plaits, not even braids, plaits in her head and glasses . . . doing this. And more than fifty . . . years later having done that, and the impact that it could possibly have on life going forward for somebody else is just amazing. I'm eternally grateful for it. I think the good Lord knows what He's doing. We just don't know, but if we do and follow Him, it all lines up. . . . He knows the path. I was on that path for a reason, as we all were. And now to be able to go back, eventually, and share that with my grandchildren is really the blessing in it all. We were brought through that . . . with God's hand, I'm sure. . . . Back then community was community. Just like I keep saying about my grandmother and great-grandmother and my parents, that was most people's household, you know? Everybody knew it took everybody to help us through a lot of things. When we had to go to the store, if I passed Ms. Ann's house and she knew I was going to the store I could—she stopped me and I'd go get whatever . . . add her to my little list. You can't do that now with people. People barely want you speaking to their children, let alone doing anything for them. But I think this, this experience, unbeknownst to me, was an excellent one, a good one, and certainly life changing for me. . . . At the time we just did what we were instructed to do and made it through—made it through . . .

Glenda Wilson

"You went, you got through it, and you got out."

What junior high school did you attend?
East Side. . . . I was there from seventh grade through ninth grade.
How many other students attended with you? African American students.
I have talked to one other person that attended with me, and we think there were nine who started in the seventh grade. We're pretty sure there were seven who actually stayed the entire three years . . . We think there were seven females and two males. All of the females . . . I think, went from seventh through ninth grade. The two males . . . we don't know if they stayed the entire first year or if they left in the middle of the year.

How did you learn that you were going to attend a majority-White school?

I don't really remember. I know that we went through a vetting process. . . . I don't know if someone called or if we received a letter. Much of this is hazy. It wasn't the most enjoyable period in my life. . . . A lot of this has been suppressed. . . . I know that my parents were involved in the process of . . . the interviews and the discussions about whether or not . . . I wanted to try to go; but how I was actually notified, I don't remember.

When you mention "vetting process" and then "interviews," is that part of the vetting process?

That's what I remember. But that could be faulty memories. I do know that we attended meetings. There were some folks . . . in my elementary school that had expressed an interest in attending. I know they weren't selected. . . . My recollection is that there was a vetting process. . . . I really don't know how they selected any of us. When I showed up that first day, I knew one other person at East Side. She had gone to my elementary school. The other folks were total strangers. So how we were selected—if they [said] . . . "You need to have these grades, and you need to have this personality; you need to have this"—I don't really know . . .

No other children went with you to school on that first day?

One person did. Myrna Davis was the person that attended the same elementary school that I did. We were both selected out of the folks who had expressed an interest that we knew. My mother drove both of us that first morning. We got out of the car. We were escorted into the building by the police. . . . I don't remember much after that. I think I only remember the police escort [because] there was a photo . . . on the front page of the paper the next morning, showing us going in . . .

Did your parents talk with you about doing anything to prepare you for that desegregation process?

I'm sure they did . . . but I don't remember specifics . . . I mean, after having watched the debacle at . . . Central a few years before, I'm sure there were discussions about how to carry yourself and what to do in case there was trouble, especially on the first day. I just don't remember specifics. . . . I remember things about elementary school that I don't remember about East Side. I remember teachers' names from elementary school . . .

Which school was that?

Booker T. Washington. On the south side of Little Rock. I can remember my principal's name. I can remember the names of teachers. If you ask me the principal of East Side, I couldn't tell you. If you asked me most of my teachers' names, I couldn't tell you. . . . They weren't people that were meaningful to me.

What made the people at Booker T. Washington meaningful to you?

It was a very nurturing environment. Everybody knew everybody else. You had the feeling that folks cared about whether or not you did well. They were pushing you towards excellence. At East Side, I felt tolerated, not . . . embraced. I didn't feel as though anybody cared if I succeeded. In fact, in some instances, I think there might have been a desire for us to fail just so they could say, "See, I told you so. You shouldn't have been here in the first place." . . . But Mrs. Floyd was my principal at Booker T. . . . I can't tell you who the principal was at East Side. I can't tell you if it was the same person all three years. I just don't remember . . .

What experiences did you have about the White community or with anyone within the White community prior to going to East Side?

In fact, I don't recall too much exposure. We lived in a very insular environment. The church my parents attended was African American. The schools we attended were African American. The social events we attended were African American. The organizations were African American. We didn't really see a need to interact with the "majority population."

So your first significant interaction . . .

Was being dropped into East Side.

"Dropped into?"

Yes.

Do you remember anything when you came home . . . during that first year and talked with your parents about that experience? Do you remember any of those conversations?

Not really. . . . We did our homework. We went to school. . . . It was one of those periods that you got through, as opposed to enjoyed. It wasn't an environment that . . . was nurturing, so you shut it out. You just got through it. You just took it a day at a time. You excelled if you could. You did your best. You felt as though the eyes of the community were on you. They sent you there. They expected you to do well, so you wanted to live up to that, but I don't recall specific conversations.

Would you talk about the things that you do remember when you were going to East Side?

Well, I think one of the . . . things that stood out was that we weren't included in many of the things that happened at the school. We couldn't attend certain events. If they had a dance, we didn't go. Or if we attended, we had to sit in the bleachers. We weren't allowed on the floor. If they had basketball games away or sometimes even at the school, we couldn't go. The away games, the other school perhaps wasn't integrated. The home games, perhaps—the school wasn't integrated, and they didn't want us there. There might be problems. At least that's what they said. So it was a sense of disassociation from the majority of the students there. Most of us were on the honor roll. Most of us excelled academically. Some of us were allowed into some of the extracurricular activities. Not the band. Again, they traveled and did things like that. But there were three of us on the school newspaper. And I think that's [because] we did well in English, and it was kind of difficult to keep us off. . . . There were certain activities that they had that we just weren't allowed to attend. Other than that . . . I have vague memories. . . . It's like you went, you got through it, and you got out . . .

I don't remember being called names. I'm sure I was, but maybe . . . it was, you just walked down the hall and you ignored them. So after a while, ignoring became the norm. . . . You just didn't pay attention to the negative comments. I was talking to a friend that I still know who started with me there, Alfreda Brown. . . . She was saying that there was one guy . . . who used to walk down the hall and call us "tar babies." I don't remember it. I blocked it out . . . but she remembered that. It's interesting, as you talk to folks who went through the same experience, what some folks remember and some folks don't; and I think mine is a don't—most of it. It was just . . . you were there; you tolerated them. . . . They weren't so meaningful that what they said impacted you that much; at least that's the way I looked at it. They weren't going to be a part of my life forever, so I just got through it. . . .

I knew that, much to my mom's chagrin, that when I left to go to college, I would never go to an all-White school. She thought that

I was regressing. I had spent six years in an integrated environment and I should just continue. I knew that, for sanity's sake, I had to go someplace where I was in the majority. But she thought I was going to get an inferior education, and I had to continually explain to her that education is more than books. It's also the socialization process. I think that for me, my social development was stunted. I attended predominately White schools. . . . You meet your first boyfriend. You go out on dates. You do all of that, and it's usually with people that you meet while you're in school. We didn't have that. In the neighborhood I lived in, I didn't know a lot of the kids there. . . . From a social development standpoint, I think I was stunted . . . Now academically, I don't know if I would have done as well had I gone to a predominantly African American school or not. Probably. But I'll never know.

You didn't interact with the neighborhood children?

I moved to a new neighborhood between the sixth and seventh grades. The kids that I would have known from elementary school were no longer in my life. I was in a new neighborhood. I didn't know them. I didn't see them in school. . . . I moved to the west part of Little Rock. So between commuting and homework and those kinds of things, I really didn't have that kind of interaction with the neighborhood folks. . . . Everything changed for me. I mean, we were involved in activities. We were part of the . . . NAACP . . . I met people there, but a lot of them were older. Some of them are my older sister's friends. So, again, I think I was socially underdeveloped as a result of the interaction.

You all remained in the same church community?

Right. But it was a small church. Not a lot of young people in the church. It was a small Presbyterian church, and there aren't a lot of African American Presbyterians in Arkansas. So even from that standpoint there weren't a lot of folks with which to interact.

Do you remember any teacher who stood out, either positively or negatively, in your junior high school?

None. . . . Well . . . I think, my homeroom teacher. . . . She was an older White woman. It used to fascinate me that you could see her veins in her hand. But that was it. I mean, it was something totally superficial. But as far as somebody reaching out and taking you under their wing and helping you to grow and develop—no one. They might have, but I don't remember. . . . It wasn't strong enough to have made an impression on me that I can say, "Oh yes, Mrs. So-and-So, or Mr. So-and-So really helped me get through this process. They were nurturing. . . . They bucked the system, and they helped me." No. Nothing.

You went on to Central?

I did.

What made you go to Central instead of to Horace Mann?

It was expected. I don't know how else to explain it. . . . The kids who went to East Side went to Central.

You didn't see that you might have had a choice to move . . . to something else?

I might have. . . . I think my parents would have been disappointed. To them I was on a path . . . I think at that time the assumption was that integration was better. I have since changed my mind about that whole premise; but it was, "You're in a school with more opportunities to grow, develop, [and] learn. Facilities are better. . . . They've got more equipment. They've got the teachers . . . have better skills." So it was expected. . . . As I became an adult, I realized . . . academics are important, but nurturing is important too. There has to be a balance between the two, and unfortunately for me, I didn't get that balance. I got the academics, but I didn't get the nurturing.

Is that also why you came to think maybe integration was not the essential thing that needed to take place?

Well, I think I saw the disintegration of the African American community in Little Rock . . . once integration hit. I mean, the businesses that African Americans owned—even the churches—are slowly dying away and people are moving towards majority organizations and institutions. I think there was another . . . kind of sense of community. . . . Prior to integration you had doctors, lawyers, plumbers, carpenters, unemployed all living in the same African American neighborhood. You had role models with which you could identify. Once integration hit and people started to move out from those neighborhoods into other places, you were kind of left with this, this void. So I don't see a lot of value in it. I think we've lost a lot. Maybe we gained some things, but . . . I think we lost so much more. . . . I look at the fact—probably when I was growing up and a little before, most of the folks were bricklayers, carpenters, all those jobs—African Americans did those. Then there was this assumption that they wanted their children to do better. So they sent us to school, and they sent us to college, and we lost all those skills. Well, the people that are making money and are never out of work are the brick masons, the carpenters, the plumbers. But . . . somebody came up with this idea that . . . those trades were beneath the professionals, and that's the most ludicrous thing. . . . A college degree doesn't guarantee success, but our parents and our grandparents, for some reason, thought that. They were told that or maybe they just wanted a better life, and it was something to try. But I don't think that's true . . .

How did attending a primarily White junior high then high school affect or influence your adult life, both personally and professionally?

I think that my social development was stunted. When I got to college I wanted to belong to everything. I mean any opportunity that came forth, I joined.

Where did you attend?

I went to Howard, in Washington, D.C. If there was a political campaign, I was part of it. If there was a club, I was part of it . . . could have been to the detriment of my academic life. . . . My grades were fine, but I probably could have . . . been on dean's list if I wasn't in everything. But I had to—I felt stunted. I felt like, "Oh wow! Now there's this buffet and I can partake of all of it, and I don't have to fight to do it. I don't have to be a first to do it. I don't have to . . . beg, borrow, whatever, to write an article for a newspaper . . . to join a club. I can just do it if I want to." So from that perspective, it kind of made me a bit more outgoing, I guess—a bit more aggressive in going out and taking advantage of opportunities that were presented. I also said that it stunted me—I don't know about the rest of the folks—on in interpersonal level, not having had dealings with a lot of African American males in junior high and high school. When I got to Howard . . . it was . . . a strange environment to me. I hadn't developed those social skills in high school and junior high. I was a slow starter . . . from that perspective.

Did it carry on later on into your adult life as well?

Well, I think the one thing that carried on into—even today—is a basic distrust of people who aren't like me. I see Caucasians and I always wonder what their agenda is. My first exposure to them was not a positive one. I never think that they look at me and see me as a person. I think they see me first as Black and then maybe as a female and then somebody to be tolerated. But I probably will never have a White

Our Stories

friend. I mean I have Whites that I know and I interact with in business and that I can socialize with anybody, but I would never have a White friend. . . . My first exposure was East Side. My continued exposure was the three years at East Side and the three years at Central, and those are very formative years. So, no—I don't trust them.

And your profession now is what?

I am basically retired. But for twenty years I had a small management consulting firm, and I guess that could be part of my need for control. (Laughs.) I was never able to really work for anybody else, so I just decided to work for myself. . . . Now I do part-time work.

But in that controlled environment you succeeded?

I did . . . For twenty years I did a lot of federal contracting. . . . I was able to pay the bills, pay other people's salaries. . . . I'm not rich or anything, but I'm comfortable.

How do you think your actions of desegregating a Little Rock junior high school influenced Little Rock, the state, and the nation?

I don't know that it had that much of an impact at all. . . . It was part of the whole desegregation of the South process that I'm not so sure benefited Black people in the long run. I look back on it and wonder if what I did mattered from . . . the big picture perspective. . . . A lot of African American schools were closed. . . . A lot of African American teachers were demoted. . . . A lot of African American children were not nurtured as much as they should be. I look at Central now and I don't see the progress that we thought would have been made with all the sacrifices that a lot of folks made. . . . Sometimes you think that maybe you were detrimental as opposed to a positive impact.

You just highlighted . . . a series of influences, even though it might not have been positive in your view . . .

I think I was trying to find a positive . . . and I didn't. I'm not finding a real positive impact. . . . Even the folks at Central in '57—I don't know whether or not their sacrifices really benefitted Black folks in the long run. . . . They pretty much started this whole process. . . . Yes, we've got some judges and we've got . . . folks in different positions, but when you look at Black folks as a whole, not a lot has changed. It's kind of like South Africa . . . after apartheid . . . Some folks over there are doing really well, but then you think about the folks in Soweto. . . . Their life hasn't changed that much, you know. . . . We went to a school and we looked at the children, and there's such hope. But you're wondering, "Are they just going to superimpose another kind of suppression on them, even though the people in the positions of power—the visible folks—have skin like theirs? . . . So sometimes I look at the South and that is the same . . . it's, "Are we any better off?" My grandparents had a farm. My mother tells me that even during the wars where they were rationing, they always had food. They always had a place to sleep. . . . Maybe they didn't have the best, but they always had the necessities. Now you look at children who go hungry every day. When I was growing up, we didn't see a lot of that. Somebody always took you in. Grandma, grandpa, Aunt So-and-So, always took you in. Now it seems like the fiber of the community has disintegrated and nobody's taking you in anymore. You know, it's like integration changed us, but perhaps not for the better.

Do you have any other comments that would help the community and the world to know more about those experiences . . . ?

I recall . . . the day Kennedy was shot and killed. We were in journalism class, and a boy ran in and this—this is this guy that my friend told me used to call us "tar baby"—and he was so excited that Kennedy was dead. He was happy. That always stuck.

How could you tell that he was happy?

Oh, he was telling us. . . . He was from an ultraconservative family. They didn't like the Kennedys. Kennedy was Catholic. He was liberal. He says, "I'm glad he's dead!" So . . . it wasn't conjecture. . . . And I was like, "Hmmm, this is who I'm in school with?" So that stuck. . . . It was . . . a . . . negative scene. . . . A person who . . . in the midst of tragedy saw joy. Those are the kind of people I was dealing with every day. . . . I'm lucky pretty much to have survived . . .

What would you tell a parent who was contemplating placing their child into a situation that would make them a minority, whether it was a race, ethnicity, or any other type . . . ?

I'd tell them not to do it, but nobody listens to me. I have cousins who—upper-middle class—have young children, and they send them to predominately White schools. They think the schools are better. I tell them, "Don't do it." But they think that in order for the children to have advantages, to meet the right people, to get the right jobs later on, that they have to put them in those environments. Maybe it's different today.

It's more accepted, and those children aren't going to be called names, but I think that they are missing out on some socialization that they can only get in environments where they are majority. But, as I said, nobody listens to me, so I just shake my head and say, "Okay, I told you." . . . The world is different from the '60s and '70s. People keep telling me they don't see race anymore. Maybe they don't, but I still do. There's always, in the back of my mind that, "You can't trust them." . . . I remember, I was little and there was a White family who moved in not too far, and they were poor—really, really poor . . . This . . . is elementary school . . . They moved in nearby where we were living . . . We were going to give them food. My mother allowed us to do it, but she also, in a subtle way, cautioned us that, "White people, no matter how poor they are, still think that they are better than you. . . . When their circumstances change they will forget the kindness . . ." It happened. . . .

In what way? . . . You gave them food and they accepted it?

They accepted it. But later on . . . I guess the parents were able to right whatever the problem was. . . . They no longer wanted to be a part of the little group. You asked me before if I'd had any experiences prior to, and that was an experience. . . . It just came to mind. . . . It just reinforced later on the fact that people will use you but not necessarily care about you. So I'm very distrustful. I mean, my little cousins, I worry about them. I worry that, later on, if they have to come face-to-face while driving while Black—face-to-face with someone who doesn't allow them to do certain things [because] of the color of their skin, that they won't have the coping mechanisms they need in order to succeed. . . . You see all these kids whose parents have money. . . . They bought them cars, and they think, "Well, nobody's going to do the things they did to you, to me. I'm protected by money and wealth." Well, money and wealth doesn't change the fact that if you're a Black person walking down the streets of Beverly Hills at night, they're going to pick you up. Even though you live in the neighborhood, they're going to pick you up and ask you why you're there. It happens all the time. . . . I don't know what neighborhoods they don't want you in Little Rock, but it happens constantly. . . . I don't think they know . . . They have a void in their history. They have no idea what happened in the '60s, and they don't want to know. It's not a part of their curriculum in schools.

It's not a part of the discussions they have with parents. They don't want to know. To them life started when they opened their eyes. They don't look back. They don't try to find out the shoulders upon which they climbed to get where they are. They don't want to know.

Do you think they need to know?

Oh, they definitely need to know. . . . This color-blind society that they think they live in is a bubble that's going to burst soon, and they're going to be the fallout. I hope I'm wrong, but I don't think I am.

CHAPTER 4

Forest Heights Junior School

One African American student desegregated Forest Heights Junior High School in 1961. As was mentioned previously in this book, another student, Ida Butler, was listed in the newspaper as being assigned to attend the school. Her parents, however, petitioned during the summer that she be reassigned to attend Dunbar Junior High School. Because the primary author is Dr. Bell-Tolliver, who is normally the interviewer, Dr. Lind conducted this interview.

LaVerne Bell-Tolliver

"I knew I had to move forward."

[My name is LaVerne Bell-Tolliver.] I attended Forest Heights Junior High School in Little Rock, Arkansas, in 1961. . . . I was the only one to attend that school for the first two years, the seventh and eighth grades. In the ninth grade, two other students attended with me, but [for] those first two years, I was the only African American student there.

Did you know the other two students who came in your ninth grade year before they attended?

I knew one of them. . . . She lived a few blocks over [from my house]. The other student, I did not know.

And you completed all three grades there?

Yes I did.

How did you learn you were going to attend a majority-White school?

I'm the oldest of six children, and some of them were born during that time . . . They loaded us into the car one day after I finished the sixth grade and drove me to Forest Heights, and they said, "This is your new school."

Did they do anything to prepare you for the change?

No. That was the preparation . . . Actually, I thought I was going to be attending the all–African American school, which is where every African American child went up until that year. . . . In . . . the sixth grade, probably the last few weeks, the sixth grade class took a walk to Dunbar Junior High School, to tour that school and to see where we would be going. . . . That was where I thought I would be attending until that time. . . . My parents, and probably many parents of that generation, were very autocratic and very structured. . . . They did not allow for much input. Questions would not necessarily be tolerated, at least in our home, and so when I found out, I didn't feel comfortable in asking, "What do you mean? Why am I going here . . . to this particular school?" I just knew, "This was it." . . . At some point along the way, my parents must have told me that one other student was supposed to attend with me. . . . It's my belief—my parents are passed away now . . . that they understood even until the first day that someone else was going to be attending, and then they learned that she was not.

Was there anybody else in your family, or in the church, or any of your relatives that helped prepare you for that experience?

No. Now I have a cousin that tells the story of an aunt who brought clothes and all kinds of things for me during that summertime. I have no memory of that. But she explained to me that she remembered my aunts bringing clothes to make sure that I looked nice for school. . . . That would have been a certain level of preparation. I had a close-knit church family, and some of my extended family members attended that church. They were all supportive of me, even though they didn't say anything to me about that particular school or that experience. . . . I felt their love and their nurturing during that particular time. At some point during the first year or two perhaps . . . I attended some meetings. . . . I can't tell you whether they were sponsored by the NAACP or others. . . . During the time that I've been doing the research for this project, I've heard several names being mentioned—meetings being held at the Dunbar Community Center, and meetings being held at one of the churches— Bethel A.M.E. . . . I think they may have been at Bethel. . . . I'm not sure . . . who would have sponsored those, but that would have been some level of preparation. I don't know if anyone understood the level of preparation I would have needed to be the only student there . . .

What . . . were your experiences . . . with the White community before you attended school?

I had no experience beyond being cursed at or treated in some harsh manner. Let me explain that. When I was in the first through the third grade, attending Stephens Elementary—I attended there . . . through my sixth grade—[for] the first few years, my family and I lived on a street just behind that school. . . . That was totally African American. That neighborhood was insulated. We had no contact with . . . the White community . . . The children didn't have contact beyond . . . the local grocery store owner . . . His store [was] right down the street from our house. Other than that, everyone else was African American. Our stores were on what is called Ninth Street here in Little Rock, and the movie theater was there, the hairdressers, the doctors—everyone was located on Ninth Street. I didn't know any different. . . . The summer of my third grade year, I believe, we moved to Twenty-Fourth Street, and everything changed. There were very few African Americans there. . . . When I'd walk to the store, that is when I was met with a lot of hatred . . . People who were driving cars [would] throw things out of their windows, call me derogatory names, and otherwise try to make life very negative. So that was my experience with the white community before I went to junior high school.

What experiences stand out in your mind from your junior high days . . . ?

You know, it's funny that it's usually the harsh ones that stand out in my mind. . . . I'll try to also think about some positive ones as well. . . . The first one was the first day of school when my mother took me to school. . . . I could tell that she was pretty anxious, pretty nervous, even though she didn't say anything during that time. She drove me to school. . . . That day I remembered her holding my hand. . . . This school . . . was in an affluent area . . . Children of privilege were attending that school. So there was not outwardly on that first day the name calling or yelling or jeering or any of that. . . . When we walked through the crowd that was standing around the door, waiting for the school to open, one little child said "Hi." . . . I could tell that my mother was calmer right then. . . . She left, but that was the last time that child said anything to me. No one else said anything . . . on that particular day. . . . The other memories that I have are of people who would . . . push one person onto me and say, "Is the color going to rub off on you?" or "Is the Black going to come off on you?" to that person's friend.

People . . . ignored me, which was more often the case . . . I don't know if anyone can express how [it] feels to be ignored for so many years. Most of the time, no one said anything to me at all other than those few people who would taunt me in different kinds of ways. . . . Now there were people in class, and I think it was maybe the second year or the third year, who might say something or talk to me, one or two people—in class—and that was about it. But they wouldn't say anything outside of class . . . There was this somewhat-understood pact that I might be talked to *inside* the class. That's as far as the students went. There were a couple of teachers that seemed to be at least—I wouldn't say friendly, but accommodating in some kind of way. I had a home economics teacher who was rather kind, and even though there were several negative incidences that happened out of her sight . . . in the home ec class, they didn't happen while she was around, so she wouldn't have known some things. It's amazing how students can find ways to do things. . . . The gym teacher—I learned years later when we were talking at some kind of reunion—seemed to have attempted to befriend me, although at the time, I didn't understand that. But she [said she] really was hoping . . . I would join some of the organizations. I had no knowledge. I did join the pep squad, by . . . the way. I had a choir teacher who allowed me to join . . . the group. I say "allowed" because I was hoarse at the time that I was trying out, both years . . . So I don't know if he ever knew whether I could sing or not, but that was so kind! (Laughs.) . . . I also remember one teacher who did a kindness. I'm not sure if she was kind, but she did a kindness . . . and that was a day when it was minus five degrees. I happened to arrive at school . . . so early that the doors of the buildings were locked. . . . She saw me standing against the wall trying to just find a way to keep warm. . . . Initially she unlocked her door and was preparing to walk in, and . . . turned around, and just told me to come on into the room. She never said a word to me or anything [during that time]. It was my teacher, by the way . . . But she never said a word to me. But she allowed me to come into the room where it was warm. That was a kindness.

You mentioned that you joined the pep squad and you were in the choir. Did you do any other extracurricular activities?

There was one year where I also actually became the Red Cross representative. . . . I know it seems so small, but when I was in the sixth grade, I was president of my student council for the student body. . . . I was shy . . . So for me to even try to run and be elected to something . . . was a major feat for me, especially in junior high school. Since no one else wanted to run, I got it. . . . It was a good feeling . . . to be that. I was in the same homeroom for three years, so at least those people knew who I was . . . So running unopposed was good.

What would you say your strengths or your resources were that helped you get to the end of ninth grade?

Oh, goodness . . . I have to acknowledge, first of all . . . that by the ninth grade I had ulcers. So I didn't quite make it totally successfully . . . But I mentioned the church already . . . My faith in God really was a strong thing for me that helped me to make it, because He was the only one that was with me during that time. I think my church family and my extended family members—really, just knowing that they were supportive of me as a person . . . helped me to do that. And I think that my parents tried to be supportive during that time. Even though they did not take the time . . . I don't think they knew how to do it . . . to ask me what was going on or allow that. In our family, we had a number of other things occurring at the same time that the desegregation was going on. So as much as they could, they were supportive of that process. But I know that my extended family was helpful to me during that time—my aunts and my uncles and those people who were involved. So my internal resources—that's a strange thing. At that time . . . I don't think that I could have identified an internal resource during that time, just determination to make it through another day. I think was my greatest strength—just that determination.

The word "resilience" comes to mind.

Resilience comes to my mind for some of the other people . . . I don't know if I was resilient . . . I think that was a very hard time . . . I think not being able to say, "No, I don't want to go . . . ," just made it so that I knew I had to move forward.

Did you attend a predominantly White high school as well?

Yes I did. . . . I attended Hall High School, and some of the school board record's meeting notes indicate that they really wanted to keep that—I don't know a polite way to say it—but as White as possible.

So . . . they deliberately did not allow very many African Americans to attend. It does not appear that . . . many African Americans wanted to attend . . . They wanted to attend Central, more than likely. And the school district lines kept changing, so that if more African Americans lived in that area, all of a sudden the school district lines changed again . . . Consequently there [were] never any more than nine or ten students . . . that were African American in that school at the time that I was there. I think there were about seven in my class, so I never attended . . . any class that had any other African Americans in the class . . . Nevertheless . . . having five to seven students [attending the school] was a huge difference to me . . . I felt much more comfortable. There were people that were sitting with me at lunch.

I forgot to mention that when I was in junior high school, absolutely no one ever . . . sat with me at lunch, except for when I was in the ninth grade and those two students were there. But I had become so desensitized to the situation, I couldn't even appreciate the fact that two students were there by that time . . . By the time that I went to high school, I knew a couple of the students, and I was just so excited to be able to have someone to sit with me. It was so different, not being ignored . . . even though the same can't be said of being in the gymnasium during assemblies or those kinds of things, because similar things would happen . . . When I was in junior high school, I would have a whole row to myself . . . because no one would sit on the row. In the high school, they would just not sit on either side of me, or they would ask for me to scoot down . . . so that their friends could sit with them. . . . I think the difference for me, being in junior high and high school, was that I knew that there were other African Americans that were there . . . and I felt better at that time.

How do you think your experiences [of] attending a White school influenced your adult life?

I think that it has had untold effects on my adult life, in that it affects the way that I need space to myself. I think . . . even if I had attended other schools, I probably would have been more of an introvert, but I need huge amounts of space. . . . I have, on the other hand, learned how to do things by myself because of the fact that I had to do them then . . . It has also affected, unfortunately, relationships . . . because I never learned how to . . . during that time, junior high and high school, is where you develop socially, emotionally, and all of those kinds of things. So it's been a challenge to learn how to relate from that social aspect. I can do very well in a work environment or where there's a purpose, something to accomplish . . . because that's what I learned in school. I learned how to accomplish tasks . . . and to move forward . . . those kinds of things . . . I have been successful in the work world and in the professional settings . . . But in that emotional setting, that's the piece that still seems to have ragged edges or gaps, no matter how hard I've worked on that piece . . .

How do you think your actions [of] desegregating the schools influenced our community and our city?

I look around this community now that I've returned to Arkansas, and I see, really, some positives and some negatives. The positives seem to be that on the surface, people do seem to get along a little bit better interracially. From time to time, there seems to be more interaction; there are people that are employed at a lot of different levels . . . There's been an African American mayor here, and there's an African American city manager. Those situations would have never occurred without desegregation beginning in the schools and in other types of areas, so that is a positive kind of thing. Even the fact that people are able to live in the [state] of Arkansas in various communities—maybe not in every community . . . that seems to be positive. On the other hand, with regard to the schools, things are in a horrible situation. There's what you call "re-segregation" in many areas. Even though—say, for instance, at Central High and in other places, people attend the schools that are Caucasian and African American . . . Latinos attend those schools—they re-segregated in certain areas. . . . There are many more charter schools and other types of private schools where many Caucasians attend. In some ways people have re-segregated. . . . Ninth Street, I just can't help but mention how our Black community was decimated . . . decimated. People lost jobs as teachers in the various schools. Businesses just completely went away because of the desegregation process. . . . I think there's a complex way of looking at it. It's not all good or all bad, but some people lost almost everything . . . I think that may also speak to why the students are not performing as well. We lost something else, culturally, that we haven't been able to regain. Whereas, in the past, the strengths of the African American families that I really hold dearly and have researched, education, and hard work ethic, and extended family—those kinds of things have taken a huge hit . . . in part as a result of the desegregation process.

As a nation, where do you think we are now?

Well, now, in 2014, we're awaiting the results of a trial of an officer who shot down a young man who was just out of his teens . . . in Missouri. . . . There's a large emphasis on the fact that race was and has been an issue there. There was a young man a couple of years ago that was killed for wearing a hood and drinking Kool-Aid . . . Those are not isolated incidences. We have coined a term, "driving—or even walking—while Black," because people are impacted in a disparate proportion because of race. . . . Racism has not gone away. Some people thought that since an African American president or biracial president was elected, that we would live in whatever was called a "postracial society." We don't have that . . . We have not arrived there. . . . We have a long way to go. I think the fact that we can talk about those issues a little bit more has been an important stand. But in some ways, we're more of a racist community . . . state and nation, now in the twenty-first century, than we were before.

What recommendations would you have for parents who were contemplating placing their child into an environment where the child will be a minority?

I would recommend to the parents that they think long and hard about that . . . and consider whether . . . they have provided that child with the proper care, confidence, consideration that they need to have in order to help that child be prepared to be okay wherever they are. Consider whether or not they as a family are able and willing and committed to talking with each other more in a democratic style, if they're committed to listening to that child. Explore that decision, and whether they're willing to support that child throughout the entire process. All children are not able to handle situations along that line. . . . Whether it's a racial issue, or whether there's something else that would place that child in a minority role, they need to have every type of emotional and spiritual support possible to be able to make that move into that community. . . . As a child, being seen as different is a reason for many people to bully them, or to cause challenges for them. . . . Some children would not be able to handle that. Making the decision to place a child, whether it's in an academic setting or in other places, might be helpful for them in terms of making progress . . . academically or physically or whatever. However, it may hamper them, as it did for me, in many other areas. So the child needs to have parents who understand the potential repercussions and are willing to provide that network of support in all those other areas. . . . They also need to have a strong faith network and a strong ability to plug into God, because . . . that child will need to be able to have that resource available. If they don't have that, I would not place that child there. Of course they would still need that wherever they're going . . . but they would need it so much more when they are intentionally placing that child in a situation where they will be . . . different, and they will be seen as different.

CHAPTER 5

Pulaski Heights Junior High School

Two students desegregated Pulaski Heights Junior High School in 1962. As mentioned in a previous chapter, no African Americans applied to attend that school in 1961. Kathleen Bell and Pinkie Thompson were, therefore, the first two African American students to desegregate this school. Interestingly enough, although these two students attended during the same year, their stories, as told through their eyes, are quite different in some places.

Kathleen Bell

"I'd bury myself in books to not have to deal with all of that. That's mostly what I did just to survive."

[I am Kathleen Bell. I attended] Pulaski Heights.

What grades did you attend there, and how old were you?

It was the seventh through the ninth. I was twelve to fourteen/ fifteen.

Were you the only African American student at Pulaski Heights, or were there others?

No, there was one other the year that I went, Pinkie Thompson. . . . We'd gone to elementary school together.

Did you know that she would be at the junior high when you got there?

Yes . . . Her mother and my mother were best friends; we had that kind of connection.

You completed ninth grade there, right?

Yes.

When did you learn that you were going to go to a majority-White school?

Probably that summer. I don't know at what point during that summer.

Did anybody talk to you about it? . . . Do you remember anything?

No.

Can you remember what your first reaction is when you walked in?

I'm sure it was "Oh God, no!" But no I don't really remember. It was not a pleasant experience, as I recall.

Describe what that feeling was like when you first walked in.

Terror. . . . It was totally new. I mean, going from elementary school where I knew most of the children anyway to junior high school—that was enough of a change, and then Pinkie and I being the only African American students at this school . . .

Did you go in with Pinkie . . . ?

No . . . I don't think so. For some reason I don't think that we went there at the same time.

You don't remember your parents talking to you about it or anything?

No . . . They decided and we went.

What experiences did you have in the White community before this junior high experience?

None. We lived on West Twenty-Fourth Street, and the most experience I had with the White community was going downtown on Fourteenth Street passing Central. . . . I don't know if I saw that on TV or if I actually saw that. But that was my first real knowledge . . . that there was a larger community out there.

Describe your neighborhood in elementary and junior high . . .

When I first started elementary school we were living on Valentine Street, which was in the block right below Stephens Elementary. . . . In '57, I would have been in the first or second grade, I moved over to West Twenty-Fourth Street. . . . LaVerne and I used to walk to school from West Twenty-Fourth over to Stephens, but we lived furthest away. The closer we got to Stephens, there were more people walking with us. I had no awareness of White people in that age because we went to a totally Black elementary. Our doctors were all Black, the movie theater we went to was down on Ninth Street before they destroyed that, and then the church. . . . My world was all African American . . . On Ninth Street was Dr. Jackson, our doctor. Dr. Townsend, optometrist. The pharmacy that we went to was down there. Gem Theater was down there. Now in terms of buying clothes and things like that, I don't remember any clothing stores and things. But the professional services that we needed were all down there. [We] took a bus down there. Our parents didn't take us. There was a library that we went to [that] was up by Dunbar, if I remember correctly. I might be wrong about that, but I don't remember going downtown to the library that they had on Louisiana until I was in junior high school. . . . I had very little contact.

How'd you get to school that first day . . . ?

We always took a bus.

You were on a bus with all White students?

No, city bus . . .

So we just want you to talk about your experiences in junior high. Anything that stands out in your memory?

I remember Pinkie and I did not have any classes together, so it was a very isolating experience. I was not a very outgoing person, and I think that being in junior high school, in that kind of situation, made me even more isolated than I was previously. When I was in elementary school I had a burn. I got burned, and I had sat out of school with my mother, and I guess a tutor. I remember that tutor. That experience had made me isolated because I couldn't do a lot of things—couldn't go outside and play—and so I was isolated in the first place. Not isolated . . . not able to join in. And so then going—that was a defining factor for me . . . going to junior high school just reinforced that apartness . . . The only person that I talked to was Pinkie when we had lunch. We had lunch together. And during the lunch period we would be separated from the other students. . . . Pinkie and I would be together . . . Beside the two of us, I don't remember anybody else. . . . I guess my focus was always on Pinkie because the rest of those people just . . .

So, any significant stories that you remember from the classrooms? What was it like to be that isolated in the classes?

It was like just being totally ignored. They were not—except for one or two instances where I think I got spat on one time, and one person actually called us names—for the most part it really was the way I remember. Now what Pinkie remembers might be something else totally different, because I did really bury myself in books about that time. That's when—on the way home—I would always go by the library, get some books, and take them to school with me. I'd bury myself in books to not have to deal with all of that. That's mostly what I did just to survive, so I only remember those two specific incidents. I think the only time that I really got recognized for anything was when I was in a classroom when they announced that President Kennedy had been assassinated. . . . Everybody in the classroom turned around and looked at me . . . I was sitting in the center of the classroom, and I remember they all turned around. That was my memory.

Do you ever remember being called on in class or being able to talk . . . ?

No . . . And that might also have to do with the fact that I was not very outgoing in the first place. I did well in school, and I remember— it must have been English class or something—two or three other students and I were put into some special group to test our reading or something. So the teacher must have known that I was a good reader . . . But in terms of raising my hand in school? No.

What are your feelings or recollections about the teachers, and how did that compare with your elementary school experience?

My gym teacher was the only one that I can remember taking any interest in me, and I can't imagine why, because I am not an athletic person—not now, not then. But the teachers were not any different from the students. They were not impolite. Not to say that any of them were rude to me or anything like that . . . The difference in elementary school was that the teachers were interested in me, interested in all of their students, interested in making sure that we learned the material. I can't say that any teacher that I had in junior high school had any particular interest in whether I learned anything or not.

Were you involved in any extracurricular activities at the school? . . . Did you ever go to any dances?

No. . . . I'm sure that they had football games or something like that, and that might have been by choice. Dances, no. I don't even know if they had them then. But I'm sure I would not have had any particular interest in going to a dance over there.

Do you remember ever participating in any class projects, or were you in choir or music or anything like that?

No. They wouldn't let me in choir. I can't sing. A little minor detail like that.

Do you remember what kind of books you read? You said you kind of hid out in books?

I read *War and Peace* when I was in junior high school. . . .I would just go through the shelves and just whatever popped out at me. I read a lot of Russian novels . . . I didn't have any particular list . . . I would just wander through the shelves at the library.

What strengths or resources did you have to complete your education? What helped get you through that isolation?

I don't know if I ever really got through it because of the fact that I was at Pulaski Heights, away from the children that I had gone to elementary school with, and because . . . there were not that many children in our neighborhood. So that increased the separation between me and the children that I had gone to elementary school with. Some of us did hook back up by the time we got to Central, but they'd had different experiences at Dunbar and West Side, because a number of kids went to West Side. So by the time we hooked back up, they'd formed other alliances. So I had friends there, but by the time I graduated from high school—I have not seen most of the people I graduated from high school with . . .

So even in high school, that isolation kind of followed you?

Right.

How many African American students were there at Central, and what year did you start Central?

1965? . . . Oh, it was a large contingent of Black folks . . . at Central. But it was like going to two different high schools. In my yearbook, there is a picture of a friend of mine walking through the hallway. They had the hallway decorated for homecoming or something, and all these people are around her being excited, and she's walking through it. And that was the way it was. She was not a part of what was going on around her, and that was the way we were.

How would you compare the junior high experience with your high school experience?

High school was a lot better for me than it was for some. Some people said it was difficult. I guess coming from Dunbar to Central . . . would have been difficult; maybe not so much West Side, but coming from Dunbar to Central would have been difficult for a lot of people. But at Central there was always other people around. There was always a companion. There were a lot of people involved in those organizations that you talked about: football and drama and choir and those kinds of things. So we were more a part of—not me so much—but they were more a part of what was going on at Central to some extent. There were still barriers, of course.

Even though you say you weren't really active in extracurricular activities, did it change how you felt about school, seeing that there were other African American students involved in things?

Yes . . . One, just because there were more people there . . . There were more people that I knew there. I didn't socialize with them after school, but while I was at school, there were people there. There was always somebody around. I think in most of my classes there would always be at least one or two African Americans, and just the fact that they were there was comforting.

Do you ever remember, in junior high or high school, either one, having conversations about desegregation?

No.

How do you think your actions or view of segregation influenced the city, community, then and now?

I can't say, honestly, that I gained anything at all from going to Pulaski Heights. I don't know what it would have been like going to Dunbar, but I do know that, based on what it was like at Stephens, that the teachers at Stephens were interested in me. They knew my mother. Some of them knew my mother because she was a teacher, and a lot was expected of me. When I got to Pulaski Heights, there was no such expectation. In fact, they did not expect us to do well. So that was a distinct difference. I think I did well just because I was a good student. I was quiet. I could apply myself and all of that.

So you say you didn't gain anything?

I don't think so.

And it sounds like you lost something. Would you say that's true?

I think I would have done well at Dunbar, maybe even better. Maybe . . . I would not have developed that sense of isolation. Maybe I would have developed friendships that would have lasted . . . And then again, it just might be my personality, because I know my younger sister, Birdie, has friends that she's had since the beginning of time. I don't know. But I do know that I can't think of anything at all that I gained from going to Pulaski Heights.

Did you ever talk to your family about any of this, or your parents at all?

Not my parents. LaVerne and I have talked about it . . . I think LaVerne has, but no, I have not. I did not ever.

When you look at the bigger picture of what that has meant to Little Rock and to education in general, what are your thoughts of desegregation, what you went through, and where we've ended up?

Just taking me out of the picture . . . I think that in terms of educating Black children . . . a lot of children probably would have been better off if desegregation had never occurred. But that the material, the facilities that went into African American schools had improved. I remember sitting . . . at Stephens, and the books that we were using came from other schools. It was stamped with the name of the other school and other children who had used them. These were second-hand, third-hand, fourth-hand books. So if the material that we were using and the facilities, the resources, had been improved, then that would have been better off. I think that the education provided would have been better.

What do you think now? What do you think desegregation has done for education?

I can't say that it's a plus. I can't. The teachers that we had back then fundamentally believed that the students in front of them were capable of learning, and they demanded that of us. I don't know that teachers nowadays do that. Again, I have not been in a classroom in a very, very long period of time. So I'm talking about what I have heard parents say. . . .

What recommendations would you have for parents who are thinking of putting their children in a school where they will be the minority?

They have to prepare the child for whatever. They have to send the child into that situation having a lot of self-confidence and knowing that there are going to be people there who do not want them there. It requires the parent to prepare the child and just don't send them blind into a situation . . . If you don't have a self-confident child, don't send them there, because children can be a little cruel. They smell blood in the water.

So you've been very successful . . . What other things do you think enabled you to be successful in the long run, considering what your junior high and high school experiences were like?

Well, school was not the end-all and be-all for me. I still had a family . . . and a church. In our church, which was this tiny little church, you were expected to do things. You were expected to participate in the programs and run the programs and speak on the programs. . . . You were up doing things and showing your abilities and being firmly reprimanded and encouraged. So I still had that kind of foundation going for me. It wasn't just school over here; I had things over here that balanced that out. So just because something was going on there at school or indifference in school—because that might have been the worst thing at all, just to go someplace for several hours a day where people were totally indifferent to your existence—except for those couple of instances, I personally do not remember anything bad that happened at Pulaski Heights. It was just the [total] indifference. That can be so destroying.

Pinkie Thompson

*"At Pulaski Heights, I had to leave me at the door to sur-
vive staying in that school. . . . At the end of the day I
would pick myself up from that entry, get in the car . . ."*

[I am] Pinkie Juanetta Thompson . . . I was born in Little Rock, Arkansas. I'm the last of six children of S. F. and E. C. Thompson. I stayed in Little Rock until I was nineteen and went to Alaska; stayed there thirty-four years and transferred with my company to Houston. . . . Upon return I moved to Reno, to try to recapture a bit of Alaska.

You were in the first class to desegregate one of the Little Rock junior high schools . . .

That was Pulaski Heights Junior High School. It was in a more affluent neighborhood and serviced the more affluent families, White families, in Little Rock . . .

Your school was actually the last of the junior high schools to be desegregated in that the first four—East Side, Forest Heights, Southwest and West Side—were desegregated in 1961 . . . Your school was desegregated in 1962. . . . No one had applied to go there in 1961 that was African American. . . . So consequently . . . you and one other person desegregated in 1962.

I did not know the reason why no one had attended Pulaski Heights prior to Kathleen and my going there. However, I did know that there was some concern about desegregating Pulaski Heights, and had been prepared that it was not going to be easy, but there would be support all around. Not only my family—which we were notorious for discussing things—but out in the city there was incredible support. There was a lady named Mrs. Townsend who owned a beauty college, and she offered to my mom that they would do my hair on a weekly basis . . . And then there was always the opportunity to connect with Mrs. Daisy Bates if there were some insurmountable things. So it was huge support in my family, but knowing that there were satellites of concern . . . really kept me going back.

Your parents told you about the people that were supportive and about the possibility of there being unrest at that school?

They did not focus on the unrest, because back in the '60s there had been sufficient opportunities to see how the people would make that split-second judgment as you enter in a door—let's say going to the drug store, trying to go to a movie, or just going into the grocery store. So we were aware as a family that there were some constraints for feeling comfortable wherever we went. Mother and Dad did not make that the big target: "There's going to be unrest when you walk in that door . . ." But they did focus on, "We're here for you. You can call us any time." My parents were educators. My dad actually became a principal. As a side note, he was very instrumental in merging the white and black principal's associations in Arkansas. . . . My parents were very "What can we do?" instead of "Why can't we do?" So going to Pulaski Heights was not an assignment, but I knew there was an underlying expectation: "Let's make this happen."

How did you learn that you would be attending Pulaski Heights?

We would hold family meetings . . . whenever there was a need to have a family meeting so that everybody had the same information at the same time. So when Mrs. Bates had communicated throughout the Black community that more representation was required at different schools, my parents came home, sat down, and talked to all of us and then said, "Pinkie, you have this opportunity to go to Pulaski Heights." Now I was sixth grade at the time, and if it was coming from Mother and Dad, it must not have been a horrific thing to be involved in. I was not sitting there thinking it was Candy Land, either. . . . After explaining what was happening in Little Rock and the process . . . I answered,

"Sure. Sure." . . . They didn't force me, but I did pick up on, "This should be done."

It felt like you were making a decision . . . although you knew that they really wanted you to?

Absolutely. And it was a decision, because if I had said no, Mother and Dad would not have forced me to go. All my brothers and sister had attended Dunbar Junior High School, so saying okay to this already separated me, made me different—that I wasn't going to follow them to Dunbar . . . My oldest brother went on to Horace Mann, but even his attendance there was interrupted when Faubus shut the schools down in Little Rock . . . He attended J. C. Cook High School because that's where my father was a teacher . . . in Wrightsville, Arkansas. But everyone else—my sister Gracetta, brother Morris, brother Traftin—completed Dunbar and went to Hall High School. . . . So once again that separated me from the family path.

There was one other person there?

Yes.

Now do you recall traveling to school with that person?

Absolutely . . . That's part of the comfort from that time in—I'm a little emotional about that . . . Kathleen Bell and I traveled to school together. It was either your parent, your mother primarily, or my brothers and sister, or my mom who would take us to school. . . . Kathleen and I would get out of the car first, then you were dropped off, and then my brothers and sister would continue on to Hall. Those rides provided normalcy beginning to my day, knowing in the back of my mind the dreaded entry into contention and hate. There was lack of support in that building.

There was no one?

There was one teacher I can recall, my Spanish teacher . . . She would keep order in the class better than any other teacher. In my home ec class it was "introduction to being organized and civil" and making pretty things . . . and sewing. . . . She kept us busy enough that those with less than congenial attitudes didn't have a lot of time to demonstrate to me they didn't want me there. So having those rides in the morning allowed me to still be me. And then when Kathleen and I would step out of the car, it was not like "every man for himself," but it was like "heads down"—not in submission, but "against the force, swimming against the current." You, you had to press through to be . . . every day, every day at that school. . . . all three years there was resistance. I can tell you on the very first day—and I don't know if Kathleen will remember this—but it was the culture of that school that when you finish lunch you had to go outside to the breezeway. Well . . . it was the parking lot between the buildings. All the kids would go there to take a break before the bell rang to resume classes, and as I was the first one out of the door, and basketballs, footballs, volleyballs, whatever balls they could get their hands on, just pummeled me as I stepped out that door. We retreated back into the building, went to the principal's office.

Was that the very first time that you went out there?

First day, first lunch . . . first exit into where all the students were required to be. . . . We went to the principal's office, and he did not have much of a reaction, but he did say, "You all do not have to go out there. You can stand in this little recessed area"—that was between the cafeteria and classrooms. And that's where Kathleen and I would go every day after finishing lunch.

In some ways that was support, but he didn't stop the children from doing what they were going to do?

That's right. The attitudes in the hallway from that day forward—they were not going to be pleasant anyway—but to constantly be placed in a, let's refer back to that moment, "We're gonna get you again. You won't know what we're going to use next time." All I wanted to do was go to class. I didn't want to go home with them—had no desire.

Did any of the teachers see the students and their actions toward you?

When adults were around . . . in the classroom, it was not as overt. But there were some who acted out. For example, I went into class . . . science or biology, and our seats were on risers. . . . Typically no one would sit on either side, directly in front or directly in back of me. I was like an island. This one student came in. He was on crutches and he sat right behind me. As he was getting ready to get settled in for class, he was going to put his crutches down and he came across and hit me . . . The teacher told him to get up and relocate. Did he get taken to the office? No. But it was almost as if, "You guys, we don't have a decision or a voice whether they were going to be here or not," but the adults communicating, "But let's not turn ourselves inside out to make them comfortable." I mean, that's the way I felt. I could not go to a teacher.

My only choice was to go to the office. . . . They had to call my parents. When my parents showed up, things began to change a bit . . . as far as my experience. . . . The very first day they had to be called because I was pummeled, and that's when they worked out for Kathleen and me to go to that recessed area. Another time when President Kennedy was killed, the math instructor was the coach and he made a very inappropriate statement . . .

He made the announcement in class that the president had been shot. "It was about time they removed him." I won't say that he used the N-word but it was the way he expressed it. . . . Being the island in any class I attended, I felt so distanced. I felt so apart. But there was laughter in the classroom. . . . So I did go to the office and call my parents. . . . My dad came up to the school at that time, and this particular teacher really had nothing to do with me after Dad came up to attend to that issue.

I shared with my brothers, Traftin and Morris, that there was this . . . one guy who never failed to harass me day after day after day. . . . On the ride home in the car, I was talking about this guy. The next morning when we went to school, this particular time my brothers dropped me off last. I had no clue they'd pulled around the corner, parked the car, and started asking for this guy by name, and they approached him. My brothers were in high school, and they have always been impressively tall, and they had a talk with this guy . . . The next day in class, somebody was about to say or do something . . . and this guy said, "Oh, uh-uh . . . Don't mess with her. She's got two *big* brothers. You don't want to mess with her."

Your parents . . . once they knew that there were problems on a daily basis, how did you all handle that?

Well, during the dinner meals everybody shared what they experienced. My sister was going through things at Hall. A year later my brother Morris joined her at Hall and he was having difficulty. . . . He joined the football team, and he used to say, "I don't have to worry about the opponents. I have to watch out for the guys on my team!" My brother Traftin came the next year . . . Gracetta had hot lunch dropped down the back of her neck. Traftin struggled with people approaching him in a very intimidating manner, and there he is alone. He doesn't have anyone immediately there to support him. So I'm hearing all this. My parents are hearing all this, and my parents were full of faith, and so that was our . . . basis, our foundation. . . . They talked us through. . . . They helped us . . . [to] be . . . sensitive to what is our best decision. . . . It was almost daily discussions about what had happened, how we handled it, what could we have done, "Did you report it to anybody . . . ?" Going to the teachers did not serve a great purpose at all.

Were there any teachers that provided anything positive towards you in terms of interactions while you were there?

They did not seem to want to make me feel comfortable, but I'm quite certain they were sensitive to the fact that there was NAACP. There was Daisy Bates; if it really came down to it, there were lawsuits. The potential of any of that, they didn't want to have happen, because Pulaski Heights was one of the more established junior high schools in the affluent area. . . . Every environment you walk in there is an established culture . . . and you have to recognize that culture and try to fit. Even as uninvited attendees or participants, you still had to learn that culture. So part of the culture I learned—these teachers were not going to let me get hurt to the point that I bled, but these teachers were not assigned to truly protect me and correct what's going on. They stopped what was going on and moved on. They kept teaching. I didn't think that they had to stop the class every time, but some of the things that were said . . . done. . . . Do you remember hearing, "I smell a 'gar?'"

I don't think so.

And then they'll sniff in disdain then keep walking by. The teacher was right there. Does that stop class? No. But does that require that teacher to demonstrate to the students that's inappropriate? . . . No, not one teacher. I cannot remember one teacher that I felt I could go to. . . . In Pulaski Heights Junior High School I did not see much motivation in the teachers to correct, to counsel. Now they may have done it after class after I walked out. But when it happened again the next day without any stronger words or actions, corrected actions, I don't believe it did happen.

You've already pointed out that my sister, Kathleen, desegregated the school with you. . . . Were [you] able to take some classes together?

You know . . . I can't remember. I believe that first year we had more classes together. The second year less classes, and the third year I don't think we had any classes together. But by our third year we had Black students in the eighth grade and seventh grades. So by the time we were in the eighth grade, we had seventh grade class students. Did it get easier? At our lunch breaks we were able to go outside then, because some of those seventh grade Black students were boys, and they were not going to have it. They were just not going to have it. . . . We would go outside and sit on the bleacher steps leading to the field, and it was just always just us. But because of the basketball goal, sometimes the basketball would come our way. Sometimes that's on purpose. Sometimes it's just basketball, that's the way it goes. But it was a different feeling when the others came.

About how many others came?

Let's see. My eighth grade year I think it was Billy Rutledge—or he might be two years younger than I am. But there were a couple of boys. I know Charlotte Perry was one of the students that came ninth grade year. She was such a trip. She was life. She was joy . . . kept us laughing . . . what a beautiful addition. But it was enough of us that no one would constantly come at us . . . You're going to have the ugliness, the bad attitudes, the bad language, the bad presence. The negativity is always going to be there.

Did all of you have lunch together?

To my memory, because Kathleen and I were the only two our first year.

Prior to attending Pulaski Heights, what exposure or experiences did you have with the White community?

Our house was located at the end of the block, immediately across the street is where the White community began. . . . We were either the end of the Black community or the beginning of the Black community. . . . Most of the White community there in the West End were in households of employees of the manufacturer that was located not too far from our home, and all the White kids are out playing in their yards and in the street playing. When I would have to go to the grocery store—I should say when "we," because mother would never allow me to walk to that grocery store in the White community by myself. But it was the closest and handy grocery store if we needed something quickly. . . . I do not remember ever being in a confrontation that stopped us in our steps, but on the way there and . . . on the way back, negative things were being said towards us. When we went to the grocery store . . . in the Black community, I could go by myself.

My parents were well regarded. My father started out as an agriculture teacher; and so . . . whenever there were injuries in the White community, they would come knocking at our door and asking my father for assistance . . . So even though I knew—as mother would say, "People can act ugly"—even though I knew there would be some ugly acting going on, I never feared for my life in that community. . . .

You had no White friends that you interacted with?

Well, the girl close to my age—she was a little older—she and I would play together sometimes. She had a brother who was close to my brothers' . . . age. They would toss football . . . and there was good communication between my parents [and] their parents. But there was never, "Why don't you come over to dinner?" . . . I guess the level of involvement of the kids was enough for them and it was enough for my parents. . . . We were all living our own lives and being very decent neighbors to one another.

Did you participate in any extracurricular activities at Pulaski Heights?

I was part of the choir. Separately I was taking piano lessons. . . . When the choir director found out that I was taking piano lessons for one of our Christmas programs . . . she had me to play the only gospel song that we sang. . . .

I came home . . . and said, "Hey, Mom . . . I'm having to play 'Go Tell It on the Mountain.'" Mother said, "At church?" I said, "No ma'am. At school." She looked at me and she said, "Wonders never cease, do they?" Mother was not going to go there and talk about how stereotypical and foundationally racist that was. She said, "Do you want to do it?" I said, "Do you think I ought to?" And she—"Does it hurt you?" "No ma'am, it doesn't hurt me. It bothers me." And she said, "Press on through." . . .

There were other songs like "Little Town of Bethlehem." My favorite Christmas song is "Noel." If she had asked me to play one of those songs, I wouldn't have been bothered at all. But all the undercurrent, the underwriting, the underlying stereotypical actions and mentality that made her feel okay to have me play the only gospel song. It made me wonder, "Why did I ever tell her I played the piano?" But I was in choir and thought that might help me relate to her better. Then it was used as a weapon against me as a child! . . . I just wanted to be a child, a student. That's all I wanted to be.

How did going to Central . . . happen?

Not only did I recognize it for the national fame, because of the Faubus involvement and the Central Nine and the majority of the nine my family knew and related to. Minnie Jean Brown lived across the street . . . Elizabeth Eckford lived behind us, one block away. . . . So we had investment in Central High School and what happened in '57 with them. When it came time for me to select which high school I'm going to go to, I could have gone to Horace Mann, but I think they were districting at that time. You just couldn't choose a school. . . . If I had pressed it, my mom and dad would have supported it. But I knew that there were Black students at Central, so I looked forward to going to Central. In my mind's eye I would have crossed over into, into normality . . . into just being a student. . . . I was not even thinking about Hall . . . After what my sister and my brothers went through, I wanted nothing. . . . There was greater representation at Central High School than at Hall. I was just tired when I left the ninth grade . . . tired of the struggle. When I got to Central High School and I saw all these Black students, my heart rejoiced. My mind relaxed. I felt like I . . . fit in this school. I could see people who look like me coming down the hallway any time I was on the campus. My ability to interact, be myself, was once again part of my life. The last time I could be myself was sixth grade.

You attended Stephens . . . and that was the last time you could be yourself?

Could be myself. I became "Pinkie" again. At Pulaski Heights, I had to leave me at the door to survive staying in that school. And at the end of the day I would pick myself up from that entry, get in the car to go home. I could not offer myself, my honest, true self, at Pulaski Heights. I brought my true self into Central.

We were still greatly outnumbered. In my graduation class. . . . Only a hundred of us Black students were in that over eight hundred class, so the same offerings even happened at Central, the struggles . . . When you would see . . . a male Black student pulled from the school for doing the very same thing a White male student would do, the injustice still gets to me. It was still a struggle. You can't do that. You must be on your best behavior. You cannot take the risk of jeopardizing yourself when they, by just the thought, can do actions—maybe get suspended for two or three days and come back. The male Black student is expelled . . . so the struggle was there . . .

How did attending a White school affect or influence your adult life personally and professionally?

Children are the cruelest things on two legs. . . . They say what they think. Their thinking has been formed by grandpa, great-grandma. . . . All that the children are doing are spouting what they've been culturally taught. And they bring it with all the energy their little young bodies can bring. When I got into the work world, there were those types of attitudes in a more sophisticated manner being shared in general and specifically . . . I shared that I had gone through everything they've ever been taught, so what they were doing was nothing new to me. "Don't waste the energy, because now as an adult I can either invite you into my world of acknowledgment or disinvite you." . . . I never . . . said, "I hate Whites." Never. Not once. The behavior of an individual will inspire me to either be drawn to them or repelled. In my personal life, living in Alaska up there—I was nineteen turning twenty, forging my own way—my mom and dad's influence wasn't there, so I had to forge my own way, and it was primarily White.

In Anchorage, Whites outnumbered Native Alaskans and out-numbered Blacks and people of color. So I had already had enough foundational experience with their culture to navigate. . . . I would say within the last ten years on the job, I became certified as a facilitator for Healing Racism in America, and I found it to be very productive and constructive in helping me better communicate on the job when I experienced the negativity. Because of that improved performance, I felt improved performance, and even my bosses would tell me, "That was a sticky situation. We appreciate . . . how you handled that, and I think that person walked away feeling attended to and heard. Thank you for handling in that manner . . ." We did Healing Racism in America classes for three straight years, and it was very professional. But the reason why I could do that was because of my experience as a child, and all of that that was still with me in the back of my mind. I did not want it to drive me into any counterproductive walk in life.

What internal and external strengths did you have that took you through that experience?

First, incredible parents . . . My family has been hugely blessed by the influence of S. F. and E. C. Thompson. . . . My mom and my dad were faith-filled parents. There was not a day I can remember that obedience, faith in Jesus, being responsible, being productive . . . My parents just made certain that we had safety, security, guidance, their presence in the home. They were very stable. . . . We discussed everything, and so Mother and Dad would discuss their approach on something, and then it was shared with us kids. . . . There was continuity in the home. Never . . . "Go ask your dad." "Go ask your mom." If one said no, just take it and go on your way. . . . Having that constancy in my life, I knew I had a safe haven always. My church, Mount Zion Baptist Church, was another place of safety, security. My parents just kept us—it was like a hedge or a corral of protection. One thing you never wanted to hear coming from my mom's mouth was to hear that whatever you've done was "in a trifling manner." That would go through me like a pitchfork, like a searing sword. If you ever thought, "Oh, I'll just do a little bit and that'll be good enough." No, no . . . With that type of parental guidance and expectations, you were always pressed to do more. Now they did not pressure us into exhaustion, except when we worked in the fields . . . every summer. But it would press you into knowing that Mother and Dad knew you could do more . . . better, even around the house. . . . Growing up with that kind of influence, and then bringing us up in the awareness and the desire for the Lord—that has been the strongest guidance in my life . . . I could hear Mother say, "So whatever you're doing, do you want Jesus to come back while you're in the midst of that?" . . . I think of it as protection—still safety, security. Making my decisions as best I can. Was I always successful? No . . . but I passed by a lot of things knowing that Jesus could come back any moment, and I love Him and I want to please Him and I don't want to disappoint him if he did come back and find me doing these things. So those were huge influences in my life.

How did your actions of desegregating a junior high school . . . influence the community, the state, the nation, and indeed the world?

That's a deep question because I always considered it more community. However . . . four of my nephews attended Pulaski Heights. So when they went there, my brother Morris had already told them, "Your aunt and a good friend of ours desegregated Pulaski Heights Junior High." And when I would come home for Christmas, my nephews, "Aunt Pinkie, tell us about . . . and did they have . . . ?" This was like a whole different world . . . than for Kathleen's and mine. So I saw it more on a community level, because then my nephews went to Hall, and then they went to Morehouse, and they have come in contact with people from all over the world because Morehouse has that type of attendance. I want to feel that my contribution to opening up Pulaski Heights Junior High School for people of color to attend has become part of their fiber without them really realizing . . . They represent the family—we're still a very tight-knit family and the expectations of our family—they represent us well. As far as my ability to go from Little Rock, Arkansas, to Alaska, or to London, or . . . Scotland, or to Mediterranean, or South America . . . I don't go expecting people to accommodate me. Pulaski Heights really taught me that. Don't expect to be accommodated at all. So when I do go to these different cultures for my company and for pleasure, I'm very open and very sensitive to, "What's that culture doing?" I'm really observant to what's going on and, "How can I fit?" Because at Pulaski Heights I was trying to fit. The way I share with people of different cultures, people seem to be attracted to me, and I've been told by people that there's a warmth, there's an understanding, there's a sensitivity, and their experience with me is not typical to their experience with other people from the United States. . . . I'm trying to be sensitive to others in the way our thinking bombards with the way other people think and live. So that's pulling Pulaski Heights forward into my adult and professional life—knowing how I felt to be disregarded, locked out of. I am absolutely not going to do that to people . . .

What recommendations would you have at this time for parents who are contemplating placing their children in a situation where the children would be the minority . . . ?

I truly believe I was given a leg up to endure by the character of my parents. In this busy . . . world, parents are unbelievably stretched to make a time, and to . . . do as my parents did—communicate with us and have meetings with us and discussions . . . In this rush . . . rush world we have at hand, it is going to put a lot on parents to take the time to do as my parents did. Maybe not everything, but if you just start with one thing and let it grow as you encourage your child to communicate. Communication is hugely important, and reacting negatively or making a child feel that they took a wrong step to bring an issue . . . is the number one wrong thing a parent can do . . . That child . . . comes home . . . knowing, "I've got a mom," hopefully, "and a dad that I can rely on." [That] makes all the difference in the world. . . . Parents, create that environment of safety, security, communication . . . with your child. Bond with them, because the world is really waiting to bond. The world's got plenty of time to mislead your child.

The other thing is responsibility or being accountable to self and family. . . . We have so much media, so many avenues to be influenced. But when the home says, "We expect this, and if that piece of media fits the mold, please pursue that." Everything isn't bad, but you've got to make choices. And every choice has a consequence. And in faith, it's not that God is mad at you that something negative happened to you. It's just that God has allowed what you started to play out. . . . His protective hand is still on you when you come to your faithful senses, and your here-on-earth obedience senses. . . . [When] you want to turn things around then, the path God has for you is going to work to your good and God's glory. But you have to be accountable for those choices and stop looking to fault any and everything that comes down to you.

[Attend] a scripture-based, faith-filled church. I start with scripture-based because . . . many churches have gone into the dramatics. . . . It's got to be a scripture-based, faith-filled and grace-appreciating church so that the children grow up knowing God is a God of relationship. He's not sitting there—"Oh, you did that wrong, and you did that." It's so important for people in every walk of life and at every age to come to know that a faith-based life is going to be one of the strongest rudders you can have that will [get] you through challenges, adversity, all of that. I believe that a faith-based life is very important. But again, parents, you've got too much to do, but you bring those babies in this world. . . . [We've] got to get back to the home being the basis of how that child grows up and succeeds. . . .

As an adult, some of the things that I had to come through on the job—I lived in Anchorage, Alaska, but I worked nine hundred miles north in Prudhoe Bay, Alaska, for quite a while . . . I eventually became a manager of two of those buildings. And some of the disrespect that I encountered as a manager was unbelievable. And even as a child at Pulaski Heights I'm asking, "What have I done?" As an adult up there in Prudhoe Bay I'm asking, "What have I done?" And so I would find myself walking away from that situation . . . singing the song—in moments like these I sing out a love song—"I sing out a love song to

You, Lord." I run to Him. I don't try to stay in the natural. I have to pull Him in a lot. So that Christian home and that scripture-based church have been incredible, just necessary for my success totally.

Are there any other comments or . . . remarks you would like to share?

From the experience of feeling like an uninvited guest at Pulaski Heights for three years to coming into myself and feeling good about coming into myself, I did recognize that my level of need for acceptance is not big. . . . From junior high school on up I have often said trying to fit into my environment has often been a waste of energy and breath. But the fact is, I am here anyway. And you will find me working hard because I'm here. Just because I'm here, and in much of what I've done in the area of diversity, there was something about tolerance—I kept hearing tolerance, and it wasn't working for me. But it was working for the majority. Oh man, we have to stop being dismissive of people. We have to find a way to tolerate, and it just was not there. So finally one day, it was in a course, I told people, "This morning when I woke up, the last thing I thought was I hope they tolerate me today." I don't want to be tolerated. Keep your tolerance and apply it in other areas. I deserve acceptance, and I will take nothing less than acceptance. I realized on that path I'm not going to meet a lot of people who will give me, share with me, and allow me to share with them, acceptance. So if I can leave this conversation with the—it's not a notion, it's the right. Stride towards acceptance. Be your best self. And those who want to feel they have the power to deny you of acceptance, find out what you need to do to fill in the gap to get past them. It's your responsibility, not their responsibility. You're accountable. They are not accountable. You have the opportunity to either strive for the best or get distracted and mess around with tolerance. You're leaving your own acceptance. Strive for the best.

CHAPTER 6

Southwest Junior High School

Two students desegregated Southwest Junior High School, Henry Rodgers and Wilbunette Walls. At the end of the year, however, only Henry remained and continued through to the completion of the eighth and ninth grades. They will share their experiences that led them to make separate choices.

Henry Rodgers

"I look back sometimes, and I wonder."

[I am] Henry Rodgers. . . . My date of birth, 1/9/49, which is January 9, so my birth date and year is one and the same . . . I was born here in Little Rock, raised here in Little Rock, attended school here in Little Rock . . . all of my life with the exception of the five years I was away at, enlisted in the US Air Force. The rest of the time I've been here in Little Rock.

What school did you attend . . . junior high school?

Southwest Junior High School here in Little Rock.

You began at the seventh grade?

Right.

How many other African American students were there?

There was only one other, Wilbunette Walls.

Did you know her prior to attending this school?

Yes, we grew up in the same neighborhood. . . . My parents and her parents were best friends, so we were good friends.

You finished the ninth grade there, right?

I was the first Black to graduate from Southwest Junior High.

How did it wind up that you were the first Black?

Wilbunette attended Southwest the first year along with me, and then she had . . . to have surgery on her feet, so she had to drop out of that. . . . I . . . finished the last two years alone at Southwest. . . . It was quite an experience . . .

How . . . did you first learn that you were going to attend Southwest?

Well they were having . . . community meetings. I think Mr. Ozell Sutton was one of the civil rights leaders at the time in some of those meetings. . . . They were asking for volunteers to attend these schools in your neighborhood. . . . Southwest was closest to me, and I decided that I would attend.

You made that decision?

Yes ma'am.

What did your parents say . . . ?

They were very supportive, especially my mom. She would take me every day. . . . We continued to have those meetings even after we had started attending school to kind of update things on how things were going at the time . . . All the students that were integrating at the time were part of the meetings. . . . We'd come together and kind of share experiences and information about what had taken place that week or whatever the time period was.

What did your parents do to support you during this process and to prepare you to go into Southwest?

Well . . . they always told me keep my head up and don't let them get me down. They knew that they would be against my attending there, so they were always supportive and concerned about my day and what happened, and how I could make things try to be a little smoother.

[Did you have] other experiences with the White community before you entered Southwest?

Yes. . . . My father had a shoe repair shop in John Barrow. It was like a magnet for the entire community. . . . The Blacks kind of lived up on the hill around Fortieth and Barrow, and the rest of the community down to Asher Avenue. . . . Most of the Whites lived down below the hill and the rest of the community north. . . . They . . . patronized my father's business and they would come together, and then after a while . . . they just started hanging out . . . Black and White. The community got along quite well. In fact, some of the teenage kids got together with the Black teenage kids and they would socialize at the club . . . the Forty-Second

Street Grill. . . . It's not there now. . . . I think they've torn it down. . . .
But for a long time it was one of the community fixtures.

That seems to be a little bit unusual in Little Rock at that time.

It was very unusual. . . . I guess my dad was just that kind of
person . . . He was raised by a Chinaman, and I think that might have
had a lot to do with it. But . . . he was just him, and everybody liked
him . . . This person owned Sings Café on Main Street for a long time.

*Given your experience in that neighborhood, your parents didn't think
there would be any problem going into Southwest?*

They didn't at first until the Central High incident started. . . . One
of the neighborhood kids from the grocery store . . . where we had
patronized, was one of the main hecklers and troublemakers. . . . We
patronized them all the time. . . . If he could do something like that . . .
the possibility [existed] that there could be others like him . . .

*So let's get down to the experiences that you had in junior high school.
Tell me what stood out for you as being positive or negative . . .*

Positive experiences were the teachers were all nice and just a few
of the students. It wasn't many; they were worried about peer pressure,
of course. And the negative part of it was being heckled every day. . . .
Some of the students would walk behind me and kind of walk on the
back of the heel of my shoes. . . . That always stood out that was something I didn't like. . . . Eventually, I started walking back on theirs . . .

Did that stop them from doing it?

Eventually it did. . . . They would always try to get me in the bathroom and talk crazy . . . "Why don't you go back to your school? . . .
Why are you over here with us?" and this type thing. The N-word was
always prevalent . . . I would never really talk to them. I think that
probably helped. . . . I would just look at them and . . . go on about my
business, which is one of the things that my parents had told me to
do. . . . It helped quite a bit.

So that means you never got into fights or anything?

I'm not going to say that. (Laughs.) Like I say, when I started walking back on their heels . . . they didn't like it either, so there were a
couple of fights. . . . We'd end up in the principal's office . . . He was a
pretty nice fellow. He . . . did what he had to do . . . [He] always let me
know if . . . I had a problem that was urgent, to let him know.

So that sounds like he was supportive?

Yeah, he was pretty supportive. . . . I think he's the other part of the reason that things went as well as they did . . . He would discipline the people whenever they ended up in his office for bothering me.

Was he the principal all three years?

Oh yes. He stayed there a number of years after I had graduated. . . . He was a pretty good principal. I have to give that to him.

Did you and Wilbunette share any classes the year she was there?

I think the first year we shared a couple of classes. I think health might have been one, and I think math might have been another one.

Did you find that to be helpful to have another African American in the class?

Yes . . . It was a little more relaxing but . . . it didn't make a great difference. . . . Coming from Gibbs Elementary where it's all Black, and going into that type of situation . . . definitely called for adjustments . . . You're in a comfort zone in a situation like that when you're at Gibbs. . . . I was a straight-A student at Gibbs. Mr. Horn was my sixth grade teacher and one of my best teachers. But, you know, after leaving that and then going to Southwest . . . you've got these other factors that you have to deal with. You're always looking over your shoulder. The folks are always messing with you. They're calling you names and trying to do things, throw things at you, this type thing. So when you have to— figuring in those other factors—then that takes away from your comfort zone. You're kind of on edge quite a bit . . . During assemblies, some- times they would . . . throw a paper at me. It wasn't bad though. . . . The teachers were in there.

Did they do something about that?

No. . . . I really didn't make a big beef about it. [As] long as they weren't putting their hands on me, I didn't really worry about that. Lunchtime, they would kind of hide around corners while I was waiting for the bell to ring and throw pennies down towards me . . .

Throw pennies?

Yeah, they'd throw pennies . . . try to hit me. But . . . hit me. I think it was just more of a just taunting type thing . . .

Did you have people to sit with you during the lunchtime?

Not really. I was mainly to myself. . . . The janitors were friends of mine. I would be with them. And that took a lot of pressure off, too.

So you would be with them during the lunchtime?

During the lunchtime at times, yes.

Okay. So they were another source of support for you?

Yes, very much so. I'd almost forgotten about that. Yeah, they were. Really were.

Did it take away from your academic . . . progress?

Yes, it did. I think the first semester I almost made straight As; then after that I kind of remained a B and C student for the most part of that. . . . Yeah, it definitely has an effect. . . . And then not being anyone else but me and the entire school, the Whites . . . it weighs on you.

You mentioned the teachers were . . . positive.

Teachers were positive. They were very good about [providing] additional instruction on things we didn't quite understand . . . I think Ms. Potter was one of my best teachers over there. She taught science, and I think I made straight As in her class—straight As in gym, of course. (Laughs.) I turned out to be a much better athlete than they thought I would. I think one time I did like twelve hundred sit-ups in forty-five minutes. . . . After that I think they kind of started taking a different look at me. (Laughs.) . . . Coach was a good teacher, too. He didn't take any stuff. He let them know that, and it wasn't going to be no stuff in there. Once I got into that, I just kept going and kept going, and ended up, I was the last one there. I was still doing sit-ups when everybody else was heading to the shower. I think I broke a record.

You mentioned the students. Were there any that you recall that were okay or positive?

Yeah, there were a couple. . . . Some of them come by my business now and patronize me. Charlie Wood. I think there was another little guy. He's a retired policeman . . . [If] he liked you, he liked you. Billy Spencer. . . .that's it. And there were a couple of others that would talk. . . . The majority of them were worried about peer pressure . . . what the others were going to say if they were talking to us . . . They'd threaten to jump on them and that type thing. . . . They would always have to watch out for that. I didn't attend any football or basketball games. Like I said, I was the only one there for the most part. . . . I think [the principal] even commented . . . about me trying to attend and possibility of what might happen, since there would be less restraints there . . .

Do you think that he was talking about the reality that something might happen?

The reality of how things really was, so—it didn't bother me. I knew there would be problems if I did. . . . There were plenty of other things in the neighborhood for me to do. I didn't have to worry about that.

Did you join any other organizations or activities within the school?
I think maybe Glee Club or something, but it wasn't much . . .

What strengths or resources did you have, either internally or from outside in your family, the community, the church . . . to make it through . . . junior high school?
You know, I look back sometimes, and I wonder. (Laughs.) I said only God could have got me through that as well as I did. But I know He was with me; [my] I guess spiritual, inner strength for the most part, and then the support of my family. . . . That's about it. I didn't really have anybody else over there to pull or draw from . . . in the school itself. So I just kept going. I guess determination was a big part of it, that I was going to make it and get out of there.

Given the fact that Wilbunette was gone, was there a time that you did think about just packing it all in and not completing that?
Not really. There were times when you feel like that, but I didn't really give much thought to it because I knew I had committed to do it and that I was going to have to do it. . . . So I didn't worry about it too much. I just continued to do what I needed to do to get through it.

You went on to attend Central High School?
Right.

What led to your decision to go to Central as opposed to Horace Mann?
Well . . . I was already . . . in the integration system, and Central was closer than Horace Mann. I would have had to go all the way across the city to get to Horace Mann. Central was a much better school . . . Just better academics, books—all of that was better. Horace Mann and most of the Black schools got the hand-me-down books. That was one reason for integration. We knew we weren't getting the education that the Whites were getting.

How did you know they were hand-me-down books?
Well, because every year (laughs) when they passed books out, they were worn out . . . "Goodness. This is a new year. Where are the new books? No new books? Oh, okay." (Laughs.)

You mentioned, just going back to your sixth grade, that you had a really, really good teacher . . . so the quality of education was good . . . ?

There was very good quality . . . of education. . . . Mr. Horn was quite a teacher. C. L. Horn . . . was one of the top teachers in the city, and very good . . .

How do you think your actions of desegregating a Little Rock public junior high school influenced the city, the community, state, and nation?

Well, just hopefully [as] an inspiration that it could be done, and it didn't have to take a lot of people to do it. You know, I did it by myself for the most part and . . . Southwest Junior High wasn't an easy school. It was one of the roughest schools in the city. After I graduated, it was like about two years, I think, before any other Blacks attended . . . That's how rough it was.

Any other way that it influenced this . . . ?

Not just that it could be done, but after it was done that . . . we could intermingle and kind of work things out and attend schools together, which is what they apparently didn't want. . . . But that, I guess, influenced the rest of the kids in the city—that others could attend as well.

How did this affect your personal life later on and your professional life?

It made me very strong within. Once I accomplished that, I went on to finish at Central in '67. [I] took my first jet flight to Washington D.C. to work for the FBI right out of high school. Then . . . that was during the time Vietnam War escalated, and I had to go in service, which was the Air Force. . . . Believe it or not, I ended up having to change the Air Force.

This was '68. Still a lot of segregation in the country, and I got my overseas tour, which was Azores, Portugal. . . . You would think that . . . would be like paradise. [I] got over there and found out that things were worse over there than they were here back in the States. There was nothing for the Black airmen to do. We couldn't even attend the Airman's Club. They didn't have music for us in there or nothing that Blacks would like to do or anything . . . just nothing in there—country and western. . . . Who's going to listen to country and western music? . . . We grew up in the soul community. . . . So myself and five other guys was involved in . . . an international incident. We were involved in a fight where fourteen White guys jumped us in a club that we had reserved for a party . . . We sent all of them to the hospital . . . Two of those guys were base commanders for the Portuguese Air Force, but they were all in civilian clothes and we didn't know it. So that's what ended up being an international incident. They had to have a congressional meeting on it in Washington D.C. I was quarantined to the island after the incident and none of us could leave, supposedly. But my grandfather died, and he helped raise me. I was determined to go to his funeral . . . and I went to his funeral. . . . After his funeral I flew straight to Washington D.C., Senator Fulbright's office. [It] took . . . most of the day to get in to see him. . . . When I did, I went in and told the secretary who I was and she informed me, "Yes, I know who you are. How did you get here?" (Laughs.) . . . I told them my grandfather had died and I attended his funeral. . . . She said, "Well, it just so happens that all of the senators and congressmen of the airmen that were involved in that incident just had a meeting, and you don't have anything to worry about. You just need to go back over there and they'll probably give you an Article 15, which is a fine, and you'll be coming back to the States probably in the next . . . few weeks." And so that's what happened. After I went back over . . . they . . . said they realized that they had a new man in the Air Force, and they needed to make changes. And that's what they did. They made changes, believe me. . . . Every week, we had soul night at the Airmen's Club, where we had soul night in the cafeteria where they served nothing but soul food. They even had chitterlings in the chow hall, which was unprecedented for the Air Force. . . . We had to show them how to clean them and cook them and everything, but they did. And so from that everything kind of worked out . . .

That's a very powerful story. . . . They . . . utilized what could have been a horrible incident and they turned it around . . .

And made it positive, right. And . . . did what they knew they should have already done . . .

Any other ways that [junior high experience] affected you throughout your life . . . ?

It just made me stronger. . . . I'm in business for myself now. That took a lot of fortitude, getting started in that and maintaining, and now I have the largest shoe repair business in central Arkansas. . . . One of the tops in the nation. I have people coming from all over the country to do business with me. . . . I started when I was six. I was my father's only son, so it was more or less me and him. He started me out at six years of age. . . . I've been doing that over sixty years. . . . Most of the other repairmen in the city, when they can't handle something, they'll send them over to me . . .

What recommendation would you have for parents who are contemplating placing their child in a situation where the child would be a minority . . . ?

Just mainly be themselves. Don't try to be someone that they're not to try to fit in . . . Be yourself. Either they're going to like you or not. And if not, then you know who you are at least, and you know your strengths and your limitations, and that's going to help you in the long run. Parents should be supportive of their kids in encouraging them . . . to carry on the way that they know that they are . . . not try to be a wannabe or somebody else just to fit in, which you find quite a bit in that situation.

Is there anything else that you would like to add with regard to any of this topic?

Yeah. We can all get along. It wasn't that difficult. It's just a matter of [being] willing to accept what was already here in place. God put us all here for a reason. He put us all here together for a reason, and when you try to detour away from that, that's where your problems start. . . . You make the problems yourself by doing that type thing. . . . Nobody's going anywhere. We're all here, and we're all going to be here till the end of time, so just be willing . . . to be acceptable of others for what they are, who they are—whatever—and I think the world will be a better place.

Wilbunette Walls Randolph

"I got tired of being ignored."

[My name is Wilbunette] Walls Randolph. . . . I was born in Little Rock, Arkansas. [I've] been here all my life. . . . [on] 10/31/48.

We are here to talk about the desegregation of the Little Rock public junior high schools and you were . . . the very first twenty-five to desegregate a school.

I thought about it as I got older, that we were the small group that never got heard. . . . I was just elated . . . to be a part of this group

What junior high school did you attend?

Southwest Junior High. That wasn't far from my neighborhood. . . . I went there in the seventh grade, and that was the only grade that I finished [there].

Only one other person attended with you . . . ?

Yes. Henry Rodgers.

Did you know him prior to attending that school?

Yes. We grew up in the neighborhood and our families were very good friends.

Did you . . . attend the same elementary school?

Yes, we did . . . Gibbs Elementary.

How did you learn that you were going to attend a majority-White school?

It was really asked of us to take home a sheet of paper, and this is what was on it. I told my mother first that I wanted to go. She talked with my father, and they both agreed. . . . They asked me if I really wanted to go, and I said, "Yeah." . . . So we signed up for it, and I got accepted. . . . I was proud of my cousin that integrated Central High . . . Carlotta Walls Lanier. . . . I guess I had an attitude about, "If she can do it, so could I." . . . She was our older cousin, and we all looked up to her back in the day. So that was really my first thought. . . . What I saw on TV as a child in the news . . . made me want to have that fight for our race also.

Your parents . . . really let you make that decision?

Yes. They let me make that decision. . . . I've always had a fore-thought of doing things, and it always turned out for the best, one way or the other. They didn't have a problem with it.

Do you remember if everyone at Gibbs received that paper that you were talking about?

I really don't know. I . . . kind of recall the teacher asking us . . . and handing out slips of paper for us to take home, but I don't remember if it was everybody or if she said, "If you want one, come by and pick it up and take it home to your parents." I can't remember that.

Did anyone else outside of your parents talk with you about that?

No.

Did your parents do anything in particular to help to prepare you for that process of desegregating?

Honestly, no. You know, back in the day the parents really didn't talk to children . . . like we do now. It was a different set of rules, and either you did it or you didn't. All they were concerned about was, "If you don't want to stay, you let me know . . ." *They* gave me the option . . .

and I took it as that. But I was determined I was going to go through that year . . . after . . . other things happened.

What experience with the White community did you have prior to going to Southwest?

None. . . . No intervention of any kind . . . That was not unusual in our day. . . . We were in separate neighborhoods.

What kind of work did your parents do?

My father worked for a bus company, which was the Continental Trailways at the time. . . . His father had businesses . . . a pool hall back in the day, and [a] cafeteria. . . . My father would help him in the evening times with that. So my father had two jobs: one that he worked out in the community, and then the one that he would come home and help his father with. . . . My mother was a stay-home mom, and then after we got a little bit larger, she would go out and work into the domestic homes.

What it was like for you to attend Southwest.

Well, it was a harrowing experience for sure. It was a scary experience on the first day. No one really said anything to me. What I recall comforting to me was my homeroom teacher, Mrs. Wilson. . . . She was an older woman . . . as I remember. She was most concerned about me . . . in my welfare. She just made me real comfortable in homeroom. That was about the best . . . on that day that I can remember. One young girl in the same homeroom. . . . said a few words to me at times, but we never had classes together. . . . She spoke to me. . . . Out of all the other children, she seemed . . . friendly enough. I sat near her in the homeroom. . . . Henry and I both weren't in the same homeroom. We were separated. . . . We had a few classes together that I recall, and of course we were separated in gym, but we had lunch hour, or half hour together. . . . He was quiet just like I was, and we really didn't say too much. We were both just afraid . . . being in that school. As far as people coming toward us or bothering us, we had a few simple things in classroom—I did—where they put thumbtacks in the seat. Henry happened to sit on them at one time and got up, and I think I might have one time, too. But I remember Henry. . . . After that incident we started checking our seats . . . before we would sit down. . . . I really didn't have any teacher that I can say really helped me any. . . . They just did their job, and sometimes I felt it was even less . . . They would ignore us when we would raise our hands. I got tired of raising my hands.

I got tired of being ignored . . . and that did deter me, a whole lot, as a child . . . I was a quiet person and I didn't bother anybody . . . it was just hard. It was. I never will forget when . . . I was asked to go to the principal's office . . . for no reason at all. . . . He intimidated me very much. "Shut the door." I'm a girl. I'm a child, behind a closed door. It was nobody but he and I in that room together. . . . Back in that day we didn't have but a few men teachers in our elementary school, and I wasn't around but one. . . . Needless to say, he was already discomforting to me, being a male, let alone being . . . of the other race. His very words were, "Why are you here? You don't need to be here. Why don't you go home?" I never shall forget that. . . . He was a tall man, big. . . . He might have not said anything that was considered . . . a part of what he was supposed to be doing [as] the principal of the school . . . I didn't even remember his last name until I asked Henry the other day. I know he had finished and I hadn't. There are things that I blocked out . . . chose not to remember at that school. . . . Going to the classrooms, passing back and forth was okay. . . . It was something new to us. We always stayed in one classroom at the time . . . I would always see the janitors and the maids in certain areas that we would pass by to go to the classroom and they'd smile, but they wouldn't say too much to us. They didn't want to get us in trouble, nor did they want to get in trouble. . . . It got to the point where we didn't want to go to the cafeteria anymore to eat, and if we wanted a hot lunch, we would slip our money to them that day, and they would bring our hot lunch to their area and we would sit down and eat in that area, and nobody messed with us. I can't remember the young lady that did that, but I wish, you know, I could see her to thank her. It really helped me as a child. (Crying softly.) . . . She gave me that encouragement during that time. It's just a shame that we couldn't sit down and be like any other normal children.

What happened in the cafeteria?

Well, Henry would get picked on more than I would. . . . He would get things thrown at him. . . . They really didn't do too much to me but call me out of my names. . . . I was "Aunt Jemima," all the time, you know, and being a child that hurts . . . And I would think of that . . . coming up. But I just . . . thank God that I was able to overcome that . . . during the year that I was there. . . . [Henry] would come and sit, too, and eat with me. . . . I don't remember how many times that we stayed in there or how long, but I don't believe it was that long . . . Nobody said nothing about where we ate. Nobody cared. . . . We weren't in there [referring to the cafeteria], so we weren't to be messed with during that time. Even if we brought our lunch, we sat in there and they [janitors] would bring us cold milk. . . . So however it went . . . they did their part . . .

That was a safe . . . space for you?

Yes . . . to protect us the best they could and still hold their job. . . . To me that was a brave moment for them to be in that position.

What was the first day like?

It was like a nonexit—like you're walking through a maze. We were both scared . . . We weren't introduced in no other room than our homeroom. Everybody . . . said their names and where they lived and that was it . . . It wasn't an exciting day no more than that . . .

You and Henry, were you in the same . . . ?

We were in different homerooms, but we were right next door to each other. When we would come out, he would know that we would have certain classes . . . Sometimes we'd walk together and sometimes we wouldn't. Henry was faster. He wanted to get out of the hall. He was being tripped and everything else. . . . Like I said, I don't believe I was picked on as much as Henry was. I was being called names and that was about it, but Henry got the worst of that. He really did.

How did the name calling affect you?

I didn't like it one bit. I saw what they portrayed as Aunt Jemima, you know. And I didn't think I looked like Aunt Jemima at all. And I had [done] nothing but walk in through classrooms and sit down and be by myself and not bother anybody . . . But you have some people that are going to be that way and when we would go to the meetings . . . what could you say?

What meetings were those?

We had . . . meetings at Dunbar Community Center for all those that attended the junior high. I recall those. And it wasn't near as many as I thought they ought to have had. If it was, we didn't attend many.

Do you know who was holding those meetings?

I have no recollection of that. But I do remember that . . . it was held at Dunbar Community Center. . . . I don't know if it continued throughout that year or . . . every month or so. . . . I can't recall that . . . They asked about how were things going, and they wanted to know also if you needed any help . . . they could provide. We lived in John Barrow Addition. [My] parents worked—one car in the family. If I needed assistance, I didn't say it, as a child. I tried to fight my own little battle with them within myself.

John Barrow, especially at that time, was pretty far out, wasn't it?

When we went to [Southwest], Henry's father would carry us. He had his own business, and he was able to take us and bring us back, so we didn't have a problem with getting home. At that time they tried to put you within a school within your walking distance. But in that day . . . you can't imagine how far that was from where we were. It was still a dangerous area for us to be walking by ourselves at that age.

During the time that Henry's father was driving, did he talk with you all about anything that was going on . . . ?

Not really. . . . We just never had a conversation. . . . They always asked if we were okay . . .

To get from your school to your home you had to go through a White neighborhood?

Yes . . . we had to go through a White neighborhood and a busy intersection . . . we had to walk on a busy street. Anybody could have driven by and thrown stuff at us, you know. We thought of that; we remember what happened in the '57 crisis . . . So we were aware of danger.

Before you went to Southwest, you were still living in that same area?

Same area.

And had you experienced any negative reactions with the neighbors?

No. Not at all.

So . . . it was just the fear that something was going to happen?

Exactly. The unknown is what scared us . . .

Did you have any other experiences with the larger White community before . . . Southwest experience?

Before I even went to Southwest? No more than we were at Gibbs Elementary. We were let out early during the crisis. It was told that the children weren't in school and they were headed our way. And our bus had to come pick us up. . . . Being little kids at the time, we were definitely afraid and that stuck on our mind. . . . But nothing happened.

That was during the Central High Crisis?

Yeah, during the Central High Crisis. . . . So that's what made me want to be a part of the junior high. . . . I felt like if the other children could make it through the high school experience, maybe I could also. I felt the need to try . . .

But once you got there the teachers were not helpful to you?

No. No.

It sounds like only that one student might have been somewhat nice.

Yes, but I didn't have a class with her, and no one else . . . chose to be a part of us at all. . . . During that time also I had a real bad experience with the math teacher. He couldn't talk good and he had a problem with his windpipe. I think he must have had cancer at one time, or something going on with him. He would always have to hold . . . his chin down to his neck like, and you couldn't understand him. . . . I raised my hand to ask for certain things, and then when he would [respond], I still wouldn't understand. So Henry was much better than I was in math, and I would go study with him . . . But it didn't help any, to be honest. We were children, and this was an experience like none other. We had never had books like that before where we were introduced to something that was already in their schools before ours. . . . I was always told, and I always felt like we didn't get any new books when we were in elementary school. We would get their used books.

You had to grasp concepts that they had already . . . learned?

Already learned in elementary. And there we were stepping into something entirely new. And it was something. I guess after that I didn't care for math at all. That was my weakest subject for sure.

Was it a good subject for you prior to that time?

No, not really. I didn't like math . . . I was doing okay in math, but the algebra? That was like French, okay? So that's what I'm talking about. We were not prepared for that all . . . We weren't taught any of that when we were in elementary. So that was hard for me to grasp. So naturally I didn't take a liking to it (laughs) one bit. But I tried. I didn't want to fail in it.

You mentioned that you did not finish there.

No.

What was the reason that you chose to move away from that school?

Well . . . it was the teachers for sure. And that year during the summer, I was going in for surgery for my feet. I was having surgery on both of my feet, and I had decided at that point I didn't want to return . . . to that school. I was going to be out for a half of a semester anyway. . . . At that time I had fallen arches, and they scared you back in the day with that . . . They offered to operate and make it better. . . . It's no fixing fallen arches, but of course we all know that now.

But that made it a little bit easier to move away from Southwest . . . you knew that you would be out a semester . . . and that would pretty much put you far behind?

Yes, it would. . . . My homeroom teacher—this is what I love about her—went to the teachers that were failing me and begged for them to at least pass me [award me with a passing grade.] I would not be back. And that's what happened.

So at the time that you left, you were not doing well?

No, I was not doing well at all . . . They wouldn't call on me. . . . And . . . one particular teacher . . . she was my social science teacher, told me so. Regardless . . . she told me she wasn't going to pass me. . . . I was surprised to hear that from a young lady. I'd never done anything but try to do my work right. . . . She'd given me one semester. . . . I ended up taking social science . . . [in] summer school. When I changed schools, I went to summer school at Horace Mann at the time. I went that year and then the next year for math. So I did two summer school sessions back to back to clear up my grade before I got into high school. . . . And therefore there was no going to Central High. I went to Horace Mann. . . . That was the purpose. I didn't want any more integration.

What was it like returning to an all-Black school?

Wonderful. (Laughs.) I felt in place, you know, like a normal child would. . . . During the time that I had my surgery and I was at home, I was being taught by the Little Rock Public School District. A teacher came out, and so I was able to keep up with everything . . . I would have my books together and ready. I was in a wheelchair, and I would be able to let them . . . I would turn in homework; and then by the time I got ready to return to school, [it] was after Christmas, and I went to Dunbar Junior High . . .

Did your grades improve?

Yes . . . they did. . . . And after I finished that, I was able to keep up with my class and I graduated from Horace Mann, and things were totally different.

The students there didn't . . . say anything to you about coming back?

No . . . no. Everybody knew—it was like, "Yeah, so you're back." Who cares, you know? . . . And you never had any questions about, you know . . .

What recommendations would you have for parents who are contemplating placing a child either in the setting . . . where they would be the minority?

I would say make very sure that they understand everything in this day and time. Things are totally different for them, but it's still not different in the real world. I have grandchildren that have grown up in that type of situation. . . . My oldest one is in college here, and I can see the difference in where her parents raised her, and I don't like it, but it wasn't me . . . to tell them. It was different. . . . Don't let them forget where you came from . . . My son was able to tell his daughter . . . what I went through. I related it to him . . . as he grew up and how different things were. When they came through school, they both went to Southwest Junior High, ironically. We moved in the neighborhood not too far, and they were surprised. They first heard me talk about it when they got to that school. . . . It's totally different, you know. And the grandchildren are even better off; but then, to me they're not living in the real world. Once they get out in the work world, it's still a hassle as their race, and they don't understand the difference yet. . . .

Let them understand that there are people that are much better than that—than it was in our day. They can help you a whole lot if you're willing to listen and take advice. There's still some good meaning people on all hands, all races. Don't classify one as they classified us. People are easy . . . to classify you as one race and not see the big picture of you. . . . It's just people, period. People are going to be different regardless . . . They're going to look at you as a human being . . . That's what we need to do: look at each other like a human being. . . . Why would you treat anybody any differently?

Is that what you mean also by your grandchildren needing to face reality . . . when they get out that they will not be seen as African American or Caucasian . . . ?

Yes . . . just go by what you do and what you have in your heart . . . and stop judging. . . . A lot of times I laugh at myself. I say, "Now why do I ask, 'What color are they?' (laughs) when they talk about their friends?" I want to ask so badly, but then I catch myself. . . . I'm thinking that . . .

How do you think this desegregation of the junior high schools, your role in it, influenced the city, the state, the nation, maybe the world?

I think we moved forward as people just in everything that we did. . . . As I get older, I want to say, "Well, did desegregation really help us as a race?" . . . I know it did, but then I felt like we lost a lot of our being. We weren't actually pushed with . . . who we were, you know? We were made to conform to what they wanted us to be. . . . I know that it's progress, and it's a slow progress, but whoever thought that I'd live to see a Black president, see? So it's still hope, regardless. I believe that we're going to have to walk and do the best we can in whatever we do in life and not let that hold us back. So many people talk about what other races don't do for us . . . but it's not about that. Stop making that a crutch for you to live on. Just do the best at whatever you do, regardless, you know. We know the world is not perfect; it never will be perfect. . . . Do the best you can regardless. . . . That's what I've tried to do in my life.

How would you say that your having attended Southwest affected your life over the years, both personally and professionally?

Well, just being who I am. I learned how to deal with people in my lifetime. My grandfather was always in business, and then my father helped him. . . . We had a malt stand . . . when we were children, and that helps you deal with people. I remember my grandfather having a cafeteria. . . . People would come in there, and the kids would buy candy and popcorn and stuff like that. . . . It's all around just dealing with people in the community all your life. It just helps me to see that there's progress regardless of what's going on in the world. . . . When I got married and had children, I tried to bring the same values that we were brought up on and to let them know that I went as far as high school and I chose not to go any further. . . . If I had a girl, I would have encouraged more out of her to be an independent person. . . . As far as my boys were concerned, I have two. I encourage them to, "Go to college. . . . If you don't want to go to college, go into the service . . ." That's what their dad did. So the oldest one stayed out a year and then he decided that he would go to a technical college. He did that and he got married. Then my youngest one went into service, and so he's out and doing well . . . I can say that I'm one of, me and my husband, one of the parents that have never had to go to jail to get their children out. . . . They're both doing well.

So even though . . . the teachers refused to call on you and the students refused, you also made the decision to return to junior high school at Dunbar . . . that seems to have been a help for you as well . . .

It was, and it just shed a different light on my area at that time. And the teachers were most helpful . . . I did well, and I'm glad to be a part of that experience. I don't regret it. . . . I figure I did make one little mark when I did integrate it. So I just hate I couldn't finish.

You had to take care of your feet, but also you had to take care of your health, it sounds like . . . mental health.

Yes. Yes, more than anything.

Making sure that . . . you move away from the part where the principal's saying, "Why don't you go home?"

Yes . . . I mean he's sitting at his desk, but he's still taller than me, and I'm sitting in the chair being a little child and you've got the door closed. You know, you're a man and I'm a little girl. I know he did wrong when he did that, but what could I say?

Did you tell your parents about that?

Yeah, I told them. . . . But back in that day . . . you just had to accept it . . .

Do you have any other comments or anything that you would like to add . . . to your story?

I respect that our community at that time did the best they could to provide for us. . . . This was a voluntary basis thing anyway, and it was just a few people that were able to come out and do it . . . It was only twenty-five of us at that time. So you can imagine what the other parents would have thought about it. They remembered the '57 Crisis, and they didn't want to be involved, which was understandable. But at that time, nothing happened to our houses. Nobody messed with us in our community. We didn't live near a White community anyway. And who was to bother us at that time . . . ? The forces had been stepped up, and even though Faubus was still alive and well, things didn't happen like that . . . And it wasn't so bad living in Little Rock like everybody had us portrayed over the news everywhere else.

CHAPTER 7

West Side Junior High School

Twelve names were listed at times as those Negro students who were assigned to desegregate West Side. One person, Felton Walker, informed me that he did not attend (personal communication, 2014). Other than that, eleven students may have first desegregated that school. The missing students or those who opted not to participate include Gary Ledbetter, Betty McCoy, Nathan Summerfield, and Dianne Threet. You will read the interviews of seven of the students who enrolled: Clarence Johnson, Alice Joiner, Kenneth Jones, Brenda Sims, Sandra Smith, Alvin Terry, and Joyce Williams. For the sake of clarification, Clarence is hearing impaired. As a result, some of the interview may appear rather disjointed.

Clarence Johnson

"If you make a . . . path, the longer you walk
on the path, it gets smoother."

[My name is] Clarence Alvin Johnson Jr.
> *Where were you born?*
> Little Rock . . . I was born and raised here . . .
> *What school did you desegregate?*
> West Side Junior High.
> *How old were you?*
> Twelve.
> *You entered at the seventh grade, is that right?*
> Correct.
> *How many . . . African American students were with you?*

Oh, about nine of us I think . . .

Did you know any of them before?

No . . . I'd never seen any of them before in my life.

What elementary school did you attend?

I went to Stephens. . . . They went to Gibbs, and other elementary schools . . . So it's the first time I ever met them.

Did you complete the ninth grade there at West Side?

Right.

How did you learn that you were going to attend a majority-White school?

I was told. (Laughs.) Just a second . . . Just looking for my old records.

I see you have report cards on that folder right there. . . . You have your name on there, Clarence A. Johnson. . . .

But how I found out about going to West Side. . . . I was assigned to West Side Junior High. . . . I didn't know nothing about it.

You even have assignment cards for free textbooks.

Well in the sixth grade they was giving us books . . . Well see, we never had any . . . dealing with White people . . . period . . . until I went to West Side. We always got used books from the white schools. See, they were sparing stuff we felt. We didn't ever get any new books.

So at Stephens Elementary . . . how did you find out they were used books?

It would be, when they bring them to you, you could tell, they were not new . . . Some of them would be old. Some of them would be ratty. . . . Even when they spared them, they were in, like, so-so condition.

One says "fair," others say "good." Oh! There was one geography book that said "new." But . . . all of the rest—oh, I see, "poor condition."

Yeah. . . . And even though they were assigning them to you, they were already in poor condition. . . . At the end of the year, you had to turn them back in . . . For the next class.

You found out that you were going to go to that school just by the report card. What did your parents say? Did they know about your being assigned to West Side?

During that time, they was going to some meetings and stuff. Different meetings. . . . And the parents was . . . putting the children up to do that . . . I didn't volunteer to do that. By no means. . . . So I was more or less forced into that situation. But I went on. Except . . .

I wouldn't ask one of my children to do something that I wouldn't do myself . . . Walking to school, they used to shoot at me and stuff like that. . . . I was going to West Side. . . . And I was walking by, let's see . . . West Side on Fourteenth and Marshall. And I'd turn on Sixteenth and they'd shoot at me and stuff like that.

My mother . . . notified the police, and then they took me down and interrogated me, asking me a bunch of stupid questions. Sat back like, if somebody pointed a gun at you, if it's a large caliber, you can see the bullets in there, you can see them. And if they shoot, you can hear the bullet go by. . . . They did like that for so long. So what I did, I went up on the corner . . . the corner called Eighteenth and Pine. . . . Okay. And on the line at Ninth Street, they had the Gem Theater, the club, stuff like that, before they closed it down. But on the corner, and on the line, you could buy anything that you wanted . . . And I was about twelve or thirteen years old. So I went up on the corner and bought me a nine-shot double deuce. And I start returning fire. And to my surprise, they quit bothering me! (Laughs.)

But you were a little boy! You were able to buy a gun to protect yourself?

The White folks wasn't. . . . And you tell some folks about that, and they wouldn't believe you, stuff like that.

You walked to school every day?

Yeah! But at first . . . they put us in meetings and stuff. . . . They told us we would have a ride to school and everything; we'd have someone pick us up and everything like that. That happened for about maybe a week. And then we had to walk. . . . After that, it was walking all of the time. . . . rain or shine.

Before you went to West Side, did you have any dealings with White people?

The only people that I knew or socialized with were Black people. I never had no dealings with White people, period. Like in '57, when the . . . soldiers come in . . . and the Airborne Division was present, some of them would take their rifles and hit those folks—White folks upside the head with them up there on Fourteenth street by Central. I saw that. . . . Most people saw it on TV. . . . But I saw it, okay, I stayed on 3116 West Seventeenth. . . . It's about six blocks—seven blocks from Central. . . . And I would be riding or walking that way . . . and you could see them.

Did your parents prepare you at all to go to West Side?

Prepare me how? Wait a minute, wait a minute. . . . How can you prepare someone, someone for a condition that you yourself don't know nothing about? How could they?

So your parents weren't around White people at all?

No! Okay, except like my . . . dad worked for the VA hospital. . . . He was around the folks he worked with . . .

When you went to West Side, what was your experience like there when you first went there . . . ?

When I went to West Side . . . it was . . . I think about nine hundred–something students . . . going to West Side. And only about seven, eight, nine of them Black—all of us being in the seventh grade. Sometimes you'd have a Black student in your class, maybe. But a bunch of classes you was in by yourself. So you didn't socialize. . . . When they was carpooling us to school, back the first month, okay, I knew the people that was riding with me. It was about three or four of us, because one girl lived up the street from me . . . Dianne Threet. . . . So she rode with me, and then there was another one. About three or four of us rode. Those were the only ones that I knew. But see I knew Dianne Threet because she grew up in the same neighborhood. But the rest of them I had never seen before in my life. It was all strangers. But when you go to a class—let's see, it was about thirty in the class—and you walk in there, and you look around first to see if you see anyone of color, and if you see them, then you all would interact. You would sit together, you know. So there'd be two of y'all there. You wouldn't be alone . . .

What was the good part about going to West Side for you?

(Laughs.) The good part. What I learned: them that's got, is them that get. . . . If you were born Black, you were at the bottom of the "get" list. I learned that the White folks had, well, some of them . . . had some well-to-do parents, and were chauffeur-driven to junior high school! And you look at them and say, "There's a prize man." Back then, my daddy had a car. But some of the parents of those twenty-five children didn't have no car. They was doing without. Just like most other Black people.

What was the worst part about going to West Side?

Well, when they were shooting at me at first, that was the worst part. But that was . . . fifty years ago. . . . Now they talk about students and stuff having guns and stuff, that's old. 'Cause I had a nine-shot double deuce and a box of shells in my locker. (Laughs.)

Everybody, even then—Black, White, tough—everybody understood that lead, everybody. . . . A couple of White groups—called, one of them was the "blue devils"—they had a '58 blue Chevrolet. . . . The other ones had kind of a gold-ish '57 Chevrolet. They used to ride around, and they'd shoot. But after you returned fire, well see, if they miss me, you hear the bullet go by—pow, pow . . . If you're shooting somebody and you're driving a car, and the bullet comes through your windshield, you think, as they should, "Doesn't it look as if he were trying to kill me? I better leave him alone!" And they do! So after that I didn't have no problems.

When you were in school, what were the other students like to you? The White students?

When I was in school, I didn't realize how dumb some White folks were. . . . Actually they were, I mean, dumb. (Laughs.) And see, they were put in a position that they should know, because they had all the material and everything that they needed . . . And like when I was going to Stephens, they had, for the sixth graders, a day when we went over to Dunbar and spent a day with them to see what they was doing . . . different classes at Dunbar, like industrial arts, where they make stuff and tables. . . . At Dunbar, they had like lumber and stuff, and plywood . . . the Black school got scraps. When I went to West Side, they was bringing in by the truckload like sheets. . . . They cut it up into scrap; they'd throw it over there. And they said, "Give it . . . to the Niggers." So . . . that's what Dunbar had, the scraps. . . . The White folks got the new material, the new and better material. . . . I went over there, the "Getting to know [you] day" at Dunbar, and I noticed the scraps and stuff like that. . . . There's a big dumpster-like that they'd throw it in there. The Black [teachers would] come over there and pick it up and take it to the—"take it to the Niggers." (Laughs.)

What were the teachers like for you at the school?

Well see, people can only do so much of whatever you are allowed. And if . . . you don't take no stuff, they don't mess with you. (Laughs.) And everybody want to be left alone. . . . I wouldn't take no stuff. I had a double deuce.

The teachers probably didn't know that, did they?

Well see, the other Black students knew I had it . . . See, like now. Show you what I got, when it first come out. Say, twelve, thirteen years ago. . . . Do you have one of them?

No, I do not have one of those concealed handgun carry licenses. So all your life, you've had some way of protecting yourself?

So what I do, in my old age, I stay at home, mind my business. . . . But when I leave the house . . . (pulls a handgun out of a Crown Royal liquor bag).

You're showing me that you still have a way of protecting yourself right now. . . . (He removes the gun from the table where we were sitting and returns it to the bag). . . . What that's showing me is that . . . from junior high school, even until . . . today, that experience influenced you, so that you still find ways to protect yourself as an adult. . . . Because during that time, you didn't have anybody to protect you . . .

If you don't protect yourself, who will? . . . Well see, I believe in minding your own business . . . When I was going to school, I wasn't bothering nobody.

Right. But people were bothering you.

That's right!

At West Side, when you were in the classroom and when you were walking to the next classrooms, did the students treat you okay then?

No, you see, they was kind of passive. . . . One time, I was in health. An eighth-grade health thing. And you know how White folks be. I guess they'd be playing. . . . They were shooting at me, these paper clips. . . . I had some staples. So I shot a staple off.

You never had any fights at school . . . ?

No, not really. In gym—I was at Central then, though. So I never really had a fight. But the coach at West Side, Bobby Hannon, he was in my seventh grade. And then he transferred to Central. . . . When I got to Central he was one of the first coaches that I met. And so me and this White boy got into a fight. . . . We was taking a shower. And I had done and dried off. So he was going to come and throw some water on me, so I go upside his head. They broke up the fight, so we had to go see the coach. Coach Hannon . . . said, "Clarence, what's the matter with you?" I said, "He was bothering me." He said, "You all get that straightened out?" I said yeah. He goes, "Y'all shake hands." And said, "Y'all all right?

Yeah? Go home." And they let us go. . . . Usually you get suspended. . . . I didn't get suspended or nothing, thanks to Bobby Hannon.

That's good. And that's the only fight you ever had?

That's the only fight I had. . . . Well see, when I went to Central. The tough White boy who's the one that was causing difficulty. . . . They're probably some of the ones that were shooting at the Black folks. . . . When I walked into Central, they knew who I was! (Laughs.)

Did you see the teachers trying to help you as a student?

Well see, my homeroom teacher at West Side . . . seventh grade, my homeroom teacher . . . also taught me English, okay. But I believe she was a die-hard segregationist. . . . All right, now this is the English teacher . . . Okay, pronounce "Negro."

Negro.

She pronounced it "Nig-ger-o." "Nig-ger-o." Now this is the English teacher that's pronouncing it, so her English should be better than that. . . . But that's the way she pronounced it, "Nig-ger-o." . . . Now that's the only teacher that I had any difficulty out of. . . . But she taught me English.

The other teachers weren't like that?

No. . . . Like, in eighth grade, I was . . . taking algebra. . . . Mr. Ademon. He was teaching algebra, and he would say, "If you have a problem, come by." He'd say, "I get here early. Come by in the morning . . . If you get [here] about, an hour early, come by and check it out." So in his class, I got a C. . . . When he gave me that C, he told me, "I know you can do better than that." You see, I got all them As. . . . He said, "I know you can do better than that." . . . He was fair. . . . Sometimes, he'd give a test and he'd say, "I may have made a mistake." So what he would do, the next day . . . he'd give you your paper. He'd say, "What we're gonna do, we're gonna work this out . . . ."

When you were at West Side, did you participate in any extracurricular activities?

No . . . When I went to West Side, I was twelve years old. And all the other Black students at that time was twelve years old. So . . . twelve, thirteen, and fourteen. . . . None of those first people . . . participated in no activities. None of them that I can remember. . . . Now when I went to, went to Central, some participated. But . . . I bet you it was at least a hundred blacks. It may have been more than that . . . Well see . . . I was doing, was trying to get my day made . . . until three thirty . . . call it a day. . . . Do what they give me . . . like my homework and stuff. I would always come home and do it. But see, some of it I didn't understand. I had to write stuff down. I know it'd be wrong, but I'd just put forward an effort, because a bunch of the instructors wanted you to turn in your homework. . . . You would . . . turn it in . . . knowing it was wrong. But I had to turn it in, because I'd get credit for turning it in.

So you knew you weren't learning all of it?

That was right. . . . But that that I know was wrong, and I wrote it down. It was wrong, but they could see where I had tried to work it . . . And they could see where I had made my mistakes. . . . Like Mr. Ademon, he said, "Let me show you what you did wrong." . . . And then . . . I said, "Okay."

What made you decide to go to Central instead of Horace Mann?

Wait a minute . . . let me see. You have to bear with me now, four, five . . . Hold on, hold on . . . What made me go to . . . Central? . . . When I went to Stephens . . . This is where I was assigned to go to West Side, you see that? . . . I had nothing to do with that! . . . They just assigned you! . . . (Looking through report cards.) Seven . . . eight . . . now you say what made me?

Oh! Because you were assigned again! (Laughs.)

I had nothing to do with it. None of that.

But you never thought about asking to go to Horace Mann . . . ?

It never crossed my mind. . . . Because Central was seven, eight blocks away, and I could walk to school . . . I was doing all right going to Central . . . You see, when I was going to West Side, before, they didn't know me. . . . But when I transferred to Central . . . those that was the troublemakers, they knew me! . . . So I didn't have no problem out of them.

How do you think your action of desegregating a junior high school has affected your life?

Back then I learned them that's got, is them that get. . . . And that's a hard lesson. Because some people be wondering, "Why is—why this? Why me?" You just ain't meant to have! . . . Either you have it or you don't! . . . Say now, I've been retired now for five years. . . . I probably got more money now than I've ever had in my life. Anything that I want, I can pay cash for it . . . At junior high . . . I learned mathematics . . . and algebra. . . . Everybody can't add and subtract. And see, that's, it's another thing. It don't make no difference how much money you got. If you don't have the sense to manage it, you'll end up broke. . . . I can take a dollar and stretch it. Everybody can't do that.

How do you think your desegregation has affected Little Rock and Arkansas and the whole world?

Okay. Like you say my integration, because . . . everybody didn't. . . . A bunch of people take credit for it, and say, "Oh we're doing this, we did that, we did . . ." They did nothing. They take the credit for it . . . but they wasn't the ones out there . . . they wasn't out there doing it, they just take the credit for it. . . . There's a difference.

How did you influence this whole community by doing that?

Well, I was doing what I had to do. Let's say I was compelled. . . . When I was going to West Side, some years, I got a perfect attendance. I mean, I went to school every day. And even went to Central. But even when I was just in the junior high school, in my life, I never played hooky. Never . . .

What recommendations would you have for parents who are thinking about putting their children in a place where they are a minority?

I would recommend everyone, man or woman, think of their off-spring first, and don't ask them to do something that they wouldn't do themselves. I think that's wrong. . . . I believe that's wrong. And like those twenty-five people that, I can't think of one of them that said it was their idea to go. But like on the thing . . . on the card, what does it say? It's assigned.

They're assigned to West Side. They're assigned to Central.

That's right. They had no choice in—they had nothing to say about it. But then how was I picked? How was those nine . . . how was those twenty-five people picked? You ask them, was it their choice to go. Has anyone told you it was theirs?

A couple did.

A couple. Well did they show you that?

You're the only one that has shown me those report cards . . . You did not choose.

I had . . . I'll say it again, no say in the matter whatsoever.

Would you . . . have desegregated a junior high school, if it had been your choice?

Yeah, I'd do it. But I would be more forceful. . . . I wouldn't take no stuff. None. Not from the students, not the teachers, nobody. . . . Before anyone is thrown into any predicament, they should be made aware of the circumstances that confront them. . . . People that haven't done nothing, they can't help you. . . . How can they? . . . But see, those that came afterwards had it much easier . . . because someone else already has paved the way. That's like if you make a . . . path, the longer you walk on the path, it gets smoother.

Alice Joiner Kimball

"I was determined that I would do well."

My name is Alice Joiner Kimball. I presently reside in Hickory, North Carolina. I was born in Little Rock, Arkansas, to Velma and Leslie Joiner. I am the youngest of five children. I attended the Little Rock Public School System. . . . I lived in Little Rock up until February of 2006, when my job transferred me to Hickory, North Carolina. . . . I attended Gibbs Elementary . . . attended West Side Junior High.

You started in 1961?

That's correct. In the seventh grade.

Do you remember about how many African Americans attended with you?

I think there were twelve other African American students along with myself, which was a total of thirteen.

How did you learn that you were going to be one of those who would desegregate that school?

I went to school one day . . . I was in the sixth grade . . . as I walked into the classroom everyone started to clap. And I was like, "Oh my God, what is this about?" I had no idea it was in the newspaper that morning, but prior to going to school, my family, I guess, hadn't read the paper. Normally my father would be the first to read it, but I guess on that particular day he didn't. . . . My fellow students started to applaud. I had this surprised look on my face, and then my teacher told me that it was in the paper that day. . . . She had brought a copy along for me to

Our Stories

see. I was really excited and a little apprehensive, because immediately I knew that I would be leaving so many of my dear friends.

That was your very first time that you had any idea you were going to attend that school?

To actually attend—now we had been tested prior to that . . . My teacher gave everybody in my classroom the same test, and she explained, "If you test out well, there was a possibility that you would be attending one of the White junior high schools." Well, of course, I didn't think by any means that I was going to be one of the ones selected, so I just kind of casually put that aside. I took the test, but there was no impact on me at that time because, "Surely I'm not going to be selected. All of these . . . really smart kids in my class—I'm probably at the bottom of the totem pole." But as it came about, I was one of the thirteen selected out of my elementary school.

Did your parents talk with you about what that might mean?

Oh yes . . . My father was a little apprehensive about me going. . . . I or my parents could have declined the opportunity, but my mother kind of pushed on that I should go, so I went.

Were you a part of that decision-making process also of whether to go or to go to Dunbar?

Not really. It was kind of like I sat in on the conversation, and I really wasn't asked. It was more my mom and my dad that made the decision. Having grown up across the street from Ernest Green and around the corner from Jefferson Thomas when the troops came in—I believe I was eight—I can remember standing at the screen door and the troops lined my street. So immediately, one of my forethoughts is, "Ooh, is it going to be like that?" But by the time they integrated the junior high schools, all of that had subsided. That was one of my thoughts, because I did see people throw bottle rockets into Ernest Green's yard. His backyard faced my front door . . . The troops actually lined the sidewalk of my home, and it was a little scary having experienced that with the Little Rock Nine. But my mom thought that it would be a good thing, and she thought it was a prestigious thing, and that it was saying, "You're smart enough to do this." So she was elated by that, and we went forward with me attending West Side.

What was that like when you walked into the classroom and received all that applause?

Oh, it was like, "What did I do?" because I had no idea initially why they were applauding. But then after my teacher explained that, it was kind of like you could kind of throw your chest out a little bit. Yes, I was happy about it. . . . That was an affirmation that I can do it, too. I always made good grades, but you never think of yourself at maybe eleven or twelve years old saying, "I'm really this smart."

What did your parents, community members, relatives, or anyone else do to prepare you to enter West Side?

Well I had people in my church, really good friends of my mother's, to come over and say, "It's going to be okay. It's in God's hands," and "God will take care of you." Of course I always know that God has been in my life and that He's brought me this far, so I didn't have any reservation about that. But I was always thinking about the mean things that people do. . . . Children normally are not that mean, but the parents kind of encourage them to do things, was my thinking. I was a little apprehensive about going.

It's so memorable to me. My mom had always attended the National Baptist Convention every year for years. This was a Labor Day event. My mom went to the National Baptist Convention, and my dad combed hair for a week because I have two sisters and two brothers. She had never flown before. They would always go by train or by bus, and this was going to be her first opportunity to fly, because she wanted to be there for my first day of school. So after I successfully completed that first day, I can recall us taking her to the airport for her flight. And then she would call back every day to see how things went.

We weren't allowed to walk to school or hang around after school. We were always just dropped off right at the door and picked up at the door, so it was just not what I thought junior high school was supposed to be like. All the fun was gone. We were there for a purpose more than just having a good time in the seventh grade.

Kenneth Jones was a neighbor, and Kenneth and I would ride to school. . . . His father, Henry Jones, and my father would take turns taking us to school and picking us up.

You were talking about your parents and church. What church was that?

Mount Zion Baptist Church . . . There were a lot of neighbors and friends that were close friends with my parents. They were coming to the house reassuring them that things will be okay and, "If you need anything, and you can't get your mom . . . you call me." . . . Yeah, a good community, close-knit. Like a big family, an extended family.

Tell me a little bit more about your experiences when you were in West Side. You talk about being driven there and then dropped off, but it wasn't quite like what you had imagined . . .

Going to West Side, I was a bit disillusioned at first . . . Before the first day I never envisioned that I would be the only little Black girl in a classroom with twenty-five White students. So that was kind of horrifying or terrifying, that I would go through most of my day not seeing anyone of color until I went to eat lunch. Of course the teachers were not all nice . . . They didn't do anything mean, but you were more or less ignored in some classes. It was just like you were not visible. They didn't just naturally call on you like they had done to some other students. . . . I was always trying to make sure that I had my lesson that I had studied, that I was prepared for the classroom each day. . . . It was a little disheartening, because in some classes I never had an opportunity to express myself.

Did you raise your hand?

Oh yes, but there were ten other hands going up at the same time, so there were several classes that I was never called on. They didn't do anything directly to me, but just the mere fact that you were ignored could be very emotionally disturbing. Then I would . . . be prepared and never have a chance to show it off. My father and I talked about it, and he said, "Well . . . it's going to be a little difficult, and that's why you were chosen—because they thought you could do it. So you're just going to have to hang in there and just go with the flow. . . . It's all for a good reason, a good cause." . . . I was like, "Why can't I go to Dunbar?" The last two years all I wanted to do was go to junior high school at Dunbar, and I never had that opportunity. . . . We weren't involved in activities at the school, so it was kind of like, go to school, come home, and maybe attend activities at Dunbar, like the football games and things of that nature. But it wasn't the life that you dream about growing up and going to junior high school.

When you talk about being ignored, was that all throughout the three years that you were there?

It got better in the eighth grade because more minorities came in. And then [in] the ninth grade, more minorities came in, so at least occasionally you'd have another person in a class . . . You had an opportunity to meet other people, make new friends, and sort of hang out during lunch. There were people that I didn't know prior to that year, so it gave me an opportunity to gain some friends and have more of a typical school day.

In the seventh grade, did you have lunch with any other African Americans?

I did. But there was more than one lunch period, and there were thirteen of us, so I'm sure that it didn't exceed five or six other students along with myself.

In that seventh grade year, do you remember having any other African American students in your classes?

I might have had Kenneth Jones in homeroom because it was by alphabet. Jones . . . I can't recall having anyone else in a class other than homeroom.

What other highs or lows do you recall having at West Side?

Well . . . the most memorable thing that I often reflect back on at West Side was my first year. I don't know at what point during the day someone put gum in my hair, and I had to get my hair cut off. I thought my father was going to go ballistic, because I had really long hair. I'm thinking maybe going up or down a stairwell that someone must have dropped a wad of gum. . . . By the time I got home, it was enough gum that they couldn't get it out . . . so I had to get my hair cut. And that's the most notable thing, my first haircut.

No one told you about your hair . . . until you got home?

No. I'm thinking during the course of the day maybe I moved my hair or something. It wasn't a lot of gum, but it was enough to stick in there and not be able to separate it from the hair. And rather than just cut a patch out, they just went around and cut my hair so that it would be even.

How did you handle it that day?

That day, it wasn't so bad because there had been times that I had asked to have my hair cut and my father was adamant that, "No, you're not going to get your hair cut." So it was like, "Well, I got my hair cut now." So I wasn't distraught or anything. . . . It became an issue some years later that someone had the audacity to put gum in my hair!

There was another occasion that I was in the cafeteria, and I can't recall if I had gotten a lunch tray at that time or not. I keep on trying to relive that . . . But I did lean down to get water from a water fountain, and this guy pushed my head into the water fountain. We kind of had a little fight there, and I got suspended for three days. So that was the next notable thing that happened.

So you stood up for yourself.

Oh yes, I did.

The school didn't see you as defending yourself?

No. . . . They said that we both were involved, and so they had to give us both the same punishment. It was three days' suspension. My parents were really upset about that.

Did they do or say anything to the school officials?

My parents did, and they said that was "just school policy"—that it was a "he-say, she-say." Well, if I was getting water, it's quite obvious that he would have had to been the one to push my head down. I mean, how could I push his head down [when] he was not getting water? . . . We knew that there would be things to happen, and it wasn't that surprising that those things did happen. I was more surprised that more things didn't happen than the two occurrences that I had. Maybe some things happened with other students that I wasn't aware of, but mine was pretty much to a minimum. I think that in the lunchroom after I started to fight back, I guess it let them know that, "Well, we shouldn't try to bother her. . . ."

Did you have some high points where . . . Caucasian students would talk with you?

Very little. On occasion someone would say something nice or speak, or I'd be sitting close to someone in a classroom and they would ask me a question or engage in conversation, but it wasn't the norm. Not by any means was it the norm . . .

Was there any particular teacher or . . . staff person that demonstrated something positive in regard to you?

No . . . nothing that would stand out to me. They weren't friendly, but they weren't necessarily negative. It was kind of a neutral ground. You turn in your paper or they'd pass out a test. They take up the test, but there was never a casual pat on the back or "How was your day today?" I don't recall anything of that nature.

Your grades, how were they?

Oh, they were good, because . . . all you had was to study. You didn't have any extracurricular activity. . . . I didn't start extracurricular activities until I went to high school.

Was there a particular reason you didn't have extracurricular activities?

I think that it was so much—the startup. . . . A lot of the kids had already . . . signed up for these things prior to your first day of school. And we just weren't on task with that. . . . Cheerleading and things like that. I didn't try to get into anything like that because it would involve someone having to take you, stay there with you, [and] pick you up. It was already, I thought, a burden on someone just getting you to school and getting you picked up. So the other extracurricular activities would involve you going to a ball game at night, which I'm sure would have been a problem at that time.

What strengths or resources do you think you had, either internally or externally, to help you make it through all three years at that school?

I think one of my strengths was that I was tall . . . A lot of times smaller kids don't lash out at a taller person . . . I looked down on most of the students because I'm five ten now, and I've always been tall. So I kind of thought that was one of my leveling points. . . . Another strength was that I was the youngest of five children, and having older sisters and brothers, the younger ones always try to keep up. I verbalized well. I played around because I was always with my sisters and brothers. . . . I was what I considered friendly and not easy to push to rage. I was kind of even-keeled, and I think that was probably considered in the choice making as well as the testing. The teachers probably had some input on that. I was a pretty easygoing person.

You would hold up your hand and . . . would not be called on . . . But you still continued . . . to do well . . . in school . . . If you had to name that strength, what do you think that might be?

Determination that I was going to make it. I was determined that I would do well. That, along with making my parents proud, I would make myself proud. Going back to living across the street from Ernest Green and around the corner from Jefferson Thomas, I saw how Ernest, even when they burned his yard and did different things and threw the bottle rockets, I still saw Mrs. Bates and others come and pick him up and take him to school every day, and he continued to go. So that was sort of a "prerun" to what I had to do. I knew that if he had done it—I . . . kind of knew what he was going through, because I was seeing it firsthand—then this is just something that you do. . . . Of course his was a lot tougher than mine, because high school children are a lot more vindictive than junior high. As they get older, they get meaner. . . . By the time you get to the tenth grade, they're either good kids or they're mean. In seventh grade a lot of them will still have that elementary mind, that they really aren't mean. They haven't grown into it as much.

You asked a couple of times, could you go on to Dunbar . . . What stopped you from going to Dunbar?

Well my parents just wouldn't allow it . . . They knew—we all knew—that the White schools were better equipped. The equipment was better; the books were better. I'm not going to say the teachers were better, because that's not true. Our Black teachers loved us, disciplined us, and they were like family. So that wasn't the case; but the science labs and the books and things I'm sure were a lot better. . . . As a whole, at that time in my life, I might have gotten somewhat of a better education . . . A better foundation to high school.

Do you think elementary school prepared you for junior high school?

In a way. It's just the normal course of study. And then, too, my parents were disciplinarians, whereas they required certain things of you and there wasn't any slacking. My father just didn't allow slacking. . . . I think a lot of it was we had been taught at early age—had good reading skills and everything. Parents worked very diligently with us with homework and things like that . . . My mother was a nurse, and she worked at night, so she would be there when we would come in, in the evening. . . . She would help with homework and everything. And then I had older siblings that, my father would say, "Go over there and ask your sister" if I had a question or something, or, "Ask your brother to help you with that" math or science. So I think along with the elementary school, the foundation at home was a great help to prepare me for junior high school.

You graduated from Central? . . . What made you decide to go there instead of Horace Mann?

I think we were assigned. I was assigned to Central. It wasn't a choice. . . . Either that was my assignment—and then I had a brother that was at Dunbar and Horace Mann and then I was at West Side and

Central . . . My parents kind of insisted that I go to Central. But . . . I was able to make a decision that I would go to a Black college. That's what sent me to a Black college. It was like, "I have had enough of this. I will be going to a Black college." And I did get a scholarship to go to Tennessee State in Nashville. . . . I went there for two years and then my father got sick with cancer. . . . We were paying out-of-state fee for me to go to Tennessee State, so I had to come home and go to the University of Arkansas at Pine Bluff. That's where I graduated from in 1971. . . . But that was a decision that I made—that I will not go to an integrated college. I wanted to go to a Black college. . . . So my parents agreed that I could go.

How did attending a primarily White junior high school and high school affect your adult functioning in life from a personal as well as a professional standpoint?

Oh, I think it was the greatest thing I could have done. Going to a White junior high school and a predominantly White high school prepared me for the workplace. . . . My first job I worked for the Arkansas Power and Light, and then my husband was a contractor, a bricklayer, and they got a job in Denver. So I had to quit that job, and I went to Denver, Colorado, and worked as an analyst for a bank. . . . We only stayed there for two years because that was the length of the job. They were doing an extension on an army base there, so we came back to Little Rock. I was looking for a job and happened to land a job that needed a Black person because of affirmative action. I can so vividly remember the interview. During the interview the man hardly talked to me, hardly looked at me, talked on the phone, and I thought, "Oh, my God, I know I won't get this job." And they called me back for the job. Later on I found out, due to them having government contracts, they needed to hire a Black person for affirmative action in order to keep the contracts, and when I went to work there, there was only one other Black lady in the office. . . . I ended up working there for thirty-four years, and that's where I retired from. I moved up through the ranks, and that's where I retired from. But having had that experience in junior high and high school, I was in a predominantly male, Caucasian environment, and I was used to that. It didn't matter to me whether you talked or not, because that's kind of what I was used to. I had been exposed to that and it didn't bother me. I could go on and work and not think that, "Oh, she doesn't like me because she doesn't talk to me." That was kind of the norm in me going to school. So it didn't impair my work habits or functions at all. I was able to move through the ranks, move up the ranks and stayed there for thirty-four years . . .

How do you think it affected you on a personal level being in that environment . . . ?

Well, I don't think it had such a big impact on me in my personal life because, number one, I had God in my life. I've always had God in my life, so I would always pray for guidance and understanding, and lead me in the direction that I need to go. There were times when I wanted to say something and I wouldn't, because I knew that there might be consequences. But that was me praying, saying, "Lead me in the direction that I should go." So I was able to get through that. Then I had such a strong family bond. . . . Going to work was just eight to five. My life really began at five. And I kind of looked at it that way. I'd leave work and pick up the kids and go by my mom's and go to the mall or whatever. Or meet friends somewhere. I always looked at it as if my life started at five p.m. I'd just get through the day the best way that I could by doing the right thing. . . . I had a social life and I had a work life . . .

You made the decision to attend a historically Black college setting. . . . Do you think that helped you . . . ?

I think it did . . . because after really attending a historically Black college, you can kind of reflect back to see that West Side and Central really wasn't that bad . . . I guess by that time I realized that people are just people. Other than the few incidences and being isolated and extracurricular activities and things of that nature, it really wasn't that bad. . . . You can be in any setting and have some of the same problems. People don't always mend together because they're the same race.

As I reflect back, especially high school, it wasn't that bad. By the time I got to Central, there were a lot of minorities there, and the teachers had warmed up. . . . You actually had conversations with teachers. . . . We were able to participate in extracurricular activities in high school. So things . . . you could just see them gradually getting better . . . So seventh, eighth, and ninth grade . . . I really didn't know everything that was out there that I could take advantage of. But by the time I got to high school, I kind of knew, "I want to play in the band, and I want to do this, and I want to do that. I want to be in the Beta Club. I want to be in the Honor Society." I . . . could select things and then if I qualified, it wasn't an issue . . . I became a part of things in high school. . . . I even went to prom, so that was nice.

Think about how your desegregation of that school influenced the city, the state, the nation . . . the world.

Well it let my city, my state, my town, my nation know that we're equally able; we have the abilities to learn and to do just like anybody. For so many years we were snuffed out and referred to as "animated people" or "baboons" or people of that nature . . . That let them know that we are human just like anybody else. We have the ability to learn. . . . In my class we have judges, doctors, [and] people of all calibers that have proven that we have the ability to learn and to function in society. . . . Somebody had to start. The class of '57, Central High . . . were the ones to open up the way, and then as it matriculated down, they went on to the junior high schools. So I'm just proud that I was one that was chosen and could come all the way through and graduate with honors. So it is a good feeling. It really is.

Way back in elementary school you didn't . . .

. . . think that I could do . . . anything. I know.

And . . . you're saying that you graduated with honors, right?

Right. Exactly. Went to college on a scholarship. And then years later, just to show you how things continued to improve, my son graduated from Little Rock Central High School in a class of six hundred–plus, and he was a graduation speaker and became a National Merit Scholar and went to college on a full scholarship out of the same high school that I came out of. . . . It was a pivoting moment in my life to just see him stand on that stage and make a graduation speech—a stage that I had walked across many years prior to him being there.

What recommendations would you have for parents who are considering placing their child in a situation where that child would be a minority . . . ?

I would encourage them to push them. Push them forward and let them do it, because that's the way of the world now. If you hold them back there, how long are you going to hold them back? Once they get into the workplace or out in the world, you can't be there to protect them. So you should try to encourage them to move forward where you're there to try to help them through the knocks and the bumps and

Our Stories

the bruises. You can encourage, pick them up, and keep them moving forward. If you hold them back and don't have standards for them, they become a lost generation . . . There are so many kids that are right in that place. They're a lost generation. Once Mom and Daddy's gone, what are they going to do? They have no idea. So I'm glad that my parents encouraged me. That my mother and father were always there with an open ear. "How did your day go today?" "Well what can we do to help you improve it?" or "Do you want to talk about it?" They were always, every day, very supportive, encouraging. "Oh, it's okay. Oh, it will be better tomorrow." . . . Thank God that I had parents with that foresight to insist that I become an independent person. This is part of putting the clay together to declare your independence. You need to go through these stages. My father was adamant about that with his girls. He spoiled his boys. But he was adamant about that with his girls . . . "You will go to college and you will be self -sufficient." . . . He spoiled the boys.

I'd like to leave you room to make any other comments . . .

Well . . . this is something that has been in my heart and on my heart for years, because a lot of people don't realize that you went through a little something. It wasn't as spectacular as the Little Rock Nine, but it was something. I don't think people shunned you for that reason. They just didn't know. . . . We were just thirteen that weren't missed because the numbers were so small; you just don't miss a person out of Dunbar when it's only thirteen. But I did maintain relationships with friends from elementary school that went on to Dunbar. We that were in the neighborhood that I would play with after four o'clock in the evening, and I'm thankful for that. We've carried those relationships on through adulthood.

I'm just so thankful that my parents taught me to persevere through—to reach for something, to have goals. To complete tasks . . . That's why I was able to be successful, because that was my early training—to complete a task. "If it's just cleaning up the kitchen, you complete that task," is what my father always emphasized. "You finish that." So when I'd go to school, I would finish my work, and my grades were always good. . . . There were a few of us that towed the road through, to open it up so that many others could . . . come through.

Kenneth Jones

*"I was going to burst on the scene as a young Black male
and prove to you that we deserve to be here in
every respect possible."*

I'm Kenneth Jones. I was born here in Little Rock, Arkansas. Grew up on Pulaski Street until I was ten. Then we moved to West Twenty-Third, still in Little Rock. I attended Gibbs Elementary, West Side Junior High, then Central.

Do you know how old you were when you began attending the seventh grade at West Side?

I was twelve. . . . I remember . . . it very well. . . . I remember watching what was going on at Central High at eight. And that was four years later. Ernest Green . . . is a friend of my family's, so I knew what was going on. . . . At some level I understood what was going on. . . . I remember that very distinctly. There were ten of us altogether. There were nine other . . . than myself. . . . Most of them I knew. We were chosen by . . . teachers to actually desegregate the schools. . . . We had to have certain grade point. Back then they also gave a grade for citizenship. . . . We had to be students who . . . they thought were intelligent enough to make it, but behaved well. . . . They asked our parents. . . . Then the parents with the teachers and some others—I don't remember who the others were—but they asked us, and we talked about it, and it happened.

Did they pull you from the classes . . . and have a discussion with you?

They did that, and they came to our homes. At least I know they . . . came to my friends' homes too . . . and talked with us about it . . . The parents sat down and talked with us. . . . They also assigned a White family to each one of us. . . . I think the White family was more for our parents to help them think about what we might be dealing with. I remember them coming to the house, and I remember speaking with them on several occasions. I don't remember very much about what we spoke about. . . . They talked with my parents quite a bit. . . . I think it was more of a coaching session for the parents. "Here's what your child may go through, and we're here to support you. . . . Here is a way that you may have to—some of the things you may have to deal with, and here are some ways that you might want to deal with it . . ."

Was it your decision or your parents'?

To attend West Side? . . . It was mine. . . . Now I was twelve, so if my parents said no (laughs), obviously there's no way I would have attended. But they did . . . allow me to make that. Once they were fairly comfortable with it, the question was, "Are you, Kenneth? Do you know what this is about? Do you understand what you might be dealing with? Will you be comfortable doing this . . . ?" I was, even at that age, pretty much aware of a lot of what was going on racially in Little Rock. As a matter of fact, I remember probably two years before that at ten, riding around on my bicycle . . . taking forms to African American homes so that they could sign up and pay a poll tax to vote . . . I knew Ernest Green and some of the others. I remember a friend of the family, John Watson, went to Central, and some of the things that happened to him. . . . So even at that age I thought it was something that I should do to help push the racial issue of desegregation and equality . . . And then another piece, you may not want to say this, there was a girl that was going that I liked and I figured I wanted to be close to her, too. (Laughs.) . . . Wherever she went, I would have gone probably.

How did you all get there?

My father drove us to school. It was myself and three of the girls. There were four of us. . . . I don't know if you remember that picture from the front page of—on that first day going into the side of West Side. . . . I was out front and they were all back here. . . . My father drove us and he picked us up. They were not going to let us walk, given the racial tension in that area during that time . . . He worked at night. . . . He would get up, take us to school, pick us up, and . . . go back home, go to sleep.

Did you find that to be helpful to have your dad taking you . . . ?

Now, it was helpful for me. As a young Black male, it was a little embarrassing! I wanted to walk. . . . You've got that macho, testosterone thing going on . . . You've got all the little girls around that you want to impress, and your daddy's taking you to school. . . . I mean that. But that was the right thing to do. . . . Absolutely.

Do you remember anything else that your parents did to prepare you for this desegregation process . . . to help you through that process?

I grew up in Mount Zion Baptist Church. . . . We always had . . . a very firm spiritual foundation. . . . That was a big piece of what my parents tried to instill in us . . . even in this situation . . . saying . . . "White people are not evil. This is what's going on in this world. By doing this you have to be . . . as Christlike as you can." . . . Those were the types of conversations. Also, my mother being a schoolteacher . . . I can't remember what grade, but I remember one day I came home and I wanted to go out and do something. . . . My mother asked had I done my homework. . . . I said, "I don't have any homework today." She said, "Well, have you read ahead several chapters in every subject?" . . . That's that only time I ever came home and said, "I don't have any homework." . . . That was not the right answer, because then I had to read ahead. . . . She wanted to make sure that if I made this decision, I was going to be there—that I was going to excel. I was going to do as well as anybody else in that school . . .

What experiences did you have with the White community prior to attending junior high school . . . ?

The only real memory of having any interaction with the White community as a child was there was a White family that lived around the corner somewhere. . . . One of their little boys would come around and play with us. . . . One day, we were out in the street playing, and his mother came around the corner just angry yelling at him, grabbed him by the hand and just dragged him back around the corner, and I never saw that kid again. . . . Other than seeing things on television . . . I really had no interaction with the White community. . . . It was . . . a totally Black experience with the exception of that one kid . . . Family, school, friends, neighborhood . . . the neighborhood store . . . It was Powell's Grocery Store right on Twentieth and Pulaski. . . . Every Saturday my father would take my brother and me to the library. We'd get a book. We would go to the barbershop. . . . The barbershop was on Sixteenth and High. . . . From the time we were, I don't know, we could read. My mother taught us to read before we were in the first grade . . .

Both of them were very involved with your life?

Oh . . . very much so. I think one of the reasons that, from a political and even a racial perspective, that at eight, nine, ten years old I understood some things is that we would sit in the barbershop and listen to the Black men talk. I mean that was a gathering place—a gathering of Black men. . . . When I grew up it was, "A child speaks when spoken to." . . . It wasn't like we could get into anyone's conversation. But to listen to what they were talking about, and then on the way home—my father was driving us home—or when we get home, we could ask him . . . "What was that . . . Mr. So-and-So said such and such. Can you explain? What did he mean about that?" . . . I remember there were some things that he would say, "Your mother will explain that to you." He was either getting ready to go to work or he needed to go to sleep to get ready for work, or whatever. But he would . . . say, "Hey, Babe," you know, to my mom, and say, "So-and-so said this at the barbershop. They want to know what that means. Could you explain it to them?" . . . Then he'd go do what he needed to do, and she'd sit down and explain it . . . The interesting thing about those memories is the fact that, here are these men who many did not have a formal education. That was one of the things my parents talked to us about. Now these are intelligent men and they can speak very intelligently and eloquently about, you know, national news, issues—I mean just everything that's going on. The racial tension that was going on . . . not only locally but nationally. They could speak on global issues . . .

So it brings us to those junior high school experiences. . . . Please tell me about those experiences . . .

Well . . . it was interesting to be in a White environment. . . . It was . . . new. It . . . wasn't very frightening, which I would . . . think people would . . . anticipate . . . I had a little bit of a chip on my shoulder, and so . . . in some respects I went in ready to fight. . . . I wasn't going to back down from anybody.

What did the chip stem from . . . ?

Well part of it is just being twelve. Part of it was seeing what happened at Central four years earlier. Part of it was knowing that we could go to Gillam Park to swim but we couldn't go up to War Memorial and swim in that pool. They would not allow us. Knowing that going to downtown, Woolworth and places like that, and not being able to sit there. . . . At some level I knew what I was at West Side, and a part of that was, "I'm going to prove to you that we're just as good as you are." That was . . . literally a part of my choice at twelve to do that. . . . I was . . . not going to be timid. I was going to burst on the scene as a young Black male and prove to you that we deserve to be here in every respect possible. Whether it was intellectually and academically, whether it was physically in terms of fighting, I didn't care . . . I could give you my spiritual side because I . . . did believe in God. . . . It was . . . just that . . . chip. . . . I was going to burst on the scene. ". . . You are not going to hold me back." It . . . just wasn't going to happen.

You had perhaps heard that, that the White society did not believe that you should be there, or that you were not prepared . . .

Oh, absolutely. Yeah. That we were inferior. Remember, we read a lot. I remember reading that Whites believed that African Americans had tails . . . those types of things. I remember . . . walking down the street and this kid couldn't have been more than two or three years old . . . a little White kid one day pointing at me saying, "Nigger." . . . I mean, that kid couldn't know what it meant. . . . It had to be from their parents, okay? . . . We did have to walk through White neighborhoods to go various places or ride your bike. . . . We couldn't go to the movie theaters. . . . There was the Gem Theater on Ninth Street, and then there was the Nabor Theater on Wright Avenue, but we had to sit in the balcony . . . I had a chip on my shoulder because of that. . . . Going to West Side for me was to prove, "That's not right . . ."

So when you burst on the scene, you were ready to dismantle . . .

The entire establishment . . .

What stood out for you there, positively or negatively, while you were there at West Side?

Negatively, I'd say, well—to balance it out, there were those White teachers who really wanted to help us, and worked very, very diligently with us as—just as they did the White students. And there were those who didn't . . . want us there. You could tell that. Likewise there were students, there were students who embraced us, who seemed to be happy that we were there. I remember this one guy in . . . my home-room. When a couple of guys wanted to fight, he jumped in and said, "No. . . . No you're not. This is not going to happen . . ." He actually stood up for me. There were those students who wanted to fight, and there were the ones who embraced us.

I think the thing . . . that bothered me the most is that . . . it was related to the academics. . . . I didn't realize this until the eighth or ninth grade, but my friends who were going to Dunbar Junior High School . . . the books . . . they were using were so outdated. . . . We were so far ahead of them. . . . That was one of the things that really bothered me.

How did you figure that out?

Well just . . . going home . . . to do homework, and talking with my friends, you know . . . "We want to go out and play baseball." I said, "Well I've got to finish such and such," and they're like, "You've got to finish what? " You know, and it's like . . . "What book do you have . . . ?" Here I am in the seventh grade reading the books that some of them don't get to until eighth or ninth grade. . . . That's when I learned. . . . That's one of the reasons . . . I chose to go to Central—to continue the continuity of the academic preparation. . . . Now I think it may have been an erroneous belief . . . but a part of my belief was that if I didn't stay on that track, that I would go backwards by going to Horace Mann. . . . My mind was made up . . .

Did you find yourself having to get into fights . . . ?

Oh, at West Side? . . . Oh, absolutely. (Laughs.) . . . I remember . . . being . . . pushed. . . . You're walking down the hall and somebody just pushes you into a locker. I . . . think their belief was that because we were in the numerical minority that nothing was going to happen. Like I said, I had a chip, and so, "You push me into the locker, and I come off the locker and hit you." . . . "Just call me a Nigger and I'm gonna bust you in the face." . . . I'm not saying that was right, but . . . I never got suspended or anything. I did have to go to the principal's office more than once. I was threatened with suspension. . . . The student I . . . mentioned . . . one of the reasons I remember him so well is because I remember the principal telling me, "You get into any more fights and we're calling your parents in, and you're going to most likely get suspended." . . . Some of the students knew that. . . . When this one guy started to pick on me, knowing that I had a temper and knowing that I was going to get kicked out of school . . . my homeroom mate . . . said, "You know he can't fight you, so leave him alone or you're going to have to fight me." . . . That . . . kind of . . . softened my chip. . . . We were sitting in assembly one day and this kid just kept kicking my seat. . . . It was like, "Stop!" you know, kick, kick . . . you know. And that goes on for fifteen or twenty minutes . . . I just turned around and smacked him one. . . . I just turned around and—pop—and that was it . . . Nothing else happened. . . . There was another instance where . . . I don't remember why this young man wanted to fight me, but it was after school and he wanted to fight. . . . I remember throwing . . . him down on the steps in the front of West Side. . . . My father was driving up to pick us up. . . . My car mates had run . . . to the car to tell him, "Kenneth's in a fight!" . . . He got out of the car, came and kind of picked me up off of this boy, and threw me in the car . . . Where the teachers were all these times, I really don't know. . . . Now, I didn't really get into fights at Central . . . But I remember students getting into fights [at West Side]. I still don't remember the teachers being around, with the exception of a couple of times when fights got bad and the coaches showed up and took some kids out . . .

You mentioned there were some teachers that were really . . . seemed to care and to teach you. . . . Was that the norm?

For me it was the norm. There were very few that outwardly, you could tell, just did not really want us there. . . . I don't know . . . what occurred to prepare them, but I really don't remember much about being—with the exception of a couple—singled out or treated any differently. As a matter of fact, I had a couple of teachers . . . I remember my French teacher. . . . She really . . . just wanted students to excel. . . . Then I went into honors . . . English, I know, in the eighth grade. . . . That teacher was a very good teacher, and she just pushed everybody. . . . She would answer questions . . .

Were there any extracurricular activities you participated in?

We weren't allowed . . . I played a clarinet in elementary school. As a matter of fact, there were times when I would . . . play second seat concert band at Dunbar when I was sixth grade at Gibbs. . . . We were in the old Gibbs building right next to Dunbar. But when we went there we just, initially, were not allowed. . . . I remember wanting to play basketball, too. . . . I think this was the eighth grade. . . . There was a guy . . . who was the point guard for the basketball team. . . . When I went out for the basketball team, I remember stealing the ball from him and going in and making a lay-up. . . . Basically I just kind of wore him out. . . . I still couldn't make the team. So, then, no extracurriculars there, at least not in those years. . . . I ended up taking private lessons from Mr. Adams. . . . I can't remember where he taught. Maybe . . . he did teach at Central, but I did private clarinet lessons with him. My parents . . . didn't want the talents to go away.

Did you pick it back up when you went to Central?

I didn't. Lot of other things but not that.

*What strengths and/or resources did you have to complete your educa-
tion at the junior-high level?*

Well, obviously my parents . . . and really the entire community. . . .
Even though we didn't all go to the same church . . . it was . . . the community, the church . . . the parents . . . not just my parents, but other
parents would . . . take us all to the library. . . . It was those types of
things. And the fact that my parents always said, "You can be whatever
you want to be. Don't listen to any of the hype, okay? Whatever you
choose to be, you can be." . . . I remember my father always saying, "I
don't care if you grow up to be a ditch digger; you dig the best ditch you
can possibly dig." That was, that was always his mantra . . . that inner
belief that . . . whatever you want to do you can do. . . . Failure was . . .
not the failure to accomplish something. It was the failure to try. . . .
From the support I had . . . at the church . . . to the . . . families. . . . At
that time when you rode your bicycle or walked through the neighborhood, if you did anything that was seen as inappropriate, your parents
knew before you got home. . . . I remember one time in high school—I
know you're talking junior high, but the neighborhood was still the
same—we put new tires on the car. I was driving now. I was sixteen . . .
new tires on the car, and they recently paved the street. And so when
I turned the corner, new tires, newly paved street, they squealed. Well
somebody called my parents before I got around the corner and got
home. . . . My father was already asking me, "What are you doing
squealing those tires?" . . . I had to explain, "Dad, you know, you just put
new tires on here. They just paved that street . . . I was not speeding. I
was not hitting the curb . . ."

Your dad worked at night. . . . What kind of work did he do?

He was a waiter. He worked at Tijuana Club, and then he went to
the Little Rock Club. . . . If you go to the Little Rock Club right now,
there's a bronze picture of him . . . We're still members, actually . . . of
the Little Rock Club because of him. . . . Even in serving . . . as being
a waiter and then becoming the head waiter and managing all of the
waiters. . . . Just how he described . . . how you do your job . . . That
applies to any job . . . If you go to the Little Rock Club now and talk
with some of the guys who were there, who remember him, they talk
about that. About his . . . push for excellence and that everything he did
was excellent . . .

Were there just two of you? . . . Your brother was a judge, or still is?

He was a federal magistrate here for thirty-one, almost thirty-two years, and he just retired a couple of years ago.

And you're an academic dean?

I'm the dean of students. I teach sociology and psychology and I have a PhD.

That message from early on just really carried you all a long way?

Absolutely.

You attended Central High School. Your decision was primarily based on the fact that this was the natural path to take?

Right, for me, the natural progression from West Side to Central. . . . because of the difference in the quality, I'd say, of education that I was able to observe—the difference between West Side and Dunbar. I kind of extrapolated (laughs) and assumed that the same disparity existed between Central and Horace Mann. . . . Then my cohort group— these are my friends. . . . What we went through at West Side together was unique, and I didn't want that bond to be broken by going some- where else.

The disparity really had to do more with—less with the fact that you thought the students would not do as well?

More with the educational system. . . . There were some of my friends that I felt were smarter than I was, but they were going to Dunbar and they were reading at a grade level or so behind. I mean that's what they gave them to read, not that that's all that those students could do. The resources that Dunbar had versus the resources that West Side had—that, to me, was the difference. It had nothing to do with the intellectual capacity of the students.

How do you believe . . . attending a primarily White junior high school and then later on high school . . . affected your life?

I think it prepared me very well to live in a majority country . . . majority White. It prepared me to excel academically and not be afraid to be the only person of color in a situation. Most of my career . . . I have either been the only or one of the few people of color . . . whether it's Asian or Latino, African American, doesn't matter. . . . When I have been in those situations, it was almost normal sometimes. One of the things I said to some of my colleagues years ago is that it sometimes . . . frightening when I walk into a room, and I'm the only person of color there and I don't realize it . . . As an organizational psychologist I did a lot of consulting . . . I'm the only person of color when I walk in the room. Or I'd go into a situation where I'm presenting to four hundred people and you can see the two or three other people of color out of four hundred. . . . I think the positive from that is that it . . . didn't negatively impact me such that . . . I couldn't do my job . . . The negative part is that it desensitized me to some of the . . . disparity. . . . It took me a few years to get to that point. . . . I was building a career . . . And one day I just went, whoa! So I . . . started [to] kind of push that issue a little bit more. "Why"—when I'm working with a leadership—"why don't you have an African American woman, or a male, or a Latino, or something?" . . . I would be able to ask those questions.

So I believe that the preparation that all of us received . . . allowed us to be role models—whether we wanted to or not—where . . . other African American children or young adults can point and say, "If that person can do it, so can I." And I think that . . . is probably one of the most positive aspects or outcomes of that whole desegregation of the junior high school piece.

When you were at West Side, do you remember having classes with other African American students while you were there?

That first year there were two of us in the same homeroom because of our name. . . . The homerooms were alphabetical. But . . . since there were only ten, I may not have had a class that seventh grade year. But by the eighth grade and the ninth grade as more students came, the distribution, the ratio changed. . . . At Central . . . what's interesting, if you look at the November issue of *Life* magazine—November 1967 . . . it's got an article about Little Rock Central ten years later. . . . I think it's from that article—it's got Bill Brooks running track, and then when you turn the page you have the prom, and the face in the middle is mine. (Laughs.) . . . I have that one at home. Oh, there was a guy . . . We . . . were in shop together in the seventh grade . . . all the way through. At Central we worked together on the crew behind the stage . . . the lighting and all of that kind of thing . . . [This guy] . . . was the head of all of . . . our lighting for the plays, and I helped him out. When the guys came from the magazine and they set up these cameras . . . and they were leaving for the day, I said, "Now tomorrow night when we have that prom, I want you to get a good picture of me," and they said, "We will." . . . At some point, I saw that same guy and he said, "I got a good one of you . . ." . . . And when this came out in November I remember I was somewhere in the house and my mother said, "Kenneth Wayne . . . Come here. When did this happen?" I looked. I went, "That guy actually did it." (Laughs.)

What recommendations would you have for parents who are contemplating placing their children in an environment that might make them a minority, whether it's race [or] some other type . . . ?

Pray. Always, always pray. I'm serious about that. . . . I think that really helped us a lot. . . . The one thing, other than having a firm spiritual foundation, is to . . . learn as much about that environment as you can. Know what the environment is, and then have a support system inside that environment as well as outside. One of the things we found in all of our research is that if a student has one adult that cares about them inside that system, that the likelihood of their academic success increases exponentially. It can be the custodian. It can be the bus driver . . . It can be one of the food service workers. . . . That student knows that somebody cares. . . . So having an internal support system, even if it's one person, and knowing that environment.

Do as much as you can to prepare that student . . . not just you as a parent . . . Figure out how to help them understand that environment also. I didn't know what I was going into. I just knew that I was angry at twelve about what White America was doing to Black folk. . . . I knew intellectually I was smart. I had . . . I don't think it was an arrogance around the intellect at that point, but my mother had taught—when we went to the first grade we could print, we could read, we had watches, we could tell time. You know, this was before entering the first grade, you know. I started memorizing the Lord's Prayer at two because my brother said the Lord's Prayer . . . I had the capability . . . to do those things. But I wasn't prepared to go into that White environment. So if I had some advice, prepare that student . . . Help them figure out what it is they're going to be facing . . . when you put them in that situation . . .

What other thoughts or comments do you have . . . ?

I'm thankful that I had them. . . . I truly believe that what we all did at that time, collectively, began to move the needle in terms of breaking down the racial barriers in this community.

Brenda Sims Clark

"I never did take into consideration the isolation."

I am Brenda Clark. My maiden name was Sims. . . . I was born and raised in Little Rock. . . . I lived at 1805 Wolfe. . . . That was . . . less than six blocks than the school that the desegregation was. . . . I was used to the area because I was born in that area. . . . Somehow certain people were selected to see if they would be interested and if their parents would let them . . . integrate the schools. . . . My parents . . . I guess, didn't think anything about it, because it was almost like a neighborhood school. They asked me, and I didn't see anything about it because I was used to White neighbors who lived across the street. . . . I said yes. Now I don't know who had contacted them, but they asked me . . . how . . . I [felt] about it. I had an older sister who was five years older than me, and she kept on saying, "You don't want to go there. You don't want to go there." . . . I think she thought a little bit more of the singleness that I would have . . . being a few . . . because she went to Dunbar . . . Perhaps she saw where I would be, in a sense, isolated from my culture and friends . . . She talked to me more about it than my parents after they asked me . . . would I consider it. . . . I said yes because I never thought about the isolation . . . and she kept on saying, "They're not going to let you be in the band. They're not going to let you be . . . on the drill team or pep squad . . ." or something like that. But my mind . . . didn't go there. I had one sister and three brothers. . . . My sister was five years older and my brothers were younger.

She went from . . . Gibbs to Dunbar and . . .

And then Horace Mann.

You attended what junior high school?

West Side Junior High, which was on . . . West Fourteenth. . . . I went there after I left Gibbs. So that was grades seventh, eighth, and ninth.

You started there in 1961 . . .

Yes. . . . We started with nine . . . Yes, we all finished with nine. In fact I think we all left West Side and went to Central. . . . We all did.

You learned from your parents about the process of desegregating. Do you remember anyone talking with you about that at school or in any other meetings?

We would have meetings periodically. Probably about every two weeks we would meet at Dunbar Community Center. . . . We would discuss, first of all grades . . . if we were having any problems. A lot of us, only being nine, we had classes . . . I had about probably three classes where I was the only Black in the class. . . . We talked about the isolation there—how we were treated and just whatever problems. I figured there were some problems going on, but . . . as students . . . we didn't talk about it. We would talk about it maybe at lunchtime: "This person did something to me," or "This person—" you know, isolation in the girl's bathroom or when we had PE . . . little things like that. . . . But that wasn't a problem that I encountered to the point of telling somebody.

Did you know those other students before getting to West Side?

I knew several of them. I knew Sandra Smith because we were in homeroom with S, you know, alphabetically. And I knew Joyce Warren, now Judge Joyce Warren. We had gone through elementary school together. . . . Our parents knew each other. . . . So the . . . activities that we had . . . at the community center or churches and things like that . . . did help; because, after a while, you begin to pick out who you knew your friends were, or who, at least, you knew you could be honest with, to talk with . . . I remember leaders like Dr. Sutton. . . . Certain people . . . would come and just . . . talk to us periodically. . . . I guess they were the ones probably more involved in the desegregation, and they wanted to know what input we could gather with them. . . . NAACP . . . and things like that.

Your parents talked to you about it. I love the fact that you said your sister might have prepared you a little bit more . . . She was five years older . . . She was really helpful towards you . . . ?

Yeah. And more of in a teenage sense—knowing the things that I would miss out on because she was involved in them. . . . In the first place, they asked her . . . would she have considered—and she told them definitely no. She said, "My attitude would be one—I wouldn't be civil. I'd go in there with a hostile attitude, and you don't want me there. You don't want me up there." (Laughs.) . . .

She was very aware of herself.

Our Stories

Very aware . . . and quick tempered . . . Yeah. But she was a lot of help. She was.

And your parents honored that?

Oh, yes. They understood her more . . . She had, in a sense, a different attitude because she wanted to be more involved in herself rather than just doing the streamlined work, seeing what things she could accomplish. She wanted to put a little bit more of herself . . . I just accepted, "You do the best you can," because I had been taught that, really from one teacher from Gibbs, Mrs. Bussey, Charles Bussey's wife. She had instilled . . . getting the best out of an education. . . . I guess that's why . . . I had no problem with it . . . I knew wherever I went, I was going to do my best . . .

So when they posed it to you, you felt included in that decision-making . . . process. You decided to go.

Exactly. . . . I never did take into consideration the isolation. . . . Unless you're involved in it, you don't think about it until you enter into it.

You lived across the street from someone . . . who was White? . . . Did you all engage in play?

On the weekends. We played dodgeball. . . . We played baseball. . . . I wouldn't say we'd become friends, but . . . our family knew families . . . across the street. . . . It wasn't a problem until I started going to school with them.

Tell me about some of those experiences in junior high school.

Well, first of all you begin to notice—which I didn't notice at the all-Black school—the differences in attitudes. Attitudes where you saw the [disparity] of people who had money versus people who didn't. . . . It was brought out . . . even in the classroom. "Will your parents be able to afford this?" versus not saying it to the whole class but singling me out by the teacher, as far as equipment [or] things within that class that I would need. So that's when I began to notice. Or even, as far as notebooks, you know, paper. ". . . Will your parents be able to get you this, because you're going to need to have this by . . ." . . . I would just say, "I think whatever I need, my parents will be able to get it." . . . Remember now my sister has already told me, "You're going to notice a difference." I was kind of like set up to understand even to the point of where I had . . . little situations . . . coming up the stairs and somebody calling you a "Nigger" . . . Teachers would be at the door. . . . When they'd get around their peers, one person can start it, then others can pick up on it. It became so obvious to me because nobody wants to be ridiculed in that way and when more than . . . three would start . . . I was okay with one, but then two and then three; and then . . . going to my classes I would see teachers standing in the door. . . . When they'd get louder and louder, I'd look over at them and they would just turn their back and go on to their class.

So they didn't intervene to assist you in any . . . kind of way?
No. No.

Was it only verbal?
Well, I had one encounter where I remember this guy. . . . He always wore like a black jacket, like he was part of a motorcycle or whatever. . . . He had called me a name, and we had gotten to the stairs and he said, "I'm going to push you down these stairs." I said, "If you push me, you're going with me, because I'm going to grab you. So we're both going to go down these stairs." There was a teacher at the door and she spoke up and said "Hey, let's cut that out." She cut that out . . . when I said . . . "We're both going down these stairs." I didn't say, "You're not going to push me." I said, "I'm going to grab you and we're both going to go down these stairs." . . .

If I notice something I don't have to point you out. . . . More than likely you know something too. [It was the] same way with . . . a guy in my homeroom. . . . He was kind of vindictive in what he said. . . . He always would come up to a part where he wanted to say more, but he would always kind of like cut it off. When I was working at the bank, at Regions Bank, I waited on him. . . . When he came up, I said, "Well hello. . . . We were in homeroom." He said "Oh yeah. Oh yeah." . . . So, like I say, it comes back. . . . It's just not anything that's going to go away. . . . You're going to remember certain things that happened to you. . . . The good thing about it is, thank God, sometimes I wasn't like my sister, because she said she would have . . . reacted to what [was] said.

Was there anyone else that stood up for you?
Not stood up. I remember because I was . . . probably the only Black in my PE class. Of course I'd always be the last one to be picked for certain games. You know how you pick certain people and then finally that

teacher would say, "Well just go over there . . . with that group," because nobody would ever pick me . . . When we had field day, I would get picked for like probably doing races . . . throwing the baseball . . . things like that. But my score would dictate how you got on these teams, not somebody picking you . . .

You were athletic . . . and you still would not be picked?

Not be picked. No, and . . . I almost got to the point of reacting to what I was feeling. We were in gym, and I was placed on a team . . . One of the little girls—and I know she was a cheerleader or something—but when I went over to hit the ball, she kind of like pushed me . . . and went to screaming, "Oh, a Nigger, a Nigger, a Nigger." . . . I was fixing to slap her, but I stopped myself. But I did scratch her down the arm with my fingernail. And of course, you know, I had to explain that was strictly an accident. I really wanted to slap her, but I didn't. We had a meeting about that at the center. . . . I guess these were kind of like counselors from the center that were meeting with us . . . every two weeks asking us . . . And I guess the purpose of that was to see if you were at a point where you needed to be pulled out or if you could . . . stand the heat. And that was explained and everything, because they got a report. I really thought I was going to be expelled and—but I didn't. . . . I don't know if that was smoothed over by . . . the status of the people . . . meeting with us . . . I . . . kind of felt like I was going to be expelled . . . but I didn't . . . I had to go to the office. . . . I was sent back to class, but . . . it got back, because within that meeting at the center, they knew about it. . . . But as far as people spitting on you . . . I never would even report that kind of stuff because . . . it was so many. . . . You'd be telling everybody every day—you know what I'm saying . . . ? You had to deal with it . . . I never had anybody within those years to even want to approach [me] like a friend. And this was the amazing thing because— remember—I said on the weekends, the Lingos over there, we'd go back to playing dodgeball and all. But then on Monday, when they got with their friend, they would say "Nigger" and this kind of thing.

These same children would play with you even during your junior high years? . . . And you would still play with them? . . . Knowing that . . .

On Monday you're going to change. When you get with your friends, you're going to change.

But you made a choice to continue . . .

To continue on . . . yeah. . . . In my neighborhood . . . it was just like you were at home . . . then on Monday when you got in school, they got with their other friends and they became bargaining chips with them. . . . So . . . for a child to even go there—and thank God I didn't put a lot of time and effort because, you know, it really could have brought about some . . . changes in my behavior or my thinking. I thought about it . . . after I left the scene. As far as being a child . . . I just said, "Well . . . they're with their peers and they're going to do what their peers are doing right now. When they get by themselves and they want to play . . ."

When you were in school did you have White people that interacted well with you . . . ?

Some were cordial. Some would eventually tell a friend, "Don't say that"; but as far as befriending me, like my sister had said, "You're not going to have a best friend up in there . . . You're not going to have anybody . . . want to have you overnight or whatever. . . . How're you going to feel . . . when you know that you're not going to be wanted around? You're going to be tolerated . . . But they're not really going to want you there . . ." She had told me about this so much, I guess it had really filtered in my mind to don't even look for it . . . But . . . it caused me to be able, I guess, to withstand . . . the name calling, spitting, and stuff like that . . . The other Blacks, if we met coming down the hall or walking . . . we'd say, "Did so-and-so do something to you today?" because we'd get it back. I'd say "Yeah. What do you think about it?" "Oh, forget about it," this kind of thing. And this not only happened to me, it happened to others. . . . So I know I wasn't the only one keeping it within . . .

So you, you got a chance to talk with them in the hall . . . and at lunch?

And also at these meetings that we had . . . We bonded . . . And then again we lived—because I remember Betty McCoy, she lived on Bishop. I lived on Wolfe. Sandra Smith lived [on what is now] MLK. They were . . . kind of in the same proximity of where we were. . . . Besides . . . even in the Black community there were certain places you could go . . . Usually these are the places that my parents would say . . . "If you're going to go over Betty's, I'm going to call to make sure you get there . . ." They just knew where you were . . .

What . . . strengths or resources helped you to make it through those three years . . . ?

I think I understood the differences in what education should be, whether you had the right resources [or] didn't have enough resources. I saw the difference in . . . the teacher saying, "Are you going to be able to do this? Are you going to be able to do this?" . . . I knew she got that idea from somewhere, because she didn't say it to the whole class. . . . It's kind of like you're looking for something to let that person down, but yet you know you've got to put it out there . . . And I think I noticed that within that framework. It's kind of like, even though you're not expected to get it, being in the midst you're going to get something. . . . At that time I saw a difference in not only the way you speak, how you look a person in the eye, how you mean what you say when you mean it versus somebody just telling you. . . . I noticed that. I noticed, coming from an all-Black [school], where they had the best thing in mind—teachers, but they're used to telling their kids, "You do this. You do that." In the White schools you have an opportunity to express yourself and you're just not told everything. You're expected to get it, but you're not expected for somebody to tell you everything. So it gives you a thinking capacity. . . . So I picked up on that.

Your teachers would allow you to . . . express yourself?

Exactly. . . . I took a speech class . . . This teacher . . . remember I said every day you could expect somebody spit at you, call you whatever? In this class she told them . . . we had to do some kind of recitation or something, and I did it. She said, "Now this was very good." . . . The whole class, she made them aware. She said, "Now did you see how she wasn't nervous? You see how she expressed herself?" And so this teacher brought that out. . . . She did that. I wasn't expecting it, you know. . . . It was kind of like an affirmation . . . of the reason I was there. . . . In . . . class they didn't . . . expect you to excel. . . . The teachers didn't . . . I expected it. . . . I came from a background where Mrs. Bussey had always said, "You do your best, wherever you are." . . . She was a tough teacher. . . . You not only said your time tables, you gave the answer. (Laughs.) Yeah, she'd lined you up against the wall. . . . You gave the answer. . . . I appreciated all of that. That's when I began to see the difference in the schools themselves. But it is an affirmation of what you think, and how you perceive it, and how you give it out.

Do you believe that Gibbs adequately prepared you to enter West Side?

I think Gibbs did. I'd say it was . . . a lot of fright. . . . They picked kids that made . . . more than adequate grades, but I think this came in out of what kind of teacher you had. It's just certain teachers that you knew you'd better get this. . . . Not only to the fact that they would call your parents, but . . . you got it, you know. . . . So that was kind of like a fear factor in there, too. . . . But I do think that it did help in some cases. I had already made up in my mind that I would always do the best that I knew how to do. . . . To some kids that already know that, [when] you keep expounding on that, it puts in a fear factor . . . It sets that up. . . . It made some things I didn't necessarily need, but I got it. . . . It didn't give you an opportunity to give up . . .

Do you think that you would have gotten that same high level of education at Dunbar?

No. . . . I don't think so. I think because, in a sense, where my education at West Side was geared towards academics, I probably would have offset some of that academics for being friendly and wanted to have a play time . . .

Whereas as West Side . . .

It was strictly, do your lessons, in getting you prepared for . . . life itself, because that's what it was. You being involved in an element of some things that you couldn't change now. . . . It was just some things in place. You had to accept them for what they were. . . . You could have your opinion, but the status quo was already set.

When you were at West Side did [you] . . . participate in any extracurricular activity?

I could have because they had drama. I remember Sandra Smith did a dance, we had a talent show, and she was great. And you could tell part of the audience wanted to clap for her, and then some of them didn't because she was Black. . . . I know she was disappointed because I know she had practiced . . . and she was good. . . . I was going to try like in drama . . . I didn't push that because I saw how she was done . . . The boos were a lot louder than the claps. . . . She didn't even try again for anything

You went on to Central High School. . . . What led to that decision?

It was just like a follow-through. After you left West Side, then you went to Central. . . . It's kind of like from junior high to senior high, and that was one of the schools.

Even though every day something was happening, there was nothing that made you want to ask your parents to let you go to Horace Mann?

No; but I tell you after Central, I felt so isolated from my own people—and I mean people at church, different organizations and things—I just felt like I was left out. . . . Even my own people . . . said, "Where [do] you go to school?" This kind of thing, or "Why [do] you always have something to say about this? How did you come up with that idea?" And I'm beginning to notice that. But then . . . I'm coming into a young adult of who I am and what I am. . . . So I can't let that belittle me in my own thinking of me.

So the experience at Central led to you feeling more isolated . . . from your own people?

Exactly. . . . From my own people.

Even though there were African Americans at Central?

Oh, yeah. A lot more to come.

How do you suppose that isolation occurred?

I don't know. I guess I didn't venture out and make more friends. I kind of . . . stayed within the area of what I thought I knew, and it just brought about . . . a sense of isolation. . . . I felt like I was missing, I don't know if it was a commonness of understanding. I was getting away from [what] most Black people knew . . . I felt like I was missing some part of me, and, you know, [there] wasn't anything I could do about it, because I chose to go that way. I became geared in a different kind of music . . . a different kind of reading books . . . Just a difference.

So there were some things you chose—because you chose to attend West Side and Central—that meant you chose not to . . .

Be involved, yeah, in my own people.

How do you think that experience of attending West Side, Central influenced your adult life both professionally and personally?

It made me center on not necessarily want[ing] to be part of a bigger group, but seeing what I could get out of something and what I'm able to contribute. . . . I'm not so geared toward what people think about my ideas as long as I'm able to express and get them to understand. . . . I don't mind having alone time. Sometimes that solitude is good. . . . A lot of people say right now, "You don't venture out." . . . Unless it's really something that I'm connected to, I just don't go along to go along . . . I've got to see some goodness in it for me in order for me to spend my time on it.

I went to UAPB [University of Arkansas at Pine Bluff]. . . . Remember I said I felt isolated from my own? . . . I told my parents I just need to be with some Black people. . . . So I went to UAPB. . . . It was a good experience, but it wasn't one that I totally appreciated. It was at a point where my parents really couldn't afford it. I was steady growing up. . . . I didn't date a lot. . . . I came back home and got involved. . . . Left home, got married. It didn't work out. Went to California and had my child . . . and came back home. Got interested in banking. Stayed there for thirty-two years and . . . just basically lived my life . . . I guess I just appreciated what was offered. I knew I had a responsibility to do what I thought was going to be best for me, and . . . that's where I've been. Even today I'm not as involved in a lot of things that people would like to have me involved in. I choose to have that solitude sometime. [I] do a lot a work at my church, Mount Pleasant. Enjoy that. . . . You have to learn to get the good out of that, and sometimes you have to leave even church. . . . You just have to develop some things out of there and see what's good for you and still not go . . . along with the crowd, even there. It's what you pull out and what you see yourself involved in and . . . what makes you pliable. I don't see happy all the time . . . But [that] makes you want to get up and take the next day.

What would you say to a set of parents or parent who are contemplating placing their child in a situation where that child might be in a minority . . . ?

I would say be thoroughly involved in your child's life. Build that child up within, where they have the stability to know that they can achieve what they put a response to. Keep them interested. Let them know that you're involved in . . . what they think about. Let them tell you some things that they're interested in. . . . Give them enough time to truly understand what education is, what life is about, how they're supposed to love and be loved, and this will keep them centered . . .

Do you have any other overall comments that you would like to make with regard to that experience?

I have an eleven-year-old . . . granddaughter . . . I take her to school and pick her up in the afternoons. . . . I am thoroughly involved in what she has to say outside of the environment in which . . . she's involved . . . It's amazing that they're going through some attitudes, probably some of the same concepts even educational now that's going to set them up or set them back. . . . What I mean by set them up—it will . . . strengthen them when a teacher tells them, "You're doing great" or whatever. It will set them back when she's told, "You didn't try your best today. What was on your mind?" and I understand that these attitudes are coming from another adult . . . She may have something else on her mind, but she's putting that on your child. It's very important that parents be involved in the educational system and knowing something about who's teaching your child.

Some of the same statements that were made to you years ago . . .

They're being made right now, and I'm not saying that it has nothing to do with the educational system and equipment and all this stuff they're having now. It's coming from individual lives the teachers are putting on our kids.

And that message will affect or influence that child?

Whether they do their best or their worse.

How do you think your desegregation of a junior high school influenced the state—the community, the state, even the nation?

I think what it did—and I think it's diminishing because we don't put a lot of focus on our kids and the education. We hear more about the bad parts than we hear about the great science projects they've been put out . . . the poems and the drawings that the kids are doing . . . I think it's . . . really exploited to a point where it becomes utmost that this is the only thing we're thinking about. . . . Neighborhoods are getting older; people are getting older. People that know this stuff, they're tired. . . . They really want to just lay back and let somebody else carry it on. But we've got to find a way to promote that to parents who are having kids now . . . Just don't set them up and send them to school and think they're going to get what they're supposed to get. You still have an involvement to make sure that everybody, not only your neighborhood, but even in your family here . . . say something encouraging. "What good things did your teacher have to say about you today? What things did she let you down on? What made you feel good about going to school today . . . ?" . . . I think it helped our community. . . . I think when you get to know people who are advocates for education or communities, I think you knowing that that's available—it enhances what you're feeling. You can . . . put a face to what you want to say.

People of the community came together . . . to assist you?

That's right.

And you don't see that as much . . .

As much now, no.

But your choosing to desegregate the school itself influenced the community?

Exactly. . . . Yeah.

So it takes both parts?

Yeah, it does. . . . And . . . knowing the responsibility, first of all to myself at that time, but then seeing how it can carry over. . . . First you'll get it yourself and then you want to give it back. Then you want . . . to give it back. And there's no hostile attitude about it. You know some people got it, some people haven't. . . . We have a responsibility to keep it going to an extent those who want to get it will get it. Now some people don't want it and ain't gonna never get it anyway, you know. But you have a responsibility to keep trying—if you care. If you care. . . . If you care.

Sandra Smith

"We were all pretty strong. We all stood our ground."

[My name is Mrs. Sandra Smith.] I was born here in Little Rock. I grew up here in Little Rock. Went to college in Chicago, Illinois . . . North Park College. It's now North Park University. . . . Before college, while I was in high school, I spent my summers in Chicago and I would always work. I could always find a summer job in Chicago. . . . My mom had a sister in Chicago and a cousin that I consider really a sister to me, so I was familiar with Chicago. . . . I spent a lot of my summers there . . . when school was out. After graduating from college I came home . . . to rest a little bit. Had plans to go back to Chicago, and I decided that maybe I would substitute because I wanted to get some money for a car. . . . They called me for a job . . . I majored in art education and minored in psychology. So then I met Mr. Smith, Mr. Lorenzo Smith, at the teacher's meeting and . . .

You mentioned that your maiden name is . . .

Smith. . . . Maiden name is Smith and my married name . . . is Smith. . . . I taught school for five years, and then I went to work for Xerox Corporation as a marketing exec. I was with them for fifteen years. . . . During that period my husband and I opened Center Stage

Music in 1987 . . . here in Little Rock. . . . We were full-line retail store. We put special emphasis on private lessons. At one time we had about six teachers teaching alone in the studio, along with our retail sales. My husband and I were always big—and always tried to emphasize to students, "This music could be your way to college"—so we were big on the private lessons. . . . A lot of times he would even help prepare students for college scholarships in music. . . . We even enjoyed working together . . . which was kind of unusual.

What junior high school did you attend here in Little Rock?

I attended West Side Junior High. . . . 1961 . . . I was probably about twelve. . . . I had a new little sister that came into my life. . . . She was born in 1961.

How many other African American students attended with you?

I believe there seven of us all together, so there were six others . . . We went to elementary school together . . . It was Gibbs . . .

How did you learn that you were going to be attending that junior high school?

Well, I believe the teacher—I think it was Mrs. Robinson. . . . I remember her talking to me about it. . . . I don't remember if she talked to us as a group, but I do remember her talking . . . to me about it . . . I gather, when I think back, that she may have said . . . "You have been selected to go to West Side Junior High." . . . I can't remember what terminology she used . . . at that time. But I . . . was aware of the crisis that had happened previously, and I knew that it was going to be . . . an all-White school. I knew that.

Do you have any thoughts or recollections about . . . what that selection [was] about?

I could not tell you. . . . Back then, I'm not really sure if I knew exactly . . . why I had been selected . . . I don't know if it had to do with my performance in school or probably my behavior, my temperament —that type thing.

What about your parents? Did they talk with you about this process?

I vaguely remember a conversation between my mom and dad about it, and then they came to me. . . . I kind of remember my dad saying, "Well, if she's okay with it, it's fine with me." I kind of remember that. . . . My grandfather and my dad owned Smith Glass and Mirror Shop. And their specialty was re-silvering. . . . He had, at that time, a lot of antique dealers coming into the store because they dealt with old furniture and old antiques, and a lot of times they'd come across old mirrors that needed re-silvering. . . . That's the only business in Arkansas that did that type of work. . . . He had a lot of White customers that came in. . . . It was, I think, established in 1939. . . . I was a child, but I would be at the glass shop sometimes, so I was used to, you know, interacting with . . . Black and White people as well. And then my mom . . . was the first Black salesperson hired on Main Street at M. M. Cohn. . . . I can remember going into the store and . . . she had introduced me to a lot of the people that worked there. So I was very comfortable—I remember walking all over that store as a child, and . . . I was very comfortable at that time. Maybe that had something to do with [it] . . .

That was with adults. With young children as well did you . . . ?

It was mainly with adults.

Was there any other type of preparation that your parents . . . or anyone did?

I vaguely remember some meetings at Dunbar Community Center. . . . I do remember some meetings at our church, because Bethel A.M.E.—we had four of the Little Rock Nine that attended Bethel. . . . Daisy Bates also attended there for a while. And another point I just thought, Christopher Mercer . . . was the NAACP attorney at that time. Now I may not have his position correct, but he was involved in driving the Little Rock Nine to Central at that time. Well, he attended our church. So I can remember vaguely some meetings . . . with Rev. Young . . .

Your church was making a statement directly or indirectly . . . by having meetings . . .

Right. So there was prayer—a lot of prayer . . . for them and the whole church and that type of thing. . . . I was young, but I kind of vaguely remember when that was happening.

Please tell me your experiences when you went to West Side . . .

I believe we had been taken over prior to school starting, so that we would be familiar with the school, the hallways and the rooms . . . I can remember that. I know on the first day the school was well guarded. . . . They did not want any problems on that first day of school. And I understand that there was a photographer up in a tree that got our pictures as we kind of went in the back way. . . . There was like a breezeway that we went in that first day . . . Some people kind of stared at you and some people made comments. But all in all it, it wasn't too bad. . . . I, as a child, had kind of been instilled, "You are just as good as anyone else. . . . As long as you treat people right, you shouldn't have a problem." So it was not that difficult . . .

You traveled with someone . . . ?

Yes. My dad and Kenneth Jones's dad would take turns driving us to school. So we all went together initially that first year. . . . We were . . . dropped off, and that first year we were also picked up after school. . . . I do remember the . . . fellas having more confrontations than the young ladies. . . . Sometimes they'd get in a little scuffle. (Laughs.) . . . Nothing real serious, but they stood their ground. I think we all did in our own way.

How did . . . the fellow students treat you during . . . those years?

Well, I made some genuine friends . . . and then, of course, there were some that still had that old stigma. . . . Children are not born with that. That's a learned . . . behavior, I think—being prejudiced. But on the most part it was, I would say . . . pretty good for that day and time.

You made friends even during that first year?

Yes . . . in class.

What stood out for you significantly during those years—positively or negatively?

Let me say this before I go any further. I believe that the education that we received in elementary school was critical. I think it was an excellent . . . basic start. . . . I think today a lot of our kids are missing that . . . We have a lot of kids that, in junior high and high school, [are] reading on a third-grade level. . . . I think that's very tragic. The teachers that we had—first grade through sixth grade—they were just excellent. . . . We were well prepared to go to school at West Side or anywhere else. I would even venture to say even in other cities. I think we were well prepared . . .

What do you think was the reason . . . your parents would have said . . . "Go to West Side," as opposed to Dunbar . . . ?

Everybody was aware of what was going—what had happened at Central, and that there was a push . . . for integration. So I think they understood that, and they both had dealt with the public. My dad was also a distribution clerk with the post office, so both of them were used to dealing with the public. . . . They both talked about, and then asked me about it. I didn't have a problem with it so . . . I ended up going.

Tell me about your relationship or the interaction with the teachers there at West Side.

The teachers were helpful. Some of them went out of their way. . . . I think they probably felt like the spotlight would be on them if something were not . . . to go as planned. . . . Did I have anyone that I felt they might be a little prejudiced? I don't really remember a teacher that I experienced. . . . I kind of do remember an incident with the gym teacher. It wasn't anything bad, but it just kind of stuck with me. We were running outside of the school. . . . Back then you had to change for gym. . . . I fell down, and she said to me, ". . . Oh, you don't scar like we do." . . . And I don't really think she meant any harm, because I had fallen. I had just a little scuff on my knee. I remember that just like it was yesterday . . . I think it meant that maybe Black people—maybe their skin is a little tougher. I believe that's what she was getting at . . .

Did you participate in any extracurricular activities?

You had music in class . . . I even had remarks. One young lady said to me, "If you weren't Black, you would be really a good friend, and I think you're very pretty. If you weren't Black you could really be popular." That . . . statement was made to me. . . . Also . . . I think this was high school, I had the gym teacher to say to me—now this is gym class—"You are a pretty little Black girl and they don't usually make good grades." That statement was made to me. . . . There were other comments made, but I kind of remember those.

At West Side, other than the falling down, there were no, just seriously negative experiences that you had . . . ?

No. Now . . . kids will be kids. . . . Even if you have a school that's completely one ethnicity, you're still going to have little run-ins. Those . . . things occurred; and those things occurred with us there. . . . But like I said, we were all pretty strong, as far as self-esteem, and we all stood our grounds, as I remember.

You had lunch with other African Americans?

Well, it depended on how your schedule was, who would be in the cafeteria. I would just get my tray and go sit down. You know, if I saw someone else . . . one of the other African Americans, we would all sit together, if we had just come from class . . . or I would just go sit wherever. . . . If there were other White students there, sometimes they would sit and sometimes they would move.

They would actually . . . get up and leave the table?

Oh yes . . . That was fine. (Laughs.)

What led you to go on to Central High School?

I think it was just, in my mind, a natural progression. So the group of us that were there . . . went on to Central.

There was no thought about going to Horace Mann?

No. I just thought about something else. . . . While we were at West Side, Dunbar . . . would have what they called track and field day, and we were able to get permission to check out of school and attend that. . . . We enjoyed it. (Laughs.)

Did you attend your own track and field day for West Side?

I don't remember them having a track and field day. . . . I think this is something that . . . would happen every year . . . with the Black schools . . .

How did attending a primarily White junior high school and high school affect or influence your adult life, both personally and professionally?

Well, I still go back to the education and the training that I received from the Black elementary school . . . I think I was prepared emotionally and as far as . . . education. I think I was prepared morally, physically. I think I was prepared for that—along with my church. . . . They say the elementary—especially the first part . . . the first grade, second—those are your formative years . . . I think I was well prepared during that time, and I felt comfortable with myself . . . Therefore, I could be comfortable with other people, no matter what type of sentiment that they had. I went on to Central High and enjoyed most of the time there. . . . Then went on to a college that, when I got there . . . had eleven Blacks on campus. I really didn't know that until I got there. . . . Since I was familiar with Chicago, and I had spent a lot of summers there, I didn't think twice about going to college there . . . It reminded me exactly of West Side. And, of course, that was the first year. And the next year they progressively admitted more students.

In junior high were all of your teachers Caucasian?

White.

What would you say was the difference between the teaching that made that experience in elementary school so profound for you?

Teachers back in those days really . . . cared about their students. They took the time to make sure that you learned whatever the educational topic was. . . . I think that's missing. . . . I really do. I think our kids are just missing out on a lot of basic instruction that I received . . . back in elementary school. It's just not there . . . the methodology, the method that is used. . . . What we . . . have learned today is that people learn differently. . . . So you might have to take a different track for some students. . . . The teachers back then were "old school." So they presented . . . the work to you, reviewed it, went over it with you, and made sure that you understood it. Made you feel comfortable in asking questions and . . . doing your work. It's just a big difference between what's going on now and what happened back then, in my opinion. Now as far as the teachers at West Side . . . we had some good teachers. . . . I think they were genuinely concerned about . . . us as students.

You didn't have to make any extraordinary measures to catch up to . . . where the rest of the students were?

Not at all.

How do you think those experiences at the junior high and the high school influenced you personally and professionally . . . ?

When I was teaching school I enjoyed that. . . . Then, I decided that I might want to do something different. So I had no problem . . . entering into corporate world from an educational world . . . which is very different. But I was up for the challenge. I wanted the challenge and I didn't have a problem . . . doing that. . . . I spent fifteen years at Xerox . . .

How do you think your actions of desegregating a Little Rock public junior high school influenced the city, the community, the state, and even the nation?

Well . . . the Little Rock Nine have received a lot of attention, and it's well that they should. . . . They were very brave at a time that was . . . difficult . . . I think the nation had all eyes on Little Rock. . . . People did not know where Little Rock, Arkansas, was. They knew at that point. And I think . . . it was just sort of the next level, I believe, for mankind to . . . try—if I can just say, "Can we all just get along?" . . . It's almost like a natural progression, I think, to go from . . . segregated fountains, segregated restaurants, segregated . . . theaters to integrate. . . . People want a fair share . . . as they did then and they still do. . . . I think there is a certain amount of prejudice today, but it's a different type. It's more sophisticated, if you will . . . There will probably be always some people that will be prejudiced. . . . It might be because of ignorance or it may be because they have not encountered any Black people. . . . Now we have Mexicans and . . . different ethnicities that have joined the fight to get a piece of the American pie. I think that's what it's all about. . . . People want to advance . . . They want to be recognized. . . . I think we all kind of want the same thing, you know? We've become a melting pot, but I think we still have some way to go. I really do.

And back to that level of "sophisticated" prejudice or racism—could you give me . . . an example of what that looks like?

Well, I'll just take the president of the United States. Now he is President Barack Obama giving an address to Congress, and some freshman representative has the audacity to holler out at him while he is up before millions of people giving an address. Now that's probably ignorant on his part, but some people probably thought, "Okay, he did the right thing in doing that." Now, that's more outward. That's a more outward type of display of prejudice . . . If you are maybe applying for a loan for a business and you go into a bank, you might run into some people that don't even want to talk to you. You understand what I'm saying? Then you have others that will talk to you and be very positive to you. . . . Smile in your face . . . but then you still don't get the loan . . .

What recommendations . . . would you have for parents who are contemplating placing their children into an environment that might still be the majority . . . racial . . . or any other type . . . ?

As far as socialization . . . the kids playing with each other and getting along . . . in this day and time . . . I don't think that's going to be a problem. The problem might come in from an educational standpoint. If the child has not had a good foundation, he or she may not be successful. They may not be successful if they have not had a basic foundation, you know, like old-fashioned reading, writing, and arithmetic. If they have not had that basic foundation, there might be some problems. I . . . wouldn't want a child that maybe didn't pick up some element of math . . . to be placed in special ed—I think they call it something else nowadays—just because of that. . . . I think that might be quickly done nowadays if the parent is not paying attention . . . if the parent doesn't get involved. . . . If there's a problem at the school . . . the parent needs to be involved. . . . They need to go up and see what is going on with that child. . . . The parent needs to be involved, period. . . . But I think basically—even I can look back [at] my sister—she's deceased now . . . when she went to Central. She went to Dunbar, but then she went to Central. . . . When she got to Central, and there's twelve years' difference as far as the socialization or the fraternization. . . . That was not a problem. . . . They all seemed to get along . . .

Do you have any other comments or thoughts that you would like to make regarding the whole desegregation experience?

Well, I think it was something that needed to happen, and Little Rock was the focal point. I understand that Little Rock, certainly at that time, was not the only place that this was taking place . . . but I think it needed to be done. . . . People want equality. . . . If they look over here and they see this group of people, they have a set of standards that they are living by or opportunities . . . that they are getting, and this group over here is not getting those opportunities . . . People want equality. . . . I think it's human nature. I really do.

Alvin Terry

"We were all part of the movement."

My name is Alvin Terry. I was born in Little Rock, July 28, 1949 . . . I attended West Side Junior High. We integrated in fall of 1961, I believe . . . seventh grade.

Do you remember how many other African American students attended with you?

I think there were nine.

There were some discrepancies . . . The newspaper said eleven, and . . . someone has mentioned that maybe one dropped out or didn't attend . . .

Yes, Felton Walker . . . I don't recall at all. . . . I know Felton Walker. I didn't know the Summerville guy. But I don't recall him ever being there . . . We were kind of forced together anyway, so everybody knew who was there. There wasn't anybody hanging out, because there wasn't anywhere for them to hang out that was safe . . . In that environment you came together for a number of reasons because there was nobody spitting on you, or throwing eggs at you, or acting hostile towards you within that nine. . . . It really didn't matter if were together or not, but I'm just saying that was the friendly environment . . . The other environment was rather hostile. . . .

Did you know these other students prior to attending West Side?

I knew a few of them from old Gibbs: Sandra Smith, Alice Joiner, Betty McCoy, Brenda Sims, Kenneth Jones, and maybe some more. . . . I think I had one year at the new Gibbs.

I don't know the distinction—"old Gibbs" and "new Gibbs . . ."

Well, on that property—and I guess it would encompass maybe four or five, six acres between Wright Avenue and Sixteenth Street and Chester and Cross—is all Little Rock School Board District land, and you'll find Gibbs and Dunbar. Where the field house for Dunbar is, is where old Gibbs was. It was a three-story structure built probably around the turn of the century—the nineteenth century—and the sixth grade attended Gibbs in old Gibbs. It was pretty nice. It was an old building, but we got to start our band early. The Dunbar music director would come over there and give us lessons starting on the flutophone and graduate to different instruments . . .

How did you learn that you were going to attend a majority-White school?

My parents probably told me. That's kind of cloudy, too. . . . My father was a member of the NAACP. He was pretty active. My mother was a schoolteacher, and my cousin was one of the nine in '57, at Central. So we were all in tune with the movement. . . . At what point I was told I was going to West Side, I don't know. . . . I don't really have a memory of that.

When you say you were told, it doesn't sound like you all sat down . . .

And discussed it? . . . Oh no. . . . It probably went something like, "We want you to do this, and we think . . . you've been chosen. We think you can do it." So it was, "Sit down and discuss it," probably. But what are you, eleven . . . twelve, whatever? We were already attuned to what was going on, because when we would leave Gibbs, we had to go through a White neighborhood, which was hostile, to get to our neighborhood. Back then, between '57 and '61, there was a great deal of hostility and there would often be fights going home . . . walking down Wright Avenue. . . . So we knew there was a crisis and that there were difficulties. As a matter of fact, I can remember on one occasion these White boys were chasing us down the street, and some of the older

Black kids came to help. . . . That was my first memory of a conflict on a physical level. But the interesting thing was the pathology in the Black community, that still exists today, was when we would encounter kids coming from Gibbs as we left West Side was, "Y'all must think y'all White, going to that White school."

Was that coming from the Black students?

Certainly.

So . . . you were getting it from both sides?

Right. . . . And it still exists today. If you're academically inclined or if you speak correct English, or whatever, then you're trying to . . . feel less of. That's unfortunate but that's the way it is.

Do you remember anything that your parents did to prepare you to go into the junior high school?

Well, I'm sure they pumped us up, and all of us to a child probably were loved and nourished to a degree our self-esteem could withstand what we had to go through. . . . There are a few that succumbed in other ways, but I don't think self-esteem was one of the issues. . . . I think we attended a few meetings, but I don't remember any play-by-play or whatever.

Since your dad was a part of the NAACP, did they have meetings . . . ?

Oh yeah . . . He attended a convention in New York in 1959. I went along—he and my uncle—went to New York with them.

You also mentioned that your cousin was part of the Little Rock Nine. Which one was that?

Ernest Green.

[Did you have] any conversations about this experience that you were getting ready to undertake?

No. If we did, I don't remember them. . . . Because he graduated in '58 . . . and he was gone. Went on to college.

Tell me about your first days as you were going to West Side.

I can tell you about the first day, but that's probably the only one. It stands out in memory because it was a mob there. And it was a "Two, four, six, eight, we don't want to integrate," type of thing, and a lot of shouting and hostility, and that's the day that stands out to me . . . I kept on going. I think we had escorts, and we were escorted into the building. . . . My dad was at work. My mother was at work, so it must have been some other parents or NAACP . . . There was a committee—a biracial committee. It may have been some of them that escorted us in. . . . There was a biracial committee that was helping to ease all of this into place.

Were there any particularly positive or negative experiences through your time at West Side?

Pretty much negative. Well, I discovered I liked woodworking. Other than that nothing stands out . . . It was not a nourishing environment. It was a hostile environment. And when I say hostile, I mean there was nobody for the most part trying to be your friend or be friendly towards you or trying to make you feel like a human being. You were either ignored or there was some outward negativity, and I just don't recall any positive experiences.

Do you remember talking with your parents about that?

Yes. It all revolved around, "You can't be a quitter," so there you were.

No matter how bad it was, "You can't quit."

Right.

So you went all the way through the ninth grade.

And on to Central.

Did you . . . make that decision?

I don't think so. Central was close. We lived on Park Street, too . . . We lived on Twenty-First, so it's seven blocks away. My mother was working, and she'd just had another child, so that made four of us. My dad was going through his travails, trying to break the color barrier at the post office. He became the first Black supervisor and went on to become the highest Black in the US Postal Service in Arkansas. So he had his work cut out for him. Interesting sidebar there: my uncle told me that 1957—and my uncle also worked at the post office downtown —that the workroom floor was cleared on that day 1957, when they integrated Central High. . . . They were at Central.

So your father really believed in desegregating?

Yes.

And he wanted to be a part of that activism process?

Yes.

Which was why you couldn't quit.

Yeah. Well . . . that's reasonable. Never want to be a quitter. It works most of the time . . . There are some situations where you should cut your losses . . . But once you get programmed one way, oftentimes you go too far in a losing situation when you should have bailed.

What about the teachers that you recall at West Side? Were there any that were particularly positive or negative?

I remember a Ms. Blackman. I think she taught science, and she may have been supportive to the degree. And a Ms. Settler, she taught French. They were supportive to a degree. And I had a woodworking instructor . . . Mr. Donald Bratton. I used to see him from time to time. He's passed on . . . But other than that I don't recall any.

Do you remember any of the students that you had an interaction with, a positive one at all?

Well, you couldn't interpret this as positive, but there was one guy, he had the motorcycle jacket and the greased hair back and he didn't refer to us as "Niggers." We were his "little Black buddies."

How did you interpret that . . . ?

Hyperbole, to put it without using any colorful language. Just a poor White boy . . . He could have used any word he wanted. There were no consequences. It wasn't meant to be complimentary but oftentimes, males especially, when they talk to each other, it's not kind words. So you didn't take offense to that. I didn't. After a while you begin to evaluate people not on what they say but, "Does this person have any malice towards me? Is this person trying to hurt me?" That's the way when you analyze a situation.

Do you think that there were people there that systematically did attempt to hurt you or to bring malice?

Well, you also had to remember you're dealing in an atmosphere— twelve-, thirteen-, fourteen-year-old boys. As a rule there's going to be horseplay and roughness and behavior that's frowned upon by the school. But then you have the race issue injected into it, and it changes things a bit. So, yeah, there were people trying to hurt you.

Was there ever a time that you contemplated not finishing the ninth grade or the eighth grade even, at West Side?

Sure. I'm sure. But that goes back to "no quitting."

What about your safe group, the students that were there? Did you all provide mutual encouragement to each other?

Mostly. Yes.

Were there times when you found . . . you had to take action, aggressive action, to protect yourself, or engage in fights or anything?

You encountered hostility on a daily basis . . . whether it grew into some physicality . . . is a different question. Most of the time it didn't, but sometimes it did. And that was in the school and outside the school. We had to walk a gauntlet to get in the school sometimes, because of different hostile acts. And then you encountered them in the school, too.

So from the point that you entered school during the morning to the time that you ended school, it could happen any time?

Yeah, inside the school . . . I was suspended twice, I think, and threatened with expulsion for fighting.

Were the other people threatened with suspension?

I assume so. I don't remember. . . . The one fight I had in particular, which was very helpful to me the rest of my time at West Side and Central, was an encounter with a guy in the stairwell. We bumped into each other and words were exchanged. One thing led to another and then we were exchanging blows. . . . He was bigger than I was. He swelled my face up pretty good, but . . . after suspension . . . I came back, my face was down, it was normal, but he had a black eye. So I guess that kind of helped take the heat off of me somewhat . . . A lot of them were going to be bullies to somebody and there was plenty cruelty around there . . .

Did you participate in any extracurricular activities while you were there?

We weren't allowed to do anything. . . . Looking back on it, it was probably because the school board felt like they couldn't protect us. Inside the school, that's a controlled atmosphere, but you go to extracurricular activities or at night, the public is allowed to attend, and probably didn't want any lawsuits.

Didn't sound like they were protecting you inside the school.

Well I don't know whether they could. I don't know that they could.

Did anyone ever try? Teachers?

Teachers intervened—break up a fight. . . . Well, I thought they did. I got taken to the office. So it must have . . . I don't recall a lot of, "You kids cut that out." There was probably some done, but I don't recall any where they would. Ms. Blackman may have done that. When they saw acts of cruelty or kids being cruel to each other, teachers understand that. I guess they've been trained to deal with that kind of stuff.

You went on to Central. Had you given any thought to the possibility of going to Horace Mann?

Yeah, I thought about it, but somewhere along the way I matured into another stage where I felt like I was part of the movement, and this is what I needed to do. I was proud of what I was doing, hoping some good would come out of it.

So you became "part of the movement." That's a powerful statement.

Well, actually, that could have happened a lot earlier, now that you make me think about it . . . Because we were all part of the movement. That was kind of a thread that ran through. You're not old enough, mature enough to process the trauma or the movement. But you knew that there was a force opposed to you exercising your rights. There was a force opposed to you becoming a full-fledged American, and you were where the rubber meets the road. That has some satisfying rewards to it.

How has that experience affected your life down through the years . . . being at West Side?

Both negatively and positively. . . . Negatively . . . because there have been instances when I've had an inadequate amount of compassion for White people—less than understanding. But as you grow older, you begin to put things in perspective, see things a little bit differently. . . . It's been a growth experience. You have to process all that trauma that you endured, and that's a whole field of weeds all by itself. They've, in talking about PTSD, how it happens upon people because when you're right in the middle of it, you don't have time to process what is actually happening. There was no introspection; you were just doing it. Of course, accumulated trauma over the years is going to take its toll. Now I guess I'd have to have a psychotherapist or somebody qualified to do that . . . try to explain it, but I don't know. It's just both positive and negative.

You refer to it as a trauma . . .

Well, I don't know how you could describe it as anything less. It's less than—no, it's equal to—assault, because you may be in fear for your life. You may be in fear of harm, and that's probably every day. So there's an accumulated trauma that goes on, and who knows what effect it has on you. It's had an effect on some ways I've dealt with White people.

But not with Black people?

No, I've got a different—we went through a lot of stuff, and now when you see it just being thrown away, people embracing ignorance—and it just makes you angry. Makes you sick. But then you realize that it's similar to when the children of Israel left Egypt out of slavery, and they had to wander in the wilderness a long time because slavery had done such a job on them. . . . They had a religion to sustain them, but a lot of them had rejected the values to it. . . . I often think of us in the terms of the new Jews because we're going through a period of time where we're being weeded out. Only the smart and the lucky survive . . .

What would you recommend to parents who were contemplating placing their children in situations where the children might be a minority . . . ?

You'd have to love them and make them feel good about themselves and build them up to where they feel like they can do anything. . . . Give them love, faith, and hope, because you can accomplish a great deal when you shoot for the stars and you land on the moon.

You would not recommend that they not allow the child to attend some environment where they're in the minority, because it sounds like even that challenge . . .

Builds character. It makes you—the old saying the hotter the fire, the stronger the steel—there's some truth to that, so it just depends . . .

So in some ways it sounds like maybe you developed some steel?

I think so. Adversity, I guess you could say, can make you or break you. We're not going to always win. We're going to fail. We're going to lose. We're going to move forward, move on.

Your attending West Side—[How] do you think it affected your life . . . professionally or personally . . . ?

I can't blame that experience for anything, to tell you the truth. I guess I'm different in a way because I'm a loner. I'm not a joiner, and those things may have come about pretty early. I'm not the one to want to follow. I like to go my own way, and those may have been traits that were formed earlier or the foundations were laid. So when you go it alone, it's a little tougher trail [than] going with the herd, for good or bad.

I just really can't assign any blame to that experience. It was a strengthening experience . . . I don't know that I could say that it was anything other than that. So I don't know how to describe it. Nobody was killed, nobody was maimed, and most of us had the tools to deal with the other kind of trauma.

How do you think your actions of desegregating a Little Rock junior high school influenced the city, the community, the state . . . the nation?

One tiny step forward. I can't call it a giant step. But that's going to take time. But it was a step forward. . . . Can't assign too much to it because there's still such a long ways to go, and people are falling by the way every day. . . . When you get old enough to really look back on the Civil Rights Movement—revolution, however you want to term it—it's interesting to evaluate it from this perspective now, because you can see how things really work. And . . . Farrakhan—the FBI paid him or influenced him to kill Malcolm X. Martin Luther King had on his staff traitors, informants. Some sort of government or quasi-government killed Martin Luther King, the Kennedys, and there may have been a few more. All the Black Panthers—well, the police did that . . . We're all led to believe you have these rights, so on and so forth, and the police will always be allowed more freedom than the Constitution gives them because order has to be maintained at all cost. When I say order, I mean the status quo. . . . Our property rights have to be protected. This whole area down here is a process of protecting property rights. Downtown was not flourishing, property rights were diminishing, so tax dollars flowed down here and our neighborhoods were allowed to go to hell. . . . It's interesting to look back on it and put it in perspective. . . . It was a tiny step forward. That's what most people are taking: tiny steps forward, and so goes the nation. We're moving ahead very slowly, one little step at a time, and trying to move toward an unattainable goal.

Joyce Williams Warren

"People may pick on you, but you hold your head up.
You do the best you can, and you can make it."

[My name is Joyce Williams Warren.] I attended West Side Junior High School. . . . I was eleven years old . . . There were nine others besides me. . . . We started out as ten and then one boy left and went to Indiana, I think. . . . He left after a short period of time . . .

Did you know these students before you attended this school . . . ?

I knew several of them. . . . Some of them went to church with me and some of them went to elementary school with me. . . . Kenneth

Jones [and] Alice Joiner went to church with me. [We] went to Mount Zion Baptist Church. I also went to school with them. [I also] went to school with Sandra Smith, Alvin Terry, and Betty McCoy. . . . I went to school with some others and went to church with some of them.

So you had a previous relationship. Do you think that helped you?

It helped immensely. . . . When you run into unchartered territories . . . I was so shy. I was a scary child. It just kind of helped when you had somebody to kind of to hold hands, figuratively, and sometimes probably literally. . . . We would ride to school together. Henry Jones's father would take us to school. I'm trying to see if somebody else would take us to school, too. I'm not sure, but I know Henry Jones's father. My mom and grandmother would take me over to Sandra Smith's house because Sandra Smith lived next door to Henry Jones. . . . I didn't live far from them. . . . I'd go over to Sandra's house in the morning. . . . Kenneth would come from his house and Sandra and I would get in Mr. Jones's car. . . . We'd pick up some more people . . . We kind of went . . . as a group to school.

Did you take classes with them?

It's fascinating you should say that. I'm thinking not at the beginning. . . . I do recall, though, the very first day. I don't remember a whole lot, but I remember the very first day we went. I had a book bag; it was more like a briefcase. . . . If I'm not mistaken . . . they put you in homerooms according to . . . your last name of the alphabet. . . . I think Mr. Jones took us. We got out and walked in, and . . . found where our homeroom was. I remember walking up and down the hall, and I'm thinking I was the only Black kid in my homeroom. . . . I remember walking up and down the hall, terrified, just scared to go in. I was just afraid. I was just a scared kid anyway . . .

My grandmother used to have to say, "You need to go in and pay this bill for me. You go and tell them you're paying this bill for your grandmother and ask for a receipt." I'd say, "I don't need a receipt." She said, "I'm writing my check. They're going to tell you, 'Your check is your receipt.' You're going to say, 'No, my grandmother wants a receipt.'" She was getting me prepared [to] look at people and talk to them. So that helped, but I was terrified. I walked up and down that hall, and then Mr. Bratton, Donald Bratton, my homeroom teacher . . . came out and said, "It's time to come in." Nice as he could be—"It's time to come in." I was just terrified. I just thought, "Me, by myself. I don't know anybody." I was walking up and down the hall and he says, "It's time to come in . . ."

He was Caucasian?

He was Caucasian. There were no Black teachers at West Side. None. . . . But Mr. Bratton was . . . very nice, very supportive. . . . I took Latin . . . about six or seven years altogether between West Side and Central, but . . . I started [in the] seventh grade, and he was my Latin teacher. . . . I don't remember many names, but I remember his. Absolutely. Eventually, we [African Americans] . . . had some classes together. Not a whole lot . . . I can't remember if we had classes together that first year, but I do recall being in class with some of my fellow Black students. . . . I'm thinking we had lunch together. . . . I don't know if they had more than one lunch period at that time or not. . . . I do recall though, the one thing we used to joke about was . . . you could clear a table. You could always find a place to sit because generally White kids didn't want to sit with you. So . . . all you had to do was just put your tray down at the end of the table. If anybody was sitting there, they'd get up and move.

How did you learn that you were going to attend West Side or a majority-White school?

I knew you were going to ask me that. I don't have a clue . . . I'm sure my momma and my grandmamma told me. . . . I do remember my grandmother saying this—she was kind of worried about how I would do, because again I was just real just scary . . . and not very talkative . . . and shy more than anything else. . . . My great-grandmother, my grand-mother's mother said, "She is going to be fine." Everyone else [was] saying, "What if somebody . . . ?" "She's going to be fine. Lord's taking care of her. She's going to be fine." . . . I don't remember any of the how I got there. I don't remember going, saying, "Can I go?" . . . I'm sure they made the decision for me, too—and probably asked me, too—but I don't remember.

I know what was helpful to me. . . . I came from . . . that strong Christian background . . . my mother and grandmother and great-aunts . . . just in church. . . . They always told me, "You can do anything you want to do." Even as unsure as I was and scared to really talk to people much . . . "You can do it . . ." I was always very respectful of grown-ups, and . . . obedient. So they just [said], "Go and . . . do the best you can. You can do anything." They just kind of drilled that into me, too. . . . "You are equal and capable as anybody else," and "You are a human being. . . . You are not defective. You are not inferior. . . . You can do it." Drilled into me . . .

Was there anyone else that poured that into you, to prepare you for that process?

No, just my family . . . My mother and father were divorced when I was young. I was like three, and my sister was one. So . . . it was just that "you can do it." . . . I came from a strong background of educators. . . . Everybody in my family eventually had masters [degrees] or almost a PhD. . . . So education was important, number one. And a good education was important, number two. They wanted us to have good education . . . a good sense of what we could do as an individual and what we could contribute to society.

Back then they made sure you went to tea. . . . You had social graces you needed to get, too. You needed to learn how to speak to people, look them in the face, be respectful, responsive; say, "Yes ma'am, no ma'am, yes sir, no sir . . ." Use your fork to eat. All that kind of stuff . . . And it was just . . . "You're going to a school that's different. . . . People may pick on you, but you hold your head up. You do the best you can, and you can make it." . . . And then the group of parents of the kids that I . . . went to church with—Alice Joiner and her mom and dad, and Kenneth Jones and his mom and dad—it was always supportive in church . . . So you looked up to the adults and you respected them. It was just like a collective. "These are all of our kids and you are all of our parents." So . . . every morning Mr. Jones would talk . . . "What happened yesterday at school . . . ?" and . . . "Just . . . do the best you can," kind of thing . . . So it was just that collective, "You can do it," and . . . "Keep going." . . . I know Kenneth Jones and Alvin Terry—I'm surprised that they got out of school, because . . . they had a fight almost every day . . . This continued until we went to Central, too. And both were little boys, you know, short, not big. . . . Sometimes, even in junior high school you can have bigger boys who play football, traditionally, that kind of stuff. But Kenneth and Alvin were short . . . but they were not afraid of anybody . . . I think they were suspended sometimes. . . . Apparently it wasn't long-term suspension, because . . . there had to be a fight three times a week. . . . I'm thinking this was West Side where Kenneth was fighting a big boy, and they were fighting and knocking each other into the lockers. But . . . they weren't going to put up with stuff. . . . If somebody hit you, they'd just hit them back. Of course, I was just a whole different thing . . . I don't remember anybody ever hitting me, but I remember people spitting on me . . . calling you bad names and that kind of stuff. . . . I do recall one day . . . it had to be past seventh grade . . . we were either coming from or going to an assembly or something because . . . we were all going in one direction . . . This White boy who was kind of tall . . . stuck out his foot to try to trip me. . . . Before I realized it . . . I took my hand . . . and balled it up into a fist, and when he passed by I hit him in the back of his back. I do remember that. And he didn't do anything. I remember thinking, "What have I done?" . . . I guess that day I thought, "I am just tired!" . . . Before I realized it I hit him, and I'm thinking, "That's not like me. What have I done?"

You do recall . . . being spit on?

Oh yes! . . . Spit on and called "Nigger" and all . . . that kind of stuff . . . "What are y'all doing here? Why don't y'all go home? You don't belong here." . . . You're sitting in class with people and . . . there'd be one or two as we call them "nice White kids" would talk to you like a human being. Not many. . . . Some, of course, wouldn't say a thing. . . . Then you'd have that group that would just be taunting. But . . . I just kept on going. I don't know what came over me that day. . . . He could have turned around and hit me, I guess, or told the principal or vice principal. . . . I think he turned around and he kept on going. . . . I tripped . . . And I'm thinking, "Oh my goodness!" I didn't fall down. . . . But . . . something deep within me—I don't know what that was—just kind of rose up. . . . I do recall also when we would go to Sandra's house [one] January. . . . It was my seventh grade year. . . . It had snowed, and ice was still on the sidewalk and the ground. . . . My grandmother and mother . . . dropped me off at Sandra's house. . . . Sandra and Kenneth lived on a hill, so . . . quite a bit of steps you had to walk up. I got out of the car and promptly fell. Leg went under me—sat on my leg and broke my right leg right above the ankle. . . . Slipped on a patch of ice. . . . They gathered me back in the car and took me—my mother was teaching at Rightsell at the time, and my grandmother was still teaching at Gibbs. . . . My mother went and . . . Mr. . . . Harry Fowler, was her principal. . . . I remember him coming around to the door and she was saying, "I think Joyce may have broken her leg; got to take her to the emergency room . . . not going to be to work on time . . ." . . . It was broken. . . . So I do recall they said, "You are not going to school on crutches, because somebody may push you down the stairs." I had a homebound teacher. . . . Nice as she could be. [She] would come to my house and teach me . . . traditionally for that six weeks I was out that . . . because they said, "You are not going to school, because somebody will knock you down those stairs." I believed them, too. I'm thinking, "You know, you might be right."

Did you enjoy that period of not attending school, or were you eager to return?

Probably eager to return. And it was still having contact with my friends, of course. I thought it was cool—and had the nicest teacher. . . . I didn't . . . get behind on anything, which was a good thing. . . . I didn't lose any credit . . . Grades didn't suffer, so it was a good thing . . .

Do you recall the . . . quality of your relationships or interactions with the other teachers . . . ?

Yes. I had a teacher . . . [name withheld]. [She] . . . was one of the teachers who would just kind of shorten the word "Negro." "Nigras," you know what I'm talking about. . . . So-and-so, and then the "Nigras . . ."

I had some good teachers. . . . I think I was in the ninth grade, and if I'm not mistaken, I think Kenneth Jones was in that class with me. It was a science class and had a male science teacher. And I'm almost wanting to say the science teacher was probably a football coach or something . . . I still was so shy. We used to have current events once a week. . . . I was standing up in front of class, and I was so nervous that I couldn't open my mouth. . . . I remember I had my . . . little newspaper clipping for whatever the current event was on science, whatever I was going to read about. . . . I stood there, and I remember my knees were shaking, my heart was beating fast, and I was holding the paper. I stood up there for what seemed like an eternity, and whatever his name was said, "That's all right you can go sit down now." And I thought, "Oh, thank you, Lord." . . . He didn't demean me or make me feel bad because I was standing up there shaking. I was just so afraid. I couldn't open my mouth. . . . And I was just up there thinking, "Oh, my Lord."

I stood there for seems like what was forever; and he said, "That's all right, you can go sit down."

Taunting wasn't going on?

Oh no, the taunting wasn't going on. . . . It was just kind of like all eyes on me. . . . Eventually I got out of that because . . . I was at UALR [University of Arkansas at Little Rock], and I took speech. Of course you had to take it . . . and I think I did well. . . . But other teachers—I don't remember anything.

Did you participate in any extracurricular activities . . . at West Side?

Oh, extracurricular, yes, of course I did. . . . I was in the Latin Club. I was in Beta Club. . . . I want to think that was in . . . was it West Side? . . . We went to dances. Of course . . . you just danced with the Black kids, because nobody else was going to dance with you . . . I went to dances . . . I'm thinking . . . "This is my school." That's what we thought: "Our school." . . . What's the whole purpose of integrated school if you're not going to participate in everything that you can participate? That's kind of . . . defeats the purpose if . . . you don't go to the dance and everybody's all White. You're integrating a school; you've got to be there, and you've got to be a presence. So we did. We went to the dances. . . . Of course my mom usually went with us. . . . Somebody went with us and chaperoned, which was what parents did anyway. And so, my mother would chaperone that stuff all the time . . . I didn't have a problem with that. . . . I remember we went in gym, of course, and in gym you played basketball. We played basketball . . . [The] gym teacher . . . was nice. It really helped to have teachers who treated you like human beings . . . and just weren't outwardly . . . just condescending and just racist.

What strengths and/or resources did you have to complete your education at the junior high school level . . . ?

Well, just coming from a background of educators who drilled into you the importance of education—"get a good solid education. Do the best you can. It's going to help you . . . knowledge is power." . . . If I needed help with homework, we had folks to help you with homework. You . . . just set aside time to study. Folks would look over your homework and give you tips . . .

Now those folks were within your family?

Yes. . . . I'm pretty sure. . . . I'm sure we did homework together some time. . . . Some of the students. It was just, "Do the best you can." . . . If you didn't do well on a paper or something, "Figure out what you did and why and straighten it out." But . . . just knowing that I could do it . . . knowing I had that support at home and whatever I needed to help me with my homework . . . My mom was . . . a music major, but she taught English on a high-school level for a while. . . . She was excellent in English. . . . Certain things you just knew . . . "This is how you construct a sentence." They reinforced at home what we learned at school. [We had] books at home and resources at home. . . . It was just a continuation. Education was just important. It wasn't a matter of, "Are you going to college?" It was . . . just a matter of, "Where are you were going?" . . . So I had the, "You can do it, and we're going to help you, and nothing you can't achieve, you can be anything you want. It's going to be hard sometimes. . . . Study hard." And it's funny, my mother, before she died, I said, "Momma . . . why did you let me take some of these classes, especially when I got to Central? Why did you let me take physics and all?" I never was strong in science and math, but I took trigonometry and I took algebra II and I took physics. She said, "Because you wanted to and I knew you could do it." I'm going, "You should have told me, 'I told you it was going to be hard.'" She didn't say, "Don't take this class because you're not going to do well." "Take physics? Sure, take physics." . . . I'm thinking, "Oh, my gosh . . . !" . . . She's going, "You can do it," and I did. I studied hard, and sometimes going, "I don't know what I'm doing." But, you know, I always got through.

You went on to Central. What led you to the decision to continue on at a predominantly White school?

That is an excellent question! . . . I've talked about that same issue over and over for a number of years. . . . I had formed a group of friendships with the Black kids that I'd known and came to know. When I finished ninth grade at West Side, I just assumed—which is a word I tell the people now we don't use in court or anywhere—I just assumed I was going to Central. Well, I assumed wrong, because at that time my mother, sister and I were living on West Thirty-Second Street, 615 West Thirty-Second in the south end. I think they had redrawn the district, and guess what? I was assigned to go to Horace Mann, and I had a fit. I'm going, "Oh no, I can't go to Horace Mann! I don't know anybody over there. All my friends are going to Central. I've got to go to Central." Of course my mother and grandmother knew that too, and they didn't want me to go to Horace Mann. They wanted me to continue the desegregation and with my friends—and go with my friends and continue that struggle of desegregating. . . . I moved in and lived with Aunt Mildred, one of my grandmother's sisters, who taught at Dunbar. . . . I lived with Aunt Mildred so I could legally be in the district, and I went to Central. In the meanwhile, my mother moved from Thirty-Second Street to the same street where Aunt Mildred lived; my grandmother was already there. So we had four . . . houses on three corners—three sisters and my mom. Isn't that incredible? So that's how I got to go. . . . I didn't have anything against Horace Mann, because I went to Horace Mann . . . to take American history in the summertime. And Ms. Nancy Ola Parker . . . taught at Horace Mann . . . Summer school was six weeks . . . and it was rough. . . . She was rough. . . . I knew Ms. Parker all my life. . . . She was a family friend but she was a rigorous teacher . . .

You didn't think that the level of education at Horace Mann would be lower?

I did not; and that was just based on some of the teachers that I knew at Horace Mann. . . . I knew those teachers were dedicated, and they did what I think a lot of teachers nowadays don't do: they ministered to the whole child. . . . They realized if a kid's having a problem in school for a particular reason, it may be that their learning style is different and you're not teaching them the way they need to learn. Or they're having problems at home. They may have had a bad sleep, may not have enough to eat, may be afraid . . . to come to school because they may not look as clean, so . . . they would talk to the parents. . . . My mom and grandmother did that. I could see that at home. And that's what Ms. Parker did. So no, I knew that . . . they were very good teachers . . .

I do wonder the reason you needed to go to Horace Mann for summer school?

It was because I was taking two languages. . . . I took Latin six years and I took French two years . . . and American history was a requirement. . . . I think I did that so I wouldn't have to worry about not taking one of the electives . . .

How did attending a primarily White junior high school affect or influence your adult life both personally and professionally?

What it did was prepare me to function in a majority-White society, because . . . they were people just like I was. . . . As sad as this is to say, I was used to being one of a few, and that is sad because you shouldn't have to be like that. . . . I went to a majority-White college . . . Rockford College. . . . I wanted a small school . . . So it just prepared me, because I was used to being around people who you want to call "different" . . . Different . . . race, different backgrounds . . . I was used to it. So I just felt comfortable. . . . I was . . . used to hearing some of the things folks say . . . [Attending a primarily White junior high school] . . . dispels some of those myths when you get to interact with people. . . . I think that's really what helped me . . . We are more alike than un-alike. We've got so many things in common. Everybody's different, irrespective of your color. So it helped me to know that people are people. [It] helped me get rid of some of my fears of speaking to people I didn't know and . . . going to meetings where I'd be the only Black person . . . I can function; I can talk. So it helped me that way, I think. . . . I just know it did.

How do you think your actions of desegregating a Little Rock public junior high school influenced the city, the community, nation . . . ?

Well, I think it just was a testament to knowing that, as an individual, people can do things that need to be done. . . . I never got a sense of . . . "I can't do it." Even though I was scared . . . to go to class that first day. . . . I think it's a testament of what the human spirit can do. . . . With the right kind of support and the right kind of encouragement, you can do it, no matter how difficult it is. That's what I tell kids in the courtroom today sometimes. "It's not easy to do things. You're scared for a lot of reasons, but you can do it. Somebody else has done it. You can do it."

You were in the first [group] "doing it."

Yes. . . . I don't even think I realized at the time that that was just four years after Central High School. It was still brand new. Still fresh. And that was the junior-high level . . . I think it just shows the world that . . . people are people—even kids can make a difference. You just trudge along every day, and you do what needs to be done . . .

I've always been spiritual. . . . I prayed a lot, "Lord just go help me through this day . . ." When I got scared or nervous . . . especially . . . if you were walking upstairs and saw a group of kids come down, you didn't know if they were going to spit on you. You didn't know if they were going to call you names. You didn't know if they were going to try to push you. You . . . just kind of went through it, "Just help me do it." . . . Then at the end of the day kind of debrief—"What happened to you today? How was your day," kind of thing—and you just kept right on going.

That debriefing seemed to be something that was an integral part, whether it was . . . Mr. Jones, or . . .

Or the other kids. That's exactly right. You . . . kind of say . . . [Examples of conversations between fellow African American students] . . . "Oh, so-and-so, he's a nice White kid because he spoke to me today. . . . I talked to him." "Okay, how was this teacher?" "She's mean." "What did she do?" "She did me the same way." "She did?" . . . We went . . . to football games, you know. "You're going to the game." " . . . Let's go to the dance." . . . Just kind of like this. And then, of course, you sit around and nobody dances with you, and then you dance with each other. So . . . you just have to have that somebody to pat you on the back, and go, "You can do it." " . . . Keep on doing it." You've got to have a cheerleader. It's like life, period. You've got to have somebody who says, "It may be difficult. It's new. You might be afraid. You've never charted these waters before, but you can do it. It's important to do it." Of course . . . I wasn't going to do anything to embarrass my family either. I'm thinking, "I'm over here. . . . I'm going to finish. . . . I'm not going to do anything except hit that boy in his back!" (Laughs.) But thank God I did not. I do remember one thing, though. I was really embarrassed. In the ninth grade, we had graduation. . . . This just came to me. At the graduation ceremony they . . . called my name. . . . My name was Joyce Elise Williams, and they called, "Joyce Elsie." . . . I was so embarrassed. I'm thinking "Elsie, that's like Elsie the cow!" . . . I was just embarrassed. I thought, "That is just awful. I am not a cow!"

And that was one of the last memories . . . ?

That's exactly right. . . . I'm trying to get my history right. . . . It was '63. It was Kennedy. . . . I remember coming down the steps and somebody was saying . . . that Kennedy had died, and "The Black folks' . . . president's gone," that kind of stuff. I thought it was awful. . . . Folks were just taunting. And I just thought that was just awful. It just was awful . . .

So it seems like . . . there was a mutual influence process . . . Other people . . . influenced you, and . . . you [had] a positive influence on the community by finishing . . . ?

That's exactly right . . . I think it influenced me in this way too, because even in high school and college and beyond, when I would be doing things and there would be opportunities to join clubs . . . and I would do it. I'm thinking, "It's my right to do it." . . . Everything shouldn't be all White all the time. . . . It was kind of like I had a mission. . . . James [husband] and I talk about that, too. It's awful to say that people, Black and White, have fought, shed blood, tears, and died for the right to vote and we don't vote. If you struggle to desegregate things . . . school . . . organizations . . . and businesses, and you don't follow through, then what have you done? You've broken a veil, but you haven't taken part in participating and making sure that things are inclusive and things can improve and things can get better. . . . I thought it was always my responsibility to go. . . . I'm going to participate because I would always say, we would be out there holding picket signs and striking and marching if they wouldn't let us join this club. . . . It's important to participate in society in every way. You don't have to join everything just because it's there, but if it's something that you want to be involved in and something that's going to be beneficial to you and others, you have an obligation to do it. It's not enough to say, "Oh, I was one of the first Black people who went to West Side." So what? . . . Did anybody benefit? What's the purpose? You do something just to put a little check down—"I'm the first. I'm the only." That's not what we're doing. We're trying to break down barriers to make things better for everybody—those in the present and those to come behind.

What recommendations would you have for parents who are contemplating placing their children in an environment where their child would be in the minority . . . ?

My advice would be . . . make sure that child knows that he or she should not be defined by anybody else. He or she should not let somebody else tell them what they can or cannot do and that they are worthy or not worthy of doing. . . . They have to have some sense of security or connection—got to have an anchor. . . . For those who believe in a higher power, that's the anchor, and then your family and friends. . . . Whatever it is, "You can do it. Don't let anybody tell you that you don't belong, that you are not equally as important as anyone else. You should not look down on other people, and you should not allow them to look down on you where they define you as less than—less than capable of doing whatever—whether it's because of your race, because of your physical ability, because of your mental ability. You can do it." . . . Tell them they are as much a part of that organization as anybody else. They have the right and responsibility to do the best they can and be respectful of everybody, irrespective of the fact that people may look at you and go, "Oh, she's stupid," or "She can't do this." Just go, "You will not define me!" . . . Words do hurt, but you have to get to the point where you go, "I'm taking it, but I'm taking it for what it's worth." You have to look at the source sometimes. . . . So many people have stopped doing what they want to do because somebody told them they couldn't do it. When . . . I was going to law school, somebody said, "Joyce is going to law school? She's too shy; she'll never be a lawyer. She won't be able to speak up and talk." . . . At one time I may have believed that, especially when I'm in there trying—too scared to go into that seventh grade homeroom class. But you can't let people define you. You just have to do . . . the best you can. . . . You cannot ask anybody to do . . . anything more than their best . . . You're going to make mistakes, but don't let those mistakes define you. . . . Let them know you . . . have [a] right to be here. You have a responsibility also. . . . You have to be respectful, responsible, and do your best, and everything will take care of itself.

III Conclusion

CHAPTER 8

What We Discovered

Five questions provided motivation for learning about the initial desegregation of the junior high schools:

1. What was the reason the entire school district was not being simultaneously desegregated?

2. What was the method of implementing desegregation of the junior high schools in 1961?

3. How did the students' parents and other important figures prepare them to desegregate the schools? Were they given the opportunity to make a decision about whether to attend that school?

4. What was their perception of the level or quality of education they received in the junior high school, perhaps as compared to what was received in their elementary school?

5. How did attending predominantly White junior high schools influence their lives as adults?

The first two questions were answered in chapters one and two. This chapter summarizes former students' responses to the remaining questions. Please refer to appendix 4 for demographic information concerning the former students.

Students' Preparation Process for Desegregating the Schools

History informs us that the Little Rock school superintendent and the school board, guided by the Pupil Assignment Law, were responsible for selecting and assigning the junior high students to the various schools.

This fact is reflected by some of the students who believed they were "selected" to desegregate their schools. Others were unaware of the process until they learned they would not be attending the only African American junior high school along with their classmates.

Chosen/Selection Process. While a very few students recalled signing some type of application to desegregate the junior highs, a significant number indicated that they were "chosen" or otherwise selected in some way to desegregate the junior high schools. Several described some of the criteria used to select them. Alice (West Side) specifically recalled taking some type of aptitude test. Kenneth (West Side) stated, "We were chosen by . . . teachers to actually desegregate the schools. . . . We had to have a certain grade point. Back then they also gave a grade for citizenship. . . . We had to be students who . . . they thought were intelligent enough to make it, but behaved well." Those who were able to recall being selected seemed to recognize this as an honor or privilege.

Decision. Eight students indicated that they made the decision to desegregate the junior highs. Four stipulated that their family made a joint decision. Five remaining students, however, stated their parents made the unilateral decision for them to desegregate the schools. As Kathleen (Pulaski Heights) stated very succinctly, "They decided and we went." On the other hand, Clarence (West Side) believed he was simply assigned to attend the junior high.

Those students who perceived or recalled themselves as being selected were also more likely to be those who participated in some fashion with their family members to ultimately feel somewhat involved in making the decision to participate in the desegregation process. Alice recalled, "My father was a little apprehensive about me going. . . . I or my parents could have declined the opportunity, but my mother kind of pushed on that I should go, so I went." Even though Alice ultimately indicated that her parents made the decision for her to attend, she also believed that she could decline. Other students, however, accepted the opportunity to attend this new environment. Wilbunette (Southwest) was one of that group. "Well, it was really asked of us to take home a sheet of paper, and this is what was on it. I told my mother first that I wanted to go. She talked with my father, and they both agreed. . . . So we signed up for it, and I got accepted."

Responses of students varied concerning the question of whether any preparation was provided for them to enter the junior high schools. Some explained that teachers, parents, or church institutions talked with them about what was happening and even provided them with the opportunity to make their personal decision pertaining to the selection of a junior high school. In a few instances, however, students indicated that there was no preparation for them at all. Clarence, for example, did not understand how his parents would have been in a position to assist him with this level of preparation. "Wait a minute, wait a minute . . . How can you prepare someone . . . for a condition that you yourself don't know nothing about? How could they?"

Family. The majority of the participants lived within intact family groupings, although some lived within multigenerational settings. Only one participant indicated a parent was divorced. Many of the participants emphasized the fact that their family provided encouragement for them to continue the desegregation process. Pinkie (Pulaski Heights) underscored the sensitivity her parents had about the children's experience. They had "almost daily discussions about what had happened . . . what could we have done." Participants whose parents actively engaged them in discussions pertaining to desegregation, civil rights, or the movement appeared to have more knowledge about civil rights and more ownership in their role in the desegregation process.

Civil Rights Organizations. Many of the students recalled being a part of various organizations or having meetings with one or more community civil rights members. Several people mentioned the names of Mr. L. C. and Mrs. Daisy Bates of the NAACP, and Mr. Ozell Sutton, a member of the Arkansas Council on Human Relations. Several mentioned Sutton in particular, as they recalled either being involved in meetings or directly involved in civil rights campaigns such as voter registration events (see appendix 5 for an excerpt of an interview with Ozell Sutton).

Wilbunette spoke of the role of at least one community organization. She said, "We had a committee that was formed that dealt with us. . . . There would be meetings and everything like that about conduct and what to do if something happened to you."

Ultimately, the Arkansas Council on Human Relations, along with the 1964 Civil Rights Act, facilitated the entry of African American students into the Little Rock public schools at a faster rate than was originally planned by the school board. Mr. Sutton and the council members sent a letter to the school board on August 29, 1963, where they confronted the board with the fact that "integration was an unfinished business" (Minutes, August 29, 1963; November 21, 1963). They confronted them with a powerful statement: "Negro pupils will compose less than three-fourths of one percent of the total enrollment of formerly all White schools when they open for the 1963–64 school year. At the present rate of two percent in nine years, it would take 450 years to completely desegregate our school system. We have yet to get to the business of integration" (Minutes, November 21, 1963, 2, 3).

Quality of Education in Elementary versus Junior High Schools

Two distinct themes appeared when students compared their educational experiences in elementary with that of junior high school. The first concerned the quality of the equipment, textbooks, and materials in the two schools. The second was related to the quality of teaching, which included the level of care, concern, or compassion of the teachers.

Inequality. Themes of inequality surfaced when students talked about segregation, unequal education, and other types of discrimination. Although the students frequently identified the various types of inequality they experienced in their larger environments (e.g., living in segregated areas of town, being treated as second-class citizens, or having to travel through racist neighborhoods to purchase goods and services), several described examples of inequality within the schools they attended. Multiple students described the sad state of their textbooks or the lack thereof, or the poor quality of the materials available to them as students within their elementary schools. They recognized the fact that textbooks assigned to African American students were sent to their schools only after they were used by European-American students. Clarence actually provided the author with his textbook cards to prove that point. "We didn't ever get any new books . . . Some of them would be old. Some of them would be ratty. And then they . . . were in, like, so-so condition." The actual textbook assignment cards this participant saved verified his statements. Books were assigned to him indicating they were in, "poor," "fair," or "good" condition. Although the majority of the assignment cards for the books indicated that the condition of the books was "poor," only one of the cards described a textbook he received was "new." This fact was repeatedly stated by the students as being one of the reasons they or their parents wanted them to attend a majority-White school. Concerning the materials in the junior high school, Alice reported, "But the science labs and the books and things I'm sure were a lot better."

Teacher Interactions. Many of the participants fondly recalled their elementary teachers, all of whom were African American. Those teachers were frequently described as caring or loving, interested, and passionate educators who were also disciplinarians. They also were able to distinguish differences between the student/teacher relationships or expectations that seemed to be missing for some of them in the junior high schools. Several students also indicated that the expectations for success and the quality of caring was, at least for them, missing in the desegregated schools.

Teacher or administrative behaviors can have significantly profound effects on students. Several students talked about the behaviors of teachers at the junior-high level. Some were described as ignoring African American students who were being ridiculed or taunted while in the hallway. Others were described as being "neutral." Interestingly enough, that term had both positive and negative connotations, depending on the perspective of the student. Other junior high educators were described as engaging in openly racist behaviors. For many students, the sheer lack of compassion, care, or concern the teachers or administrators displayed for them was deeply painful. A few students encountered educators who were perceived to be positive and supportive of them.

Teachers or administrators who engaged in ignoring interactions were occasionally described as those who would turn their backs on the behavior, would delay entering a classroom, or would find a way to remain neutral or minimize an adverse situation. Brenda (West Side) recalled situations in which teachers would turn their backs as they saw students crowding around her as they engaged in racists slurs and taunts. While Alvin (West Side) and Kenneth remembered teachers or administrators being conspicuously absent during fights "unless they got too bad," Equilla (East Side) came to realize that her homeroom teacher would frequently find a reason to enter the class "at the last minute," therefore allowing students to engage in negative behavior without having to admit knowledge of it happening.

Other teachers ignored the hands of African American students who wanted to respond to teachers' questions. Surprisingly, this behavior occurred in several of the schools. LaVerne (Forest Heights) recalled raising her hand to answer a question only to eventually realize she would not be called on by the teacher. Similarly, Wilbunette found the same to be the case. Not surprisingly, it tended to shut down the performance and esteem of some of the students. Brenda, who recalled always being "picked last" in gym to play on a team, inadvertently pointed to the failure on the part of the educator to provide a method to select team members without causing some to be ostracized.

Those teachers and administrators who were described in a neutral sense were those who Alfreda (East Side) described in her full interview as not being "outwardly mean. . . . I think some of them, maybe, tried as best as they could . . . to be impartial, and not show their . . . preferences for being in . . . all-White schools." "Tolerated" was the most positive descriptor Glenda (East Side) could use for the way her teachers responded to her. Several students became aware that they weren't "expected to excel." Kathleen shared a similar sentiment. "The teachers were not any different from the students. They were not impolite. . . . the difference in elementary school was that the teachers were . . . interested in all of their students, interested in making sure that we learned the material. . . . I can't say that any teacher that I had in junior high school had any particular interest in whether I learned anything or not." Although the teachers' treatment of these students was not considered openly racist, the effect was powerful and potentially long lasting.

Another group of teachers or administrators engaged in behaviors that were perceived to be racist. Alfreda, for example, described a situation in which all of the Caucasian students were in a home economics class learning the lesson content of the day, while the African American students were assigned the task of cooking cakes for the holiday. Joyce (West Side) and Clarence recalled the distinct pronunciations teachers and others used for the term "Negro." Clarence described a situation in which the English teacher never pronounced the word "Negro" properly. Instead, she—among other teachers—would pronounce the word as either "Nigra" or "Nig-ger-o." In gym classes, African American children were not allowed to touch or dance with others. They frequently were made to sit on bleachers to prevent any encounters with the other race. Some teachers actually graded the papers incorrectly and were quite irritated when confronted. Some students such as Shirley (East Side) and Equilla were threatened with punishment or were ridiculed when they were ill. Shirley refused to ignore the behavior of a teacher who singled out the African American students and watched them specifically to make sure they were not cheating on tests.

Teachers who were seen from a more favorable vantage point tended to be few in number. Nevertheless, they seemed to stand out in the life of the students who encountered them. This group of teachers who engaged in positive interactions appeared to take an interest in, demonstrate compassion or kindness toward, protect—or at least intervene—"when it got to a certain point," encourage, or otherwise affirm the students. Alvin and Joyce recalled several teachers who Joyce said were "as nice as they could be" when they displayed acts of kindness. One act occurred on her very first day of school, when she was terrified to enter the classroom. The homeroom teacher, who later taught her several years of Latin, gently let her know it was "time to come in"—into her homeroom on the first day of school. Alvin described several of his teachers as being supportive. Equilla, who described her teachers as "really good," also used the term "impartial," but viewed that behavior in a positive light. Equilla recalled being affirmed by the teacher when she was asked to serve as a greeter in her home economics class because her use of etiquette was so much better than that of others. Clarence recalled the amount of time a math teacher invested in him to help him understand various concepts.

Support within the Academic Environment. Participants directly or indirectly provided recommendations to school staff and others outside of the direct role of teaching students. Wilbunette described the impact the janitors had on her life as they invited Henry (Southwest) and Wilbunette to eat in their janitorial area. Those persons even took the time to purchase the food for them in order to allow them to avoid being harassed. Kenneth added, "if a student has one adult that cares about them inside that system, the likelihood of their academic success increases exponentially. It can be the custodian . . . the bus driver . . .

one of the food service workers. . . . That student knows that somebody cares."

Interestingly, both Henry and Wilbunette exemplified the effect of the internal academic support team on their academic success. They were both students attending Southwest Junior High in their seventh grade year. Henry, who believed he had that support, completed his junior high career at Southwest, while Wilbunette did not. Henry perceived his principal to be very positive. The principal made himself available to Henry and checked with him on a regular basis to find out how things were going, offering support to him if needed. This same principal was described by Wilbunette as being terrifying and intimidating. He asked her why she was even attending the school and told her she needed to go to the African American junior high school, which she did in her eighth grade year. Henry's belief that he knew someone in a position of power, namely the principal, at the school cared about him and his success contrasted just as strongly with Wilbunette's perception that this very same person did not.

The Influence of Attending a Predominantly White Junior High School on the Students' Adult Lives

There was a somewhat startling mixture of responses from the participants related to this question. The majority of the participants indicated that this experience helped them to achieve professionally in a majority race society. Of the seventeen participants who completed predominately White junior high and high schools, all have achieved some level of professional success. Two judges, an organizational psychologist, three business owners/entrepreneurs, a college professor, several mid- to upper-level management persons, and a health professional are counted among this group. Comments from the participants regarding the influence of desegregation on their personal lives included descriptions of the experience being very helpful, preparing them to live and work in a majority-White society even when they were still working in areas where few or no other African Americans were working. Others, such as Kenneth, believed that the experience allowed them to excel academically. Joyce and Shirley also believed that the experience allowed them to dispel myths about Caucasians, and facilitated their understanding that "people are just people," according to Joyce, or that they are "no better than me, and I am no better than them," according to Shirley.

Some participants, such as Kenneth, also saw themselves as being breakers of racial barriers for other persons, particularly when they did not see very many African Americans in their professional environments. "I . . . started [to] kind of push that issue a little bit more. . . . 'Why don't you have an African American woman, or a male, or a Latino or something?' . . . I would be able to ask those questions." Like Kenneth, Joyce also took on the role of breaking barriers and remaining actively involved in desegregating other systems:

"If you struggle to desegregate things . . . school . . . organizations . . . and businesses, and you don't follow through, then what have you done? You've broken a veil, but you haven't taken part in participating and making sure that things are inclusive and things can improve and things can get better."

A significant number of students believed the experienced caused a delay for them, particularly from a psychosocial perspective. Glenda, for instance, believed that the experience "stunted" her social development "on an interpersonal level, not having had dealings with a lot of African American males in junior high and high school." At least six other participants voiced similar beliefs about the costs of desegregation on their psychosocial development (never having married, being alone or an introvert, needing space, feeling different from others, etc.).

Early on, Wilbunette identified her involvement in desegregation as a potentially negative outcome on her social development and explained that this was one of the reasons she transferred to the African American junior high school. She later married and had children. She cited this as her idea of success.

At least five students opted to attend a historically Black college or university (HBCU) to regain what they believed they lost in terms of building an African American identity. Myrna (East Side) cited negative costs involved in her junior high experience as her motivation for attending HBCU. "I didn't get to do anything. We didn't integrate socially at Central. If I didn't earn it I didn't get it. . . . It was still very, very Caucasian." Even when the African American high school student population was larger in number than in the junior high schools, some continued to experience a sense of isolation and separation from their peers who attended the African American school.

Trauma. Although some participants such as Alvin, Equilla, LaVerne, and Myrna introduced the subject of trauma into the conversation about the influence of desegregation on their lives, it was clear that others described the effects of such an experience in their lives in similar ways. Myrna explained, "A lot of people have it [a rude awakening] when they go through traumatic experiences. . . . It's almost like when you've hit something like this and a lot of information is thrust at your brain at one time." Words or phrases such as "untold effects," "painful," "damages you," and simply "trauma" described the effect of racism on these participants. Alvin identified both positive and negative aspects of this experience, and described this long-term outcome of being a childhood victim of trauma: "You have to process all that trauma that you endured, and that's a whole field of weeds all by itself."

Several participants mentioned the traumatic effect the experience of being ignored or isolated had on their lives. For some, the effects continued to linger into adulthood. The report of trauma was the same for these students, whether they entered junior high as the only African American or as a part of a larger group. These students were frequently the only African American students in individual classrooms.

What was most startling is that even when the students appeared to have extremely difficult experiences during the desegregation process, a few were able to find positive ways in which it influenced their adult lives. Pinkie, for instance, experienced so much hostility that she would not take her "real self" into Pulaski Heights; however, she realized that as an adult, she could use those challenging experiences to help her deal with career-oriented difficulties. "But the reason why I could do that was because of my experience as a child, and all of that that was still with me in the back of my mind. I did not want it to drive me into any counterproductive walk in life."

CHAPTER 9

Recommendations

For Future Generations

This final chapter provides recommendations primarily to parents and family members from the perspective of these participants. These suggestions will also be applicable, however, to educators, churches, and members of the community. The participants have traveled down a long road and now want to improve that journey for future students who may encounter similar opportunities for rejection, isolation, and discrimination. To prevent confusion, this chapter will refer to the students who desegregated the junior high schools and were interviewed as "participants," as opposed to current or future students.

For Parents

The participants were asked to provide recommendations for parents who contemplated placing their minority children into a majority setting. The settings could be based on a number of levels other than race or ethnicity, although race was not excluded. They offered the following suggestions: (1) build secure relationships, (2) assess the child's level of self-esteem, (3) fully prepare the child for the change, and, finally, (4) ground the child in faith.

Build Secure Relationships. Participants believed it would be important for parents to maintain secure and loving relationships with their children prior to sending them to any minority environment. The process of building secure relationships with children includes consistently and actively communicating with the child, listening to what the child is saying, observing what the child is doing, and being thoroughly involved in the child's life. This allows the child to know on a consistent basis that the parent is truly interested. Other recommendations included having family meetings or conversations or informal times to talk with children. Participants emphasized that trust in the parents was built and maintained through this consistent relationship-building activity. "Parents, create that environment of safety, security, communication . . . with your child. Bond with them, because the world is really waiting to bond. The world's got plenty of time to mislead your child."

Assess the Child's Level of Self-Esteem. The child must have achieved a high level of self-confidence, which included self-esteem and positive sense of identity. This theme was verbalized in multiple ways through such words as "confident," "capable," and "self-esteem." The sentiment expressed was that children need to feel confident about themselves as individuals and to believe that, as one student frequently voiced, "You can do this." In other words, children must believe they are capable of accomplishing the tasks at hand, whether it is in an academic environment, sports arena, or any other setting.

From a developmental standpoint, children who are entering the seventh grade may not have established their own identity—a sense of who they are or what they believe in as an individual. They should, however, have successfully met previous developmental milestones from a psychosocial standpoint so that they will be ready to master the previously daunting question of "Who am I?" Children who struggle with the desire to be accepted to the extent that they may either engage in dangerous or risky behaviors or may withdraw from the group because of the fear of being rejected may find navigating a minority situation intimidating. "My advice would be to . . . make sure that child knows that he or she should not be defined by anybody else. He or she should not let somebody else tell them what they can or cannot do and what they are worthy or not worthy of doing."

Participants wanted to emphasize to the parents that they needed to assist the children in completing these tasks. "Build that child up within, where they have the stability to know that they can achieve." "You'd have to love them and make them feel good about themselves and build them up to where they feel like they can do anything." Otherwise, "If you don't have a self-confident child, don't send them there, because children can be a little cruel." "Make sure before that child leaves them that the child is rooted and grounded in themselves and they know who they are."

Fully Prepare the Child for the Change. Preparation was the main word offered by this group. The participants stated emphatically that the child must be included in the decision-making process. It is essential that the parents actively prepare the child for the move to a minority situation. "They have to prepare the child for whatever. . . . Don't send them blind into a situation. . . . Send the child into that situation having a lot of self-confidence and knowing that there are going to be people there who do not want them there."

Children need to understand what they might face. They need to know it ahead of time in order to prepare for how to deal with this experience. "Sit down and be frank with the child. You know you don't have to frighten them, but tell them the truth, and tell them . . . what to expect. . . . If you don't know what to expect, do some fact finding." One participant strongly encouraged the parents to explore the environment and to evaluate the amount of support their child might have available to them.

They also emphasized the fact that once the move has occurred, the work is not over. The words "supportive" and "support" were mentioned on several occasions. The recommendation was for parents to be the consistent and loving part of the children's support system. Support was described in various ways. "Give them love, faith, and hope, because you can accomplish a great deal when you shoot for the stars and you land on the moon." "Don't send your children to school; take them to school." Participants said children may not be able to verbalize what they need to say, so parents must make themselves available to listen. "They may or may not want to talk about it. It may just be too painful. . . . Be nice to them. . . . But . . . just being kind and being loving goes a long way."

For parents who believe their children are ready to move forward, the recommendation was "try to encourage them to move forward where you're there to try to help them through the knocks and the bumps and the bruises. You can encourage, pick them up, and keep them moving forward." On the other hand, a word of caution was offered to parents who were entertaining this decision: "I would recommend to the parents that they think long and hard about that . . . and consider whether . . . they have provided that child with the proper care, confidence, consideration that they need to have in order to help that child be prepared to be okay wherever they are." The unspoken statement includes the suggestion of reconsidering the potential placement if parents don't have the time on a consistent basis to be supportive of their children in this environment or don't believe the child has the necessary confidence to be able to manage a minority setting alone. This may be a painful realization for a parent to face. On the other hand, the child might otherwise experience emotional damage if he or she is placed there without these preparation factors.

Ground the Child in Faith. This advice should come as no surprise to the reader, as participants mentioned it earlier as one of their primary sources of strength. Their recommendations, therefore, complemented what they said regarding how they successfully completed their desegregation experience. The following words or phrases were frequently voiced by the participants: "Pray. Always, always pray . . . having a firm spiritual foundation"; "emotional and spiritual support"; "strong faith network and a strong ability to plug into God because" they've "got to have an anchor;" and "that's really the foundation they need to be able to draw upon at any time." The emphasis for many participants was the need for parents to provide a strong spiritual foundation for their children, although some recommended that the parents and children attend a physical church. "[Attend] a scripture-based, faith-filled church. . . . It's got to be a scripture-based, faith-filled and grace appreciating church so that the children grow up knowing God is a God of relationship."

For Educators, Community Members, and Others

There is a loud message that lies within the pages of this book for educators, community members, and other professionals who are truly interested in contributing to the success of a child. The description of those teachers and staff who demonstrated positive behaviors included those who were patient with the students, asked about their progress in school, expected them to achieve or excel in school, and even advocated for them at times. The latter was demonstrated in the previously mentioned situation with the janitors at Southwest Junior High School.

While it is not surprising that students need a nurturing and stimulating environment to succeed in school, what was surprising was the fact that students recognized when they were not being challenged and when they were not expected to do well. This serves as a reminder that students need to be challenged and expected to do well. Many students want to do well. It is important to keep in mind that many, if not all, of these students completed various tests in order to qualify to be selected to attend these schools. Many reported they were performing well academically in their classes while they attended elementary school. Although some indicated that they were challenged to perform well academically, others did not believe this was the case because the junior high school teachers' expectations of them were low.

On the other hand, those students who struggled in various areas may not have received sufficient support to effectively master the learning content. While Clarence was a positive example of what happens when teachers make themselves available to assist the students, Wilbunette was not. Her teacher indicated that she would fail her even if she was successful in completing the classwork. Given the fact that she had difficulty understanding the content, this rendered Wilbunette powerless to complete her assignments.

Neighbors and other community people could serve as wonderful sources of support by becoming actively involved in the life of a child. Such activities might include volunteering in the schools, asking the child about their regular activities, and otherwise serving as the child's cheerleader, mentor, or coach. The church community could serve in a similar fashion. Indeed, the church community and civil rights organizations as a whole were reported to be actively involved in the lives of several of the children. Some held regular meetings to discuss the process of desegregation, to listen to and make plans for addressing any potential problems the students were facing, and even to advocate on behalf of some of the students.

Church and community organizations are still needed in the twenty-first century. Students need a great deal of support (e.g., tutoring classes, youth groups, prevention and intervention classes that focus on a variety of subjects, among others). The participants believed church and family provided them with a strong foundation of values.

You have read the stories of eighteen courageous students who entered five primarily White junior high schools in 1961 and 1962. (Please refer to appendix four for demographics details of all of the students.) Sixteen of the eighteen students were selected from a group of eighty-four by the Little Rock School Board to attend four junior high schools during 1961. In 1962, the final two students were placed into Pulaski Heights. A secondary selection process occurred in some of the schools when teachers or community civil rights leaders approached special students with the request to enter a majority-White junior high school.

You learned that not every student was involved in the decision-making process to attend these schools. In spite of the varying manners in which that assignment was made, 100 percent of the participants strongly recommended that parents thoroughly prepare their children for entering a minority environment. Even though these participants explained that their parents discussed the situation with them and included them in making that decision, many were among those also said they needed more preparation.

You discovered that seventeen of the eighteen completed their entire three-year stay and went on to attend predominantly White high schools. Although one of the seventeen students moved to Detroit prior to her senior year at Central High School, she completed her senior year in a desegregated school.

Families, civil rights organizations, and some communities and church communities were all found to be strong sources of support for the majority of this group of students. Teachers, administrators, and other school staff were measured, and many were found wanting, to take a page from Scripture. Many of the students recalled the level of caring and compassion, along with the high standards of expectation to succeed, that they received from their African American elementary teachers, as contrasted negatively with many of their junior high teachers. Although a few encountered people who seemed to care about them and encourage them to do well, the majority believed the teachers were neutral at best and openly racist at their worst. The fact that students were in school for the majority of their weekdays for three years and faced this type of reception from teachers as well as students yet still succeeded in their adult lives is a tribute to those influences that protected them from being crushed.

As I draw to a close on the final chapter, I find it necessary to make a personal comment on the thoughts and emotions I've experienced during this process of interviewing the majority of the participants and analyzing their rich material. I've found it helpful to dialogue with my contributors in order to process my emotions and thoughts. As one of the twenty-five, I've frequently heard perceptions of experiences that were totally opposite mine. On occasion, however, others seemed to have beliefs and opinions that definitely resonated with me. As a result, these fellow cohorts have helped me grow emotionally through the sharing of their perceptions of the events. Listening to the stories of others helped to confirm for me that while this was a significant part of my life, it was not the whole story. As Joyce so aptly stated, what really matters is how we contributed to the lives of others. Fitting words of encouragement and challenge are offered by Clarence: "If you make a . . . path, the longer you walk on the path, it gets smoother."

I offer one final note: when I was interviewed, I indicated that I did not see myself as being resilient. As a result of hearing the interviews and after talking with my niece Khiela, who is a clinical psychologist, I've come to the conclusion that "resilience" is actually a continuum. I now realize that, as a result of having an incredible support team consisting of family and my faith community, I was able to survive the experience to the point that I am now able to thrive in many aspects of my life as an adult. For that, I am truly thankful.

Study Method

A phenomenological research approach was used to ask general guiding questions of the students about their perspectives of their desegregation experience. Software known as Ethnograph 6.0 (http://www.qualisresearch.com) was helpful in confirming major themes that were frequently repeated by the students. This approach provided an understanding of these events the students shared during their interviews (Miles and Huberman 1994).

Ecological theory and the resilience, family stress, and coping framework were the two major frameworks utilized for understanding what was happening to the students as they desegregated the schools and continued throughout their adult lives (Bell-Tolliver, Burgess, and Brock 2009; Bronfenbrenner 1986). Ecological theory offers a look at the factors that influence the child within various levels or subsystems of the child's life (McCabe, Clark, and Barnett 1999). The child is considered the microsystem within the context of the family. While much of the child's human development occurs within the context of the family, Bronfenbrenner (1986) argues that systems external to the family are also of potential signifcance to the growth and development of the child.

The mesosystem consists of those layers of the environment with which the child came into direct contact (Bronfenbrenner 1986). For the purpose of this study, that would include school, transportation, church, neighborhood, community civil rights organizations, and so forth. The exosystem consists of the entities that directly influenced the parents but that indirectly influenced the children of the parents. Examples consist of the parents' sources of employment and any other organizations in which the parent was directly involved.

A final subsystem that has bearing on this current subject is the chronosystem. This subsystem allows us to view a historical event that occurred at some point in time and influenced the students. In this case, the incident of interest is that of junior high desegregation. Spencer and colleagues revised the ecological framework a bit and identified their model as the "phenomenological variant of ecological systems theory (PVEST)," (Spencer et al. 2001, 24). This approach allows observation of such variables as culture, context, and other psychological considerations, along with those subsystem levels as previously identified by Bronfenbrenner (Spencer et al. 2001). This method proved to be quite useful when studying the desegregation of African Americans in majority Caucasian junior high schools.

The framework of resilience, family stress, and coping has been a particularly suitable way of considering how such an event as desegregation affected this unique group of students. The concept of resilience suggests that while a major event may happen to a group of people, some may rebound without experiencing significant adverse outcomes. Strengths or protective factors such as confidence, a cohesive and supportive family, the perceptions of a supportive community, a strong religious orientation, and supportive church community were found to deter or negate some of the potential negative outcomes of adversities facing children and youth (Bell-Tolliver, Burgess, and Brock 2009; Li, Nussbaum, and Richards 2007; Skowron 2005).

Arkansas's Constitutional Challenge to Block Desegregation

What became known as Amendment 44 was filed with the Arkansas Secretary of State on July 3, 1956, and became an official amendment to the Arkansas Constitution on November 6, 1956. Amendment 44 stated:

> From and after the Adoption of this Amendment, the General Assembly of the State of Arkansas shall take appropriate action and pass laws opposing in every Constitutional manner the Un-constitutional Desegregation decisions of May 17, 1954, and May 31, 1955, of the United States Supreme Court, including interposing the sovereignty of the state of Arkansas to the end of nullification of these and all deliberate, palpable and dangerous invasions of or encroachments upon rights and powers not delegated to the United States nor prohibited to the States by the Constitution of the United States and Amendments thereto, and those rights and powers reserved to the States and the People thereof by any department, commission, officer, or employee of such department or commission of the Government of the United States . . . Said opposition shall continue steadfast until such time as Un-Constitutional invasions or encroachments shall have abated or shall have been rectified. (*Dietz v. Arkansas* 1989)

Amendment 44, therefore, opposed the ruling of the United States Supreme Court by attempting to strengthen the states' rights and legalize the spirit of Jim Crow laws. It also authorized the forfeiture of office or position of anyone who attempted to violate the amendment (Goss 2011).

Until this amendment was repealed in 1989 (*Dietz v. Arkansas*) it was clear that the governor and the state of Arkansas believed they could operate under their own rule and authority. This amendment supported decisions made by Govenor Faubus both for bringing in the National Guard to preserve the peace of what he understood to be the citizens of the state of Arkansas against the students attempting to desegregate the schools and for closing the high schools in 1958–1959.

Other examples of such segregation acts included:

- Act 4 of Extraordinary Session of 1958: Empowered the governor to close the public schools (Sarah Alderman Murphy Papers 1951–1994, 1, 2, 3). This act was in direct defiance of the ruling of the United States Supreme Court. The governor closed the four high schools located in Little Rock for the 1958–1959 school year: Central, Horace Mann, Vocational Technical, and the new high school, later named Hall, that was to open in the fall of 1958. Ultimately, the three-panel board of the federal district court ruled that the closing was found to be illegal (*Aaron v. McKinley* 1959). Act 5 and Act 151 of 1959 were ruled unconstitutional by the US district courts. These acts would have permitted the transfer of funds from one school disctrict to another when students requesting to attend a different school did so if their school was closed. (Sarah Alderman Murphy Papers 1951–1994, 1).

- Acts 84 of 1955 and 236 of 1959 stated that children would not be required to attend public schools against their will if both African American and Caucasian children attended that particular school (Sarah Alderman Murphy Papers 1951–1994, 1).

- Act 461 of 1959 established what was later identified as the Arkansas Pupil Assignment Act, a most significant piece of desegregation legislation. Criteria for admission included:

  available space and teaching capacity in the schools . . . transportation . . . the effect of the admission of new pupils upon established or proposed academic programs; the suitability of established curricular for particular pupils . . . the adequacy of the pupil's academic preparation for admission . . . *the scholastic aptitude and relative intelligence or mental energy or abiliy of the pupil*; the psychological qualification of the pupil for the type of teaching and associations involved; the affect of admission upon prevailing academic standards at a particular school; the psychological affect upon the pupil of attendance . . . the possibility of breaches of the peace or ill will or economic retaliation within the community . . . the morals, conduct, health and personal standards of the pupil; the request or consent of parents or guardians and the reasons assigned therefore. (Sarah Alderman Murphy Papers, 1951–1994, 1, 2; emphasis added)

Arkansas Pupil Assignment Law

The following is an excerpt of the Pupil Assignment Law, as found in *Aaron v. Tucker* (1960).

The following procedure shall be applicable for each school year after the 1959–1960 school year:

During the month of May of each year, the Superintendent of Schools shall submit to the Board his recommendations as to the assignments for the next school year of each child enrolled in the schools of the District. Thereafter, but prior to the close of the school year then in progress, the Board shall assign each child in the schools of the District to a school for the next school year. Notice of the assignment shall be given by noting of the same on each child's Progress Report Card which is delivered to the child at the close of the school year then in progress. If, for any reason, a child does not receive a Progress Report Card, written notice of the assignment shall be mailed to the parents of such child at the address reflected by the official records of the District.

APPENDIX 4

Demographic Information

Eighteen of a potential twenty-five students were interviewed for this book. As with any study, participation was voluntary. Although an additional person was located, the individual chose not to follow up for the purpose of being interviewed. Various efforts were made to locate all of the former students. Recruitment examples included such activities as word of mouth/snowball sampling, flyers, radio interviews, a community program, local phone directories, and people locater services on the Internet.

Of the eighteen participants, four were male. In essence, five of the male students who were identified as being selected by the school district to desegregate the schools were not included in the interview process. Several of the female East Side students reported that the two males, Larry Davis and Jessie Walker, who began the first school year with them left before that first year ended.

Three male students, aside from those who participated in the interviews, were assigned to attend West Side. As mentioned earlier, one student, Felton Walker, reported that he never had the opportunity to attend, as his parents changed their minds when their house was "rocked" several times during the summer prior to enrolling in the school (personal communication, 2014). As a result of this low number of African American males who completed the desegregation process, the number of African American females to complete was significantly disproportionate to that of the males.

One factor to consider that led to the loss of these male students may be the matter several students addressed concerning the unfair nature of punishment. They explained that African American students were not believed and were punished more harshly for a similar infraction committed by Caucasian students.

One of the fourteen female participants interviewed, Wilbunette Walls, did not complete her assigned junior high school. She requested to be reassigned to Dunbar at the conclusion of her seventh grade year for two reasons: health and because of the treatment she received at Southwest. Thirteen female students and four males completed a predominantly White or Caucasian high school. Of those remaining students, seventeen attended and completed Central High School. Only LaVerne Bell attended and completed Hall High School.

Although the eighteen participants were not specifically asked a question concerning their highest levels of education, thirteen of the eighteen reported attending college. One-third, or six of those, attained at least a masters degree. Again, although the participants were not specifically asked about marital status, several made reference to it. At least six participants were separated or divorced, five were never married, and three were remarried. Four participants were married to their first spouses; one of the four was widowed.

APPENDIX 5

Excerpt of Interview with Mr. Ozell Sutton

School desegregation in Little Rock did not occur in isolation from desegregation of other areas. A December 5, 2014, interview with Mr. Ozell Sutton (December 1925–December 2015) revealed that he and/or members of the Arkansas Council on Human Relations, along with students of at least one college—Philander Smith—actively participated in the 1960–1962 sit-ins of such department store restaurants as Woolworth's, Gus Blass, and McClellan (Kirk 2013).

> At Woolworth I remember we marched in with the kids from . . . Philander Smith College. Every day at noon we'd march downtown. . . . I remember the first time this old White guy put some ice on my back. I was sitting at the counter; I got up and pulled my shirttail out, let it fall off, then sat back down. The second day, he—this is terrible. He spat in my face. And he chewed tobacco. And he hit me right up here with a big thing of tobacco. And it ran all down in my eyes. The kids had to take ten minutes before I could see again. . . . Then the third day, he . . . walked over where I was. And I said, "Mister, let me make one thing clear." He said, "What's that?" I said, "I am not a nonviolent soldier." He said, "I know. I don't get you mixed up with Martin Luther King." I said, "Well please don't, because I'm not nonviolent . . . I was in the Marines, during World War II, and you are looking at a Marine Raider. And sir, I could whip you before you could turn around, and I will, if you bother me this day. . . ." He didn't bother me anymore.

BIBLIOGRAPHY

Aaron v. Cooper, 143 F. Supp. 855, 1956 U.S. Dist. Lexis 3048 (E.D. Ark. 1956).

Aaron v. Cooper, 261 F.2d 97 United States Court of Appeals (8th Cir. 1958). http://law.justia.com/cases/federal/district-courts/FSupp/143/855/1417618/.

Aaron v. McKinley, 173 F. Supp. 944, 1959 U.S. Dist. Lexis 3173 (E.D. Ark. 1959).

Aaron v. Tucker, 186 F. Supp. 913 (E.D. Ark. 1960). http://law.justia.com/cases/federal/district-courts/FSupp/186/913/2374035/.

Arkansas Democrat. 1961. "Jr High Mixing Pushed." May 16.

Arkansas Democrat. 1954a. "Cherry Says Arkansas to Meet Requirements." May 18. Butler Center for Arkansas Studies, Little Rock, AR.

Arkansas Democrat. 1954b. "South, Border States Face Vast Problems after Court Voids School Segregation." May 18.

Arkansas Democrat. 1955. "Protest Segregationist Bill." February 23. Butler Center for Arkansas Studies, Little Rock, AR.

Arkansas Democrat. 1961. "Capacity Enrollment Expected in Schools." September 4. Butler Center for Arkansas Studies, Little Rock, AR.

Arkansas Democrat. 1961. "Schools All Quiet as Classes Resume." September 5. UALR Ottenheimer Library.

Arkansas Democrat. 1961. "Everything Normal as Schools Convene: Integration Extended." September 6. UALR Ottenheimer Library

Arkansas Democrat. 1961. "Court Approves L.R. Integration; Board Gratified." September 10. Butler Center for Arkansas Studies, Little Rock, AR.

Arkansas Gazette. 1956. "Here Is the Text of Judge Miller's Opinion in the Little Rock Integration Case." August 29. Butler Center for Arkansas Studies, Little Rock, AR.

Arkansas Gazette. 1957. "Bills on Segregation Defended as Legal, Deplored as Unjust: Crowds Public Session." February 19. Butler Center for Arkansas Studies, Little Rock, AR.

Arkansas Gazette. 1960. "Fall Integration May Be Limited to 12 Negroes: School Board Bases New Assignments on Preference, Test." May 21. Butler Center for Arkansas Studies, Little Rock, AR.

Arkansas Gazette. 1960. "39 Negroes Seek Integration in Fall at Jr. High Level." June 14. Butler Center for Arkansas Studies, Little Rock, AR.

Arkansas Gazette. 1961. "Quiet Opening Expected Today for Schools." September 5. UALR Ottenheimer Library.

Arkansas Gazette. 1961. "All Quiet as Integration Expanded at Little Rock; 46 Negroes in 8 Schools." September 6. Arkansas History Commission.

Arkansas Gazette. 1960. "With Values Resurgent the South Rises Again." September 10. Ottenheimer Library.

Arkansas Gazette. 1962. "249 Negroes in integrated state schools." September 30. Butler Center for Arkansas Studies, Little Rock, AR.

Bell-Tolliver, Laverne, Ruby Burgess, and Linda Brock. 2009. "African American Therapists Working with African American Families: An Exploration of the Strengths Perspective in Treatment." *Journal of Marital and Family Therapy* 35 (3): 293–307.

Bronfenbrenner, Urie. 1986. "Ecology of the Family as a Context for Human Development." *Developmental Psychology* 22 (6): 723–42.

Brown v. Board of Education, 347 U.S. 483 (1954). http://caselaw.lp.findlaw.com/scripts/getcase.pl?court=US&vol=347&invol=483.

Brown v. Board of Education, 349 U.S. 294 (1955). https://www.courtlistener.com/opinion/105312/brown-v-board-of-education/.

Cooper v. Aaron, 78 S. Ct. 1401, 358 U.S. 1 (1958). http://www.princeton.edu/~ereading/cooperaaron.pdf.

Daily News. 1957. "Take the FBI Out, Faubus Warns Ike: Won't Be Responsible, Ark. Governor Says." September 5. Butler Center for Arkansas Studies, Little Rock, AR.

Davis, T. 1955. "Growth of Negro Area Strains Social and Economic Customs." *Arkansas Gazette*. September 25. Butler Center for Arkansas Studies, Little Rock, AR.

Dietz v. Arkansas, 709 F. Supp. 902, 1989 U.S. Dist. LEXIS 3290 (E.D. Ark. 1989). http://law.justia.com/cases/federal/district-courts/FSupp/709/902/1586817/

Dove v. Parham, 196 F. Supp. 944, 1961 U.S. Dist. LEXIS 2776 (E.D. Ark. 1961). http://law.justia.com/cases/federal/district-courts/FSupp/196/944/1690651/

Faubus, Orval. 1957. Personal Communication to Mr. Winthrop Rockefeller, 426 Union National Bank Building, Little Rock, Arkansas. April 16. WR: 1957–1959 Little Rock School Situation, Butler Center for Arkansas Studies, Little Rock, AR.

FBI: Little Rock Crisis Reports: UALR 0044, Box 1, File 10, Director's Brief 2673, Volume II, Exhibit 3: Little Rock School Board plan of gradual integration. UALR Center for Arkansas History and Culture.

FBI: Little Rock School Crisis, UALR.MS.0044, Director's Brief 2673, Volume 1, Box 1, File 2. UALR Center for Arkansas History and Culture.

FBI: Little Rock School Crisis, UALR.MS.0044, Director's Brief 2673, Volume 1, Box 1, File 4, pages 1–40 of 217. UALR Center for Arkansas History and Culture.

FBI: Little Rock Crisis Reports. November 25, 1957. UALR.MS.2673, Director's Brief, Volume I, Integration in Public Schools Little Rock, Arkansas Civil Rights Contempt of Court, Volume I, Summary A1, Box 1, File 2.

Fine, Benjamin. 1957a. "Little Rock Sets Integration Date." *New York Times*. September 1. Butler Center for Arkansas Studies, Little Rock, AR.

Fine, Benjamin. 1957b. "Little Rock Board Seeks Stay in School Integration." *New York Times*. September 6. Butler Center for Arkansas Studies, Little Rock, AR.

Foreman, G. 1956. "Faubus: It's Different This Time." *Arkansas Gazette*, 12 A. July 29. Butler Center for Arkansas Studies, Little Rock, AR.

Forster, Bobbie. 1960. "3 Judges Played Major Roles in LR School Case." *Arkansas Democrat*. September 5.

Forster, Bobbie. 1961. "Negroes Placed in White Jr. Highs." *Arkansas Democrat*. May 25. Butler Center for Arkansas Studies, Little Rock, AR.

Fort Worth Herald Tribune. 1957. "Little Rock Integration Bar Lifted." September 1. Butler Center for Arkansas Studies, Little Rock, AR.

Frick, Margaret. 1956. "Little Rock's 'Gradual' Integration Approved." *Arkansas Democrat*. August 28. Butler Center for Arkansas Studies, Little Rock, AR.

Garrison, Jerol. 1962. "11 School districts to be integrated; 225 Negroes in All." *Arkansas Gazette*. August 30. Butler Center for Arkansas Studies, Little Rock, AR.

Goss, Kay C. 2011. "Amendments to the Constitution of 1874." In *The Arkansas State Constitution*. The Oxford Commentaries on the State Constitutions of the United States, ed. G. Alan Tarr. Oxford: Oxford University Press.

Jacoway, Elizabeth. 1976. Interview with Vivion Lenon Brewer. October 15. MC 1481. Elizabeth Jacoway Oral History Transcripts, folder 2, 4007: G-12. Special Collections, University of Arkansas Libraries, Fayetteville, AR.

Kirk, John. 2011. "Not Quite Black and White: School Desegregation in Arkansas, 1954–1966." *Arkansas Historical Quarterly* 50 (3): 225–57.

Lawrence, W. H. 1957. "President Warns Governor Faubus He'll Uphold Law." *New York Times*. September 6.

Li, Susan Tinsley, Karin M. Nussbaum, and Maryse H. Richards. 2007. "Risks and Protective Factors for Urban Youth." *Journal of Urban and Community Psychology* 39:21–35. doi:10.1007/s10464-007-9088-1.

Little Rock Board of Education's Plan of School Integration Approved by U.S. District Court, Little Rock, Arkansas. August 8, 1956. Little Rock School District Records MSS.13.75 100. Butler Center for Arkansas Studies, Little Rock, AR.

McCabe, K.M., R. Clark, and D. Barnett. 1999. "Family Protective Factors among Urban African American Youth." *Journal of Clinical Child Psychology* 28 (2):137–50.

Miles, Matthew B., and A. Michael Huberman. 1994. *Qualitative Data Analysis*. Thousand Oaks, CA: Sage.

Miller, B. 1957. "Arkansas Uses Troops to Bar Negro pupils: Governor Acts Despite U.S. Court Order." *World Telegram & Sun*. September 3.

Minutes of the Little Rock Board of Education Special Meeting (March 21, 1960). *Resolution of Board of Directors, Little Rock School District*. Little Rock School

District Records MSS.13.75 100. Butler Center for Arkansas Studies, Little Rock, AR.

Minutes of the Little Rock Board of Education, Executive Session (May 23, 1961). Little Rock School District Records MSS.13.75 100. Butler Center for Arkansas Studies, Little Rock, AR.

Minutes of the Little Rock Board of Education, Special Meeting (July 12, 1960). Little Rock School District Records MSS.13.75 100. Butler Center for Arkansas Studies, Little Rock, AR.

Minutes of the Little Rock Board of Education (June 28, 1961). *Hearings on Reassignment Requests*. Little Rock School District Records MSS.13.75 100. Butler Center for Arkansas Studies, Little Rock, AR.

Minutes of the Little Rock School District Board of Directors Executive Meeting (November 21, 1963). Little Rock School District Records MSS.13.75 100. Butler Center for Arkansas Studies, Little Rock, AR.

Norwood v. Tucker, 287 F.2d 798, 1961 U.S. App. Lexis 5170 (8th Cir. 1961). http://0-www.lexisnexis.com.iii-server.ualr.edu/hottopics/lnacademic/.

Sarah Alderman Murphy Papers, 1951–1994. MC 1321, Box 9, File 9. "A Summary of Arkansas Laws Dealing with Integration 5." In *Land of (Unequal) Opportunity: Documenting the Civil Rights Struggle in Arkansas*. University of Arkansas Libraries. http://digitalcollections.uark.edu/cdm/compoundobject/collection/Civilrights/id/594/show/593.

Skowron, Elizabeth. 2005. "Parent Differentiation of Self and Child Competence in Low-Income Urban Families." *Journal of Counseling Psychology* 52 (3): 337–46.

Spencer, Margaret B., Elizabeth Noll, Jill Stoltzfus, and Vinay Harpalani. 2001. "Identity and School Adjustment: Revisiting the 'Acting White' Assumption." *Educational Psychologist* 36 (1): 21–30.

Dougan, Michael B. 2016. "Francis Adams Cherry (1908–1965)." In *The Encyclopedia of Arkansas History and Culture Online*. Central Arkansas Library System, 2006–. Article last updated June 8. http://www.encyclopediaofarkansas.net/encyclopedia/entry-detail.aspx?entryID=91.

Kirk, John A. 2013. "Sit-Ins." In *The Encyclopedia of Arkansas History and Culture Online*. Central Arkansas Library System, 2006–. Article last updated December 20. Accessed March 1, 2017. http://www.encyclopediaofarkansas.net/encyclopedia/entry-detail.aspx?entryID=6921.

Valachovic, Ernest. 1955. "Negroes Take Aim at School Bill." *Arkansas Gazette*. February 23.

US Equal Employment Opportunity Commission. 2015. *Title VII of the Civil Rights Act of 1964*. http://www.eeoc.gov/laws/statutes/titlevii.cfm. Retrieved June 26, 2015.

Walker, Felton. 2014. Personal telephone communication. December 2.

INDEX

Index

Ferguson, Missouri, 70
Fields family, 101, 102
Fisk University, 64
Floyd, Mrs., 112
Forest Heights Junior High, 20, 24, 25, 121–29
Forest Park Elementary School, 20
Forster, Bobbie, 22
Fortieth Street, 154
Fort Roots VA Hospital, 39–40
Fort Smith, 10
Forty-Second Street Grill, 154–55
Fourteenth Street, 132, 175, 205
Fowler, Harry, 236–37
Fulbright, J. William, 160

G

Gem Theater, 132–33, 175, 198
Gibbs Elementary School, 156, 162, 166, 174, 182, 194, 211–12, 225
Gillam Park, 197
Girl Scouts, 46, 73, 77
Glasscock, June and Jean, 76
Granite Mountain, 53, 57, 58, 86
Granite Mountain Elementary School, 53–54, 55, 100, 101
Green, Ernest, 183, 188–89, 194, 195, 226

H

Hall High School, 125–26, 140, 142, 146, 149, 272
Hammond, Indiana, 100
Hannon, Bobby, 177–78
Harper, Mrs., 43, 52
Healing Racism in America, 147
Hendrix Teacher's College, 43
Hickman, Shirley, 23; attendance at Central High School, 91, 92, 93–95, 98, 99; on effecting racial change, 98–99; experiences at East Side Junior High School, 86–90; extracurricular activities, 89–90; family relationships, 86, 88, 89, 92–93, 95–96; on the first day of school, 87; friendships, 89;

guiding thoughts and lessons learned, 99; impact on adult life, 254–55; on interactions with the White community, 88–91, 95–96; negative experiences, 90; phone company job, 96–97; on preparation for the desegregation process, 87–88; on self-defense and standing ground, 86–88, 89, 92–99; sense of self, 92–96; on strengths and resources, 92–93; on the student selection process, 86; on teacher behaviors and interactions, 89–91, 93–95, 97–98, 253
Hickory, North Carolina, 182
high school desegregation, 5, 13, 24–25. *See also* Central High School; school desegregation
High Street, 196
historically Black colleges or universities (HBCU), 77, 191, 255
Holbert, Claude, 34
Hollywood, California, 82
Honor Roll, 38–39, 40, 43, 44, 78, 113
Horace Mann High School: Alfreda Brown, 62; Alice Joiner Kimball, 189; Alvin Terry, 230; Brenda Sims Clark, 205, 212; Clarence Johnson, 180; desegregation resistance, 268; Glenda Wilson, 47, 115; Henry Rodgers, 158; Joyce Williams Warren, 239–40; Kenneth Jones, 199, 202; Myrna Davis Washington, 75, 80, 82, 83, 86; outdated textbooks and materials, 158; Pinkie Juanetta Thompson, 140, 146; Sandra Smith, 221; Sarah Ellen Jordan Talley, 105; Shirley Hickman, 91; Wilbunette Walls Randolph, 168–69
Horn, C. L., 156, 159
hostile attitudes and environments, 53, 206, 216, 224–27, 229, 256
Howard University, 80, 81–82, 116
Hoxie, 10

used textbooks. *See* outdated textbooks and materials

V

Valachovic, Ernest, 11
Valentine Street, 132
Van Buren, 10

W

Walker, Felton, 23, 173, 224, 271
Walker, Jessie, 23, 29, 86, 271
Walls, Wilbunette. *See* Randolph, Wilbunette Walls
Warren, Earl, 11
Warren, Joyce Williams, 24; attendance at Central High School, 239–40; on broken leg, 236–37; bullying, 236; church attendance, 233, 235; college attendance, 238, 241; on educational foundation, 235, 238; on effecting racial change, 241–43, 255; elementary school experience, 233; experiences at West Side Junior High School, 233–37, 242; extracurricular activities, 238; on faith and spirituality, 234, 241–42; family relationships, 233, 234–40; fellow students, 206, 232–33, 234, 237; on the first day of school, 233–34, 241, 253; guiding thoughts and lessons learned, 243–44; impact on adult life, 240–41, 243, 254–55; on preparation for the desegregation process, 32, 234–35; on racism/colorism, 236, 241–42; on social skills, 235; on strengths and resources, 238–39; on the student selection process, 234; summer school at Horace Mann High School, 240; on support systems, 234–35, 238–40, 241–44; on teacher behaviors and interactions, 233–34, 237–38, 240, 252, 253
Washington, Myrna Davis, 23; attendance at Central High School, 79, 80–81; on awakening moments, 78; bullying, 75–76; on childhood trauma, 71–72, 75–76, 78, 256; church attendance, 73; college attendance, 81–82, 255; dance background, 78–79; experiences at East Side Junior High School, 43, 71–76, 78–80, 83, 86; extracurricular activities, 46, 60, 73, 78–79; family relationships, 70–71, 74–75, 77; fellow students, 36, 76, 100, 111; on the first day of school, 74–75; friendships, 30, 38, 40, 44, 46, 60, 70–74; guiding thoughts and lessons learned, 83–86; impact on adult life, 81–83, 255; on integration impact to Black community, 81–82; on interactions with the White community, 70–71, 73–74, 76; negative experiences, 77, 255; newspaper staff, 43; on peer pressure, 74; on preparation for the desegregation process, 73; on racism/colorism, 74, 79, 81–82; sense of self, 73, 76, 77–78, 79, 82–83; on social skills, 81; on the student selection process, 72; on teacher behaviors and interactions, 77, 79–80; as top student, 72, 73, 77
Washington University, 65
Watson, John, 195
Wayne County Community College, 107
Wayne State University, 107
Webb, Equilla Banks, 23; on abusive behaviors, 37, 38, 40, 44, 45, 49–50, 51; on being in survival mode, 50–51, 53; bullying, 36–37, 41, 43; church attendance, 39, 46, 48; on desire to attend Central High School, 30–32; on effecting racial change, 51–53; experience at Central High School, 47, 51, 52; experiences at East Side Junior High School, 35–38, 40–47, 49, 51, 86; extracurricular activities,

LAVERNE BELL-TOLLIVER is an associate professor at the University of Arkansas at Little Rock School of Social Work. She has worked in the fields of mental health and child protective services and is senior pastor of Bullock Temple Christian Methodist Episcopal Church in Little Rock.